'This thought-provoki[barcode obscures text]eaders an exciting taster of the issues anc[barcode obscures text] and substance of EU law.'

[barcode obscures text] of Cambridge, UK

'A lively and accessible book which introduces students to key issues and controversies in EU law, through vivid examples and lucid analysis. It is an appealing text for all those who are new to the subject, and who seek to learn about EU law in a way that is engaging and fun.'

– **Gráinne de Búrca**, *New York University, USA*

'A great little book for students who are eager to learn through lively analyses of core dilemmas and tensions taking their roots within EU constitutional law. *Great Debates in EU Law* is pedagogical, concise and fun to read!'

– **Xavier Groussot**, *Lund University, Sweden*

'European Union law has always been a battle ground for opposing ideas and arguments about the nature and future of Europe, and this new book excellently explores the great debates that have shaped the Union and its law.'

– **Robert Schütze**, *Durham University, UK*

'This book doesn't simply offer a fresh approach to the substance of EU law, it provides a new way to structure teaching and learning. Its vivid treatment of case studies and practical examples illuminates the animating tensions and central themes in the development of EU law. It is written with compelling flair and insight.'

– **Stephen Weatherill**, *University of Oxford, UK*

Great Debates in Law

Series Editor
Jonathan Herring, Professor of Law, University of Oxford

Commercial and Corporate Law
Andrew Johnston & Lorraine Talbot (eds)

Company Law
Lorraine Talbot

Contract Law
Jonathan Morgan

Criminal Law
Jonathan Herring

Employment Law
Simon Honeyball

Equity and Trusts
Alastair Hudson

European Convention on Human Rights
Fiona de Londras & Kanstantsin Dzehtsiarou

Family Law
Jonathan Herring, Rebecca Probert & Stephen Gilmore

Gender and Law
Rosemary Auchmuty (ed)

Jurisprudence
Nicholas J McBride & Sandy Steel

Land Law
David Cowan, Lorna Fox O'Mahony & Neil Cobb

Medical Law and Ethics
Imogen Goold & Jonathan Herring

Great Debates in Law

Great Debates in EU Law

Jeremias Adams-Prassl
Professor of Law
Magdalen College, Oxford

Sanja Bogojević
Associate Professor of Law
Lady Margaret Hall, Oxford

•HART•
OXFORD • LONDON • NEW YORK • NEW DELHI • SYDNEY

HART PUBLISHING

Bloomsbury Publishing Plc

Kemp House, Chawley Park, Cumnor Hill, Oxford, OX2 9PH, UK

1385 Broadway, New York, NY 10018, USA

29 Earlsfort Terrace, Dublin 2, Ireland

HART PUBLISHING, the Hart/Stag logo, BLOOMSBURY and the Diana logo are trademarks of Bloomsbury Publishing Plc

First published in 2021 by Red Globe Press
Reprinted by Bloomsbury Publishing, 2023

A catalogue record for this book is available from the British Library.

A catalogue record for this book is available from the Library of Congress.

ISBN: HB: 978-1-352-01241-5
PB: 978-1-352-01209-5

Typeset by Compuscript Ltd, Shannon
Printed and bound in Great Britain by CPI Group (UK) Ltd, Croydon CR0 4YY

MIX
Paper | Supporting responsible forestry
FSC® C013604

To find out more about our authors and books visit www.hartpublishing.co.uk. Here you will find extracts, author information, details of forthcoming events and the option to sign up for our newsletters.

To Sergej Ezra
SB

To Abi
JAP

Contents

Cases

EU

3 Glocken GmbH and Gertraud Kritzinger v USL Centro-Sud and Provincia autonoma di Bolzano (C-407/85) [1988] ECR 4233, 192n70
Foster and others v British Gas plc. (C-188/89) [1990] ECR I-3313, 112n89
Advocaten voor de wereld VZW v Leden van de Ministerraad (C-303/05) [2007] ECR I-3633, 157n101
AGS Assedic Pas-de-Calais v François Dumon and Froment, liquidator and representative of Établissements Pierre Gilson (C-235/95) [1998] ECR I-4531, 122n34
Albany International BV v Stichting Bedrijfspensioenfonds Textielindustrie (C-67/96) [1999] ECR I-5751, 31n87
Albert Ruckdeschel & Co. and Hansa-Lagerhaus Ströh & Co. v Hauptzollamt Hamburg-St. Annen and *Diamalt AG v Hauptzollamt Itzehoe* (117/76 and 16/77) [1977] ECR 1753, 103n41
Alfa Vita Vassilopoulos AE and Carrefour Marinopoulos AE v Elliniko Dimosio and Nomarchiaki Aftodioikisi Ionninon (C-158/04 and C-159/04) [2006] ECR I-8135, 194n86
Åklagaren v Hans Åkerberg Fransson (C-617/10) [2013] ECR I-9011, 82n40, 107n65, 157n100, 195n88
Åklagaren v Percy Mickelsson and Joakim Roos (C-142/05) [2009] ECR I-4273, 122n41, 194n86
Aktien-Zuckerfabrik Schöppenstedt v Council (5/71) [1971] ECR 975, 61n19
Amministrazione dell'Economia e delle Finanze, Agenzia delle Entrate v Fallimento Olimpiclub Srl (C-2/08) [2009] ECR I-7501, 89n84
Amministrazione delle Finanze dello Stato v Simmenthal SpA (106/77) [1978] ECR 629, 128n86
Andrea Francovich and others v Italy (C-6/90 and C-9/90) [1991] ECR I-5357, 84n52
Andrea Raccanelli v Max-Planck-Gesellschaft zur Förderung der Wissenschaften eV. (C-94/07) [2008] ECR I-5939, 98n13
Andy Wightman and others v Secretary of State for Exiting the European Union (C-621/18) EU:C:2018:999, 121n29
Antje Köhler v Finanzamt Düsseldorf-Nord (C-58/04) [2005] ECR I-8219, 192n67
Arcelor SA v European Parliament and Council (T-16/04) [2010] ECR II-211, 130n99
Armando Carvalho and others v European Parliament and Council (T-330/18) EU:T:2019:324, 147n45, 207n30
Asma Bougnaoui, ADDH v Micropole SA (C-188/15) EU:C:2017:204, 146n38
Asóciacion Profesional Elite Taxi v Uber Systems Spain SL (C-434/15) EU:C:2017:981, 210n56

Yassin Abdullah Kadi and Al Barakaat International Foundation v Council and European Commission (C-402/05 P and C-415/05 P) [2008] ECR I-6351, 49n91, 60n14, 142n16, 142n17
Yvonne Van Duyn v Home Office (41/74) [1974] ECR 1337, 82n39

Zuckerfabrik Suderdithmarschen AG v Hauptzollamt Itzehoe and *Zuckerfabrik Soest GmbH v Hauptzollamt Paderborn* (C-143/88 and C-92/89) [1991] ECR I-415, 63n33, 89n83

ECHR

Bosphorus Hava Yollari Turizm Ve Ticaret Anonim SIrketi v Ireland [2005] 42 EHRR 1, 155n87
Matthews v United Kingdom [1999] 28 EHRR 361, 155n86
Young, James and Webster v United Kingdom [1981] 4 EHRR 38, 99n16

Cases from Other Jurisdictions

Benkharbouche v Secretary of State for Foreign and Commonwealth Affairs [2017] UKSC 62, 152n68
R (ClientEarth) v Secretary of State for Environment, Food and Rural Affairs [2015] UKSC 28, 92n97, 122n37
R (ClientEarth) v Secretary of State for Environment, Food and Rural Affairs (No 3) [2018] EWHC 315 (Admin).
R (ClientEarth) v Secretary of State for Environment, Food and Rural Affairs (No 3) [2018] EWHC 398 (Admin), 92n98
R (Factortame Ltd) v Secretary of State for Transport (No 2) [1991] 1 AC 603.
R (Miller) v The Prime Minister [2019] UKSC 41, 46n66
R (Miller and another) v Secretary of State for Exiting the European Union [2017] UKSC 5.
Thoburn v Sunderland CC [2002] EWHC 195 (Admin).
BVerfG, 12.10.1993 – 2 BvR 2134/92, 2 BvR 2159/92 (DE), 16n10, 133n114
BVerfG, 5.05.2020 – 2 BvR 859/15 (DE), 134n120
BVerfG, 30.06.2009 – 2 BvE 2/08 (DE), 24n46, 52n109, 133n117
BVerfG, 6.07.2010 – 2 BvR 2661/06 (DE), 133n116
Manfred Brunner and others v European Union Treaty (Cases 2 BvR 2134/92 & 2159/92) [1994] I CMLR 57 (DE), 34n98
Re Wunsche Handelsgesellschat [1987] 3 CMLR 225, 265 (*Solange II*) (DE), 133n115
UfR 2017.824H (Case no. 15/2014, *DI, acting on behalf of Ajos A/S v Estate of A*) (DK), 100n22, 132n108
Arrêt Nicolo, CE, ass, 20 oct. 1989, n° 108243 (FR), 130n95
Dom nr 89/09, Mål nr A 268/04, 2009-12-02 57 (SE), 125n63

Acknowledgments

Our enthusiasm for EU law was inspired, first and foremost, by our teachers: Eloise Scotford, Steve Weatherill, Paul Craig, Sionaidh Douglas-Scott, and Andrea Biondi. They introduced us to so much more than just the rules, looking behind the Treaties, Regulations, and Directives to the broader context of the Union's evolution. From political tensions to the social and economic quirks of EU law: thank you for making the subject come to life.

This explains our ambition for the book. The law is often presented as a static snapshot. Over years of discussions in seminars and tutorials, however, we found that, to truly enjoy the subject, one needs to understand the contestations and tensions which have shaped its rules. So here it is: a tour through the weird and wonderful characters, institutions, and accidents that explain how EU law works. Ultimately, we hope that you will come to enjoy the subject as much as we do.

A number of colleagues have kindly taken the time to read previous drafts and discuss our arguments, including Michal Bobek, Ulrika Carlsson, Stefan Enchelmaier, Liz Fisher, Sacha Garben, Xavier Groussot, and Steve Weatherill. Jessica Allen and Aislinn Kelly-Lyth provided excellent research assistance, supported by the Faculty's research support fund. We are grateful to Jonathan Herring and the entire team at Macmillan, as well as our law colleagues at Magdalen and Lady Margaret Hall, Katharine Grevling, Roderick Bagshaw, Joe Sampson, Hannah Smith, Helen Scott, and the entire EU law teaching team at Oxford.

When we sat down over coffee in early 2020 to draft a proposal for this book, little did we know how fundamentally things were about to change. With us, right from that very moment, was baby Sergej Ezra, who kept us entertained, inspired, and in Gruffalo quotes. We could not have done without the help and love of our partners, Abi and Kristijan. Most importantly, we want to thank each other: from puzzling over how best to explain horizontality to learning more about the intricacies of jungle ecosystems and dogs that cannot bark, it has been a joy!

Jeremias Adams-Prassl
Sanja Bogojević
Oxford, Spring 2021

CHAPTER 1

From Rome with Love
The European Union's New Legal Order

Sovereign states have signed international treaties for centuries, regulating bilateral relationships and creating international organisations. After World War II, Europe saw a flurry of new transnational collaborative projects concerning such matters as reconstruction aid and human rights.[1] The trend caught on globally: there are more than 100 international organisations in the world today, from the United Nations and the International Labour Organisation to the Central Commission for the Navigation of the Rhine and the World Vegetable Centre.[2]

At first glance, then, the meeting of government representatives from Belgium, France, Italy, Luxembourg, the Netherlands, and (what was then) West Germany in Rome on 25 March 1957 does not seem all that extraordinary. The delegates signed a treaty establishing a common market – the European Economic Community – in order to facilitate trade between their respective countries. That meeting, however, kicked off a process of economic and legal integration which continues to this day in what is now the European Union (EU). The Treaty of Rome, as quickly became clear, had not merely created another international organisation: it was the founding stone of 'a new legal order'.[3]

But what does this mean? What makes the European project special – distinct from nation states, federations, and traditional public international law? In this chapter, we provide a quick overview of the key features of the EU,

[1] This includes the creation of the European Convention of Human Rights (ECHR), as detailed in E Bates, *The Evolution of the European Convention on Human Rights: From Its Inception to the Creation of a Permanent Court of Human Rights* (Cambridge University Press 2010). We discuss the role of the ECHR in EU law in Chapter 8.

[2] For an overview of the history, functions, and structures of international organisations, see J Katz Cogan, I Hurd, and I Johnstone (eds), *The Oxford Handbook of International Organizations* (Oxford University Press 2016).

[3] As proclaimed by the Court of Justice in Case 26/62 *NV Algemene Transport – en Expeditie Onderneming van Gend en Loos v Netherlands Inland Revenue Administration* [1963] ECR 2. We return to this point in Debate 2.

beginning with its historical evolution and governance structures (Debate 1). We then turn to the two doctrines that set the Union apart from other creatures of international law: direct effect and supremacy; powerful mechanisms that confer rights on individuals (Debate 2). These developments, however, have not been without controversy: the ensuing tensions create three fault lines that run throughout our Great Debates (Debate 3).

Exploring the Union's new legal order is a fascinating journey through novel legal constructs, as well as innovative approaches to long-standing constitutional and economic questions. It is like nothing you will have encountered in domestic law, and yet replete with similar motives – from the role of the judiciary to tensions between different governance levels. What makes the study of this new legal order so absorbing is that EU law traverses a uniquely broad range of the curious, the bizarre, and the outrageous. We will ensure that you encounter many of the colourful individuals, hazards, and vagaries which have shaped the Union's legal order as much as the Member States and EU institutions – from enterprising feminists and tax fraudsters to importers of dubious sex toys, fake aristocrats, and German beer lovers.

Debate 1

How did the European Economic Community become the European Union?

After the end of World War II, the European continent was exhausted. The horrors of two wars had provided ample demonstration of the dark, destructive forces unleashed by unbridled nationalism. Against this backdrop, European leaders set out to tame sovereign states in the hope of replacing conflict with collaboration. Among the most ambitious was Winston Churchill. The only remedy for 'the tragedy of Europe, this noble continent', he argued in 1946, was the creation of a 'United States of Europe': a common 'structure under which [countries] can dwell in peace, safety and freedom.'[4]

Abandoning nation states entirely, however, proved a step too far. The most ambitious plans for full-on political and defence communities quickly floundered. Jean Monnet, a senior French civil servant, realised that another tack was required. Full-scale integration could only be achieved in piece-meal fashion, with collaboration in key economic sectors as the first step. This idea was enthusiastically taken up by Robert Schuman, the French Foreign Minister, who was to become the 'Father of Europe'.[5] On 9 May 1950 – a date cele-

[4] W Churchill, 'Speech on a United States of Europe' (Zurich, 19 September 1946), https://perma.cc/JV5D-AMNH.

[5] A titled bestowed on him by the European Parliament at the end of his term as President in 1960.

brated to this day as 'Europe Day' – he declared that 'Europe [was] not [to] be made all at once, or according to a single plan'. The first step was merely to pool Franco-German production of coal and steel under the control of a common high authority. This, he hoped, would

> immediately provide for the setting up of common foundations for economic development as a first step in the federation of Europe [...] The solidarity in production thus established will make it plain that any war between France and Germany becomes not merely unthinkable, but materially impossible. The setting up of this powerful productive unit [...] will lay a true foundation for [...] economic unification.[6]

The European Coal and Steel Community was duly established just over two years later;[7] its High Authority chaired by one Monsieur Monnet. Whilst formally in place until 2002, the mantle of European integration was passed on much sooner: on 1 January 1958, the Treaty of Rome entered into force.

(A) Integration Through Economics – and Law[8]

Monnet's master plan was clear: peace in Europe was to be established through an open-ended process of market integration. Why limit trade to coal and steel, when a common market allowing the free movement of goods, services, capital, and persons would bring manifold benefits? And why not support that market with harmonised rights for consumers, workers, and the environment – and potentially even a common currency? For these ambitions to be realised, however, more than starry-eyed economic projections was needed. Only a legally robust framework, placing the Member States under the control of a centralised governance regime, could ensure the long-term success of Europe's dynamic integration process.

From Market Integration to a Constitutional Legal Order

The bedrock of Europe's integration are the Treaties. Neither the Union nor its predecessor institutions enjoy any power in and of themselves: under the principle of 'conferral' (to which the next chapter is dedicated), the Union can only exercise those competences conferred on it by the Member States.

The considerable growth of Union powers is the direct result of Treaty reform. Since 1957, national governments have continued to negotiate new

---

[6] European Union, 'The Schuman Declaration – 9 May 1950', https://perma.cc/ZVJ5-93RB.

[7] Treaty establishing the European Coal and Steel Community (adopted 18 April 1951, entered into force 23 July 1952) 261 UNTS 140.

[8] With apologies to M Cappelletti, M Seccombe, and JHH Weiler (eds), *Integration Through Law:Europe and the American Federal Experience* (Vol. 1, De Gruyter 1986).

Treaties, both in order to confer significant additional powers on the Union and to enlarge its geographic reach.[9] The result is a long and rich historical tapestry with twists and turns far beyond the scope of an introductory chapter. Let us nonetheless look at a few important highlights that mark the constitutional development of the EU.[10]

In the beginning, such milestones were few and far between. The overarching structures set out in the Treaty of Rome remained largely unchanged for three decades despite significant political changes, including the first direct elections to the European Parliament in 1979, and successive waves of enlargement (the original six members were joined by Denmark, Ireland, and the United Kingdom in 1973, Greece in 1981, and Spain, together with Portugal, in 1986).[11] There was nonetheless a sense that – apart from the case law of the Court of Justice of the European Union (CJEU) – the Union's initial momentum had ground to a halt. In 1987, the first major Treaty revision entered into effect: the so-called Single European Act.[12] 'Completing' the single market became a key priority, with powerful legislative innovations deployed to that end,[13] and a number of new policy areas (including environmental protection) added to the Union's competence.

The Member States soon accelerated the pace of change. In 1993, the Maastricht Treaty entered into force, bringing about a series of major institutional reforms.[14] The details are complex. In essence, the Treaty of Rome was amended to turn the 'European Economic Community' into the 'European Community'; a new Treaty on European Union was added to the edifice; and a series of cooperation mechanisms were established in areas including both foreign policy and home affairs.[15]

Geographical expansion continued with Austria, Finland, and Sweden joining in 1995. The first major Treaty revision for the 'EU-15' brought about comparatively few changes in substance but a major nightmare for lawyers and law students: the Treaty of Amsterdam (in force from 1999) streamlined and consolidated existing provisions, requiring a complete renumbering of both

[9] As a result of this approach, actual Treaty texts usually read more like an instruction to printers ('remove this', 'add that') – which is why we normally work with the 'consolidated version' (i.e. one where the necessary changes have all been made).

[10] For an excellent overview, see P Craig, 'Integration, Democracy, and Legitimacy' in P Craig and G de Búrca (eds), *The Evolution of EU Law*, 2nd edn (Oxford University Press 2011).

[11] For an overview of the accession agreements and their impact on the construction of the internal market, see S Bogojević and M Drenovak-Ivanović, 'Environmental protection through the prism of enlargement: Time for reflection' (2019) 56(4) CML Rev 949.

[12] European Parliament and Council Directive 2001/42/EC of 27 June 2001 on the assessment of the effects of certain plans and programmes on the environment [2001] OJ L197/30.

[13] Including the predecessor to Article 114 TFEU, which we will encounter in detail in the next chapter, and the adoption of new legislative and voting procedures to increase the role of the European Parliament and Qualified Majority Voting (QMV), respectively.

[14] Treaty on European Union [1992] OJ C191/1.

[15] These additional 'pillars' were (fortunately) absorbed into the EU in 2009.

the Treaty on European Union (TEU) and the Treaty establishing the European Community (TEC).[16]

Four years later, the Treaty of Nice entered into force, paving the way for the Union's major – and historic – enlargement.[17] On 1 May 2004, ten countries (the Czech Republic, Cyprus, Estonia, Hungary, Latvia, Lithuania, Malta, Poland, Slovakia, and Slovenia) became Member States, followed by Romania and Bulgaria in January 2007.

The next round of Treaty revisions was supposed to be the most ambitious yet, but ended in acrimony and failure. In the early 2000s, the Convention on the Future of Europe proposed nothing short of a Treaty Establishing a Constitution for Europe.[18] Its fate was sealed after voters in both France and the Netherlands rejected the sweeping changes envisaged, with further ratification abandoned in 2005.

From the Constitution's ashes rose a phoenix: the Treaty of Lisbon. In force since December 2009, it created the EU as a unified institution, based on the TEU, the Treaty on the Functioning of the European Union (TFEU), and the Charter of Fundamental Rights (CFR).[19] We will encounter their specific provisions throughout this book. For now, a bit of unfortunate news: rather than the neat single structure proposed by the Constitutional Treaty, the TEU and TFEU continued the layer-cake approach to Treaty reform, involving another round of reorganisation and renumbering. The preliminary reference procedure, for example, is today found in Article 267 TFEU, whilst it had been located in Article 234 TEC since the Treaty of Amsterdam, and in Article 177 EEC before then. This can be particularly confusing when reading older case law: watch out when taking notes.

The Union's impressive geographical expansion and increase in competence has repeatedly prompted the question of whether there are limits to its growth. There is potential for tension between widening the Union by including additional Member States, or deepening collaboration and thus increasing the scope and strength of the EU's powers.[20] At the time of writing, no further Treaty revisions or immediate enlargement plans are in the making. This is not to say that there have not been momentous changes and further challenges to the EU legal order, as discussed in the concluding chapter. Croatia joined in 2013, whilst 'Brexit' reduced the number of Member States to 27 following the United Kingdom's referendum on continued EU membership on 23 June 2016.

---

[16] Treaty of Amsterdam amending the Treaty on European Union, the Treaties establishing the European Communities and certain related acts [1997] OJ C340/1.

[17] Treaty of Nice amending the Treaty on European Union, the Treaties establishing the European Communities, and certain related acts [2001] OJ C80/1.

[18] Treaty establishing a Constitution for Europe [2004] OJ C310/1.

[19] P Craig, *The Lisbon Treaty: Law, Politics and Treaty Reform* (Oxford University Press 2010).

[20] Whether there is a necessary trade-off between the two is an important question. See, e.g. RD Kelemen, A Menon, and J Slapin, 'Wider and deeper? Enlargement and integration in the European Union' (2014) 21(5) J Eur Public Policy 647.

Centralised Governance

The Treaties confer a wide range of competences on the Union and set out its unique centralised governance structure – inspired by the European Coal and Steel Community, which featured a High Authority, Council, Assembly, and Court. Title III TEU provides a helpful starting point for understanding the Union's institutional framework, with Article 13 TEU listing nine institutions and committees.

The *Commission*, first, 'shall promote the general interest of the Union' and 'ensure the application of the Treaties'. It also enjoys the exclusive right to make legislative proposals.[21] The Commission President and her team (or 'College') of Commissioners, one from each Member State,[22] oversee a wide range of portfolios – from 'A Europe Fit for the Digital Age' and the Internal Market, to 'Innovation, Research, Culture, Education and Youth' and (somewhat controversially) 'Promoting our European Way of Life'.[23] It relies on the work of more than 30,000 civil servants,[24] including policy experts, researchers, lawyers, and translators – a comparatively small bureaucracy considering that it serves nearly 448 million citizens.[25]

The *Council*,[26] on the other hand, consists of Member State ministers, supported by their respective national diplomats, who meet as the Committee of Permanent Representatives (COREPER). Its task is to 'exercise legislative and budgetary functions' and to 'carry out policy-making and coordinating functions'.[27] In practice, there are a number of different configurations to reflect the subject matter under discussion. When animal welfare legislation is to be voted on, for example, Member States will send their ministers of agriculture, and so on. Unanimity has mostly given way to qualified majority voting (QMV) – a complex system designed to ensure equal representation across small and large countries.[28]

The *European Parliament* is made up of 705 Members of the European Parliament (MEPs) – representatives elected directly by the citizens of Europe.[29] Organised in pan-European groups across the political spectrum, MEPs scrutinise and vote on legislative proposals and 'exercise functions of political control and consultation' – including, notably, the election (and if necessary, the removal) of the Commission.[30]

---

[21] TEU, Article 17(1)(2).

[22] This is notwithstanding Article 17(5) TEU, and embodies a political compromise following the Irish Referendum on the Lisbon Treaty.

[23] European Commission, 'The Commissioners', https://perma.cc/YR9H-RBJ2.

[24] European Commission, 'Commission staff', https://perma.cc/B5N5-TQ29.

[25] Eurostat, 'Population on 1 January 2020', https://perma.cc/6GXS-6Q6N.

[26] Not to be confused with the *European Council*, a bi-annual agenda-setting meeting of heads of state and government (Article 15 TEU), or the *Council of Europe*, an entirely independent international organisation tasked, *inter alia*, with overseeing the ECHR.

[27] TEU, Article 16(1).

[28] The full details can be found in Article 283 TFEU.

[29] European Parliament, 'About MEPs', https://perma.cc/UVJ8-A3RX.

[30] TEU, Article 14(1). Note also its budgetary functions.

This triptych of political institutions is joined by the CJEU, tasked with ensuring 'that in the interpretation and application of the Treaties the law is observed.'[31] Members of the Court include one judge from each Member State, sitting in small groupings known as 'Chambers' – or, in the case of particularly important issues, as a larger Grand Chamber. A number of Advocates General support the Court's work with 'Opinions' on cases heard. The Treaty also provides for a General Court (previously known as the Court of First Instance) and 'specialised courts' – although none existed at the time of writing.[32]

These, then, are the central institutions that govern the EU. Add to this the European Council,[33] which provides general political direction (although it has no legislative powers) and consists of its President, the President of the Commission, and the heads of state or government of the Member States.[34] In addition to these institutions, there are a number of further bodies and agencies with specialised functions – from the Economic and Social Committee and the European Committee of the Regions to the European Central Bank, the European Ombudsman, and, most recently established, the European Labour Authority.[35]

Over the course of this book, we will learn a great deal more about these institutions. For now, two important points should be noted. First, the Union's institutional arrangement does not reflect the traditional separation of powers familiar from domestic constitutional law. The legislative function in particular is shared among the three key political actors: the Commission, the Council, and the European Parliament. This institutional design seeks to ensure the separation and balanced representation of competing interests: the Commission acts as the 'guardian of the treaties', representing Union interests;[36] the Council is where national governments represent their individual domestic agendas, as a result of which negotiations are not infrequently 'characterised by all the warmth of a love match in a snake-pit';[37] the European Parliament, finally, serves as the direct representation of EU citizens.

Second, there is the dynamic nature of their relationship, which in turn tells us a lot about the evolution of the Union's legal order. Over the decades, there have been significant shifts in power relations amongst different institutions. Key developments to watch out for include the growth in powers of the European Parliament (particularly when it comes to legislative involvement),

[31] TEU, Article 19(1).

[32] TEU, Article 19(2).

[33] Not to be confused with the Council of Europe, a different international organisation independent from the EU; see note 1 supra.

[34] TEU, Article 15.

[35] The directories of these organisations are available online at https://op.europa.eu/en/web/who-is-who.

[36] European Commission, 'What the European Commission does in law', https://perma.cc/6MQ7-HW7A.

[37] G Mancini, 'The making of a constitution for Europe' (1989) 26(4) CML Rev 595, 598.

a shift of powers from the Commission to the Council, and the role of the CJEU as the interinstitutional arbiter (to which we return in Chapter 7).

Debate 2

A new legal order?

Having surveyed the Union's history and key institutional features, you might wonder whether they really are different enough from other international treaties and organisations to merit the grand claim that the EU constitutes a 'new legal order'. The World Trade Organisation (WTO), for example, is similarly based on Treaties, comes with its own adjudicative mechanisms, and continues to evolve over the decades.[38]

But it is not just a novel institutional setup that makes the EU unique. Most importantly, the Union is an international legal order deeply intermeshed with national systems. As a result, the Treaties do not just bind sovereign states and their governments together: EU law directly grants rights to individuals.

(A) Beyond Dualism: Supreme Rights for Individuals

As a matter of orthodox public international law, the domestic effect of international agreements is left to national constitutional arrangements. So-called monist legal orders automatically incorporate duly ratified international law into the domestic legal system. The majority of countries, on the other hand, are dualist legal orders and treat international law as an entirely distinct system. Treaty obligations float like a layer of oil on top of water: they are only binding on the government. Domestic measures, such as implementing legislation, are required in order to make international rights effective for individuals.[39] With a mix of monist and dualist Member States, the CJEU was soon faced with a crucial question: How should the relationship between EU law and domestic legal systems be understood? In early landmark cases establishing the doctrines of direct effect and supremacy, the EU court firmly went beyond the prevailing orthodoxy by establishing the Treaties as a source of supreme rights for individuals.

Direct Effect

The recognition of direct effect 'revolutionised European law'.[40] In *Van Gend en Loos*, the Court spelled out the implications of the Union's 'new legal order

[38] For an overview, see A Narlikar, *The World Trade Organization: A Very Short Introduction* (Oxford University Press 2005).

[39] B de Witte, 'Direct effect, supremacy and the nature of the legal order' in P Craig and G de Búrca (eds), *The Evolution of EU Law*, 2nd edn (Oxford University Press 2011), p. 324.

[40] M Rasmussen, 'Revolutionizing European law: A history of the *Van Gend en Loos* judgment' (2014) 12(1) Intl J Const L 136.

of international law for the benefit of which the states have limited their sovereign rights'. This was no mere international Treaty: its subjects included

> not only Member States but also their nationals. Independently of the legislation of Member States, Community law therefore not only imposes obligations on individuals but is also intended to confer upon them rights which become part of their legal heritage.[41]

This is a powerful statement. EU law takes on a unique *sui generis* life, independent of both international law and national constitutions. If the Treaty grants you the right to, say, move freely to another Member State, that is it: there is no need for any translation into domestic law, or worrying whether the domestic legal system is dualist or monist. Direct effect guarantees the uniform application of EU rules across the Member States and, as such, elegantly cures the 'infant disease'[42] of the Treaty of Rome.[43]

Supremacy

One immediate problem that arises in consequence is a potential clash of norms. What if the Treaty grants you a particular right but national law contains a provision to the opposite effect? In *Costa v ENEL*, the Court of Justice laid out the solution. Due to the principle of supremacy, EU law was to enjoy primacy over any conflicting domestic rules:

> The law stemming from the Treaty, an independent source of law, could not, because of its special and original nature, be overridden by domestic legal provisions, however, framed, without being deprived of its character as [Union] law and without the legal basis of the [Union] itself being called into question.[44]

Subsequent cases, explored in depth in Chapter 7, flesh out the contours of supremacy. There were to be no exceptions – not even for Member States' constitutional fundamental rights guarantees – and the duty to disapply conflicting national law was incumbent upon all national courts.[45]

(B) Dual Vigilance

Nor are individuals alone in enforcing their rights. In another move beyond orthodox public international law,[46] the Commission, as 'guardian of the

[41] *Van Gend en Loos* (n 3), p. 12.
[42] P Pescatore, 'The Doctrine of "Direct Effect": An Infant Disease of Community Law' (1983) 8 EL Rev 155.
[43] Some scarring remains. There are detailed rules about the contours of direct effect, which we explore in detail in Chapter 5.
[44] Case 6/64 *Costa v ENEL* [1964] ECR 585, pp. 593–94.
[45] Note that the duty is to disapply the relevant law, rather than strike it down; national law remains valid outside the scope of EU law.
[46] R White and A Dashwood, 'Enforcement Actions under Articles 169 and 170 EEC' (1989) 14(6) EL Rev 388.

Treaties', can bring so-called infringement proceedings under Article 258 TFEU against Member States who fail to comply with their Treaty obligations.[47] The country in question is put on notice by a reasoned opinion delivered by the Commission. If compliance is not forthcoming, the matter is brought before the CJEU.[48]

The purpose of infringement proceedings is clear: they are necessary for the Union's continued existence as a 'community of law' ('*Rechtsgemeinschaft*'), bound by rules that Member States agree upon as co-legislators and promise to implement in their national system. Most importantly, however, they are 'key to ensure that EU policies become a reality for people in their every-day lives'.[49]

Taken together with the principles of direct effect and supremacy, the Union's legal order is thus characterised by what Weatherill has termed a 'system of dual vigilance'. The '"vigilance" of individuals [highlighted by the Court of Justice in *Van Gend en Loos*] supplements that of the Commission … in securing the enforcement of EU law'.[50]

As a result, the promise of integration, free movement, equal treatment, and many other rights writ large in the Treaties is not merely another *séduisante mais lointaine abstraction intéressant seulement les gouvernements*. Instead, EU law has become *une réalite effective et par conséquence créatrice de droits*.[51] The Treaty had left the question unresolved, but it did not take the Court of Justice long to decide upon '*une certaine idée de l'Europe*':[52] the Union's 'new legal order' would be firmly committed to the effective protection of individual rights.

Debate 3

An ever closer Union?

In the Treaties, the Member States commit themselves to creating 'an ever closer union among the peoples of Europe'.[53] The result is a dynamic process of integration, the growth of an ever-changing Union. As one French minister is supposed to have told then Prime Minister Edward Heath during Britain's

[47] Most legislative measures contain an obligation on Member States to report back on their implementation, and there is also an online form allowing citizens to report states for breaching EU law. See https://ec.europa.eu/assets/sg/report-a-breach/complaints_en/index.html.

[48] Member States can also sue each other (Article 259 TFEU), but such actions are very rare in practice.

[49] European Commission, 'Monitoring the Application of European Union Law: 2019 Annual Report' (European Commission, 31 July 2020), https://perma.cc/W68Z-643R.

[50] S Weatherill, *Cases & Materials on EU Law*, 12th edn (Oxford University Press 2016), p. 85.

[51] In translation: EU law is not an abstraction, relevant to the Member States only, but a creator of rights. See R Lecourt, *L'Europe des Juges* (Bruylant 1976), p. 248, as cited by Weatherill, *Cases & Materials on EU Law* (n 50), p. 101.

[52] Pescatore (n 42), 'The Doctrine of "Direct Effect"'.

[53] TEU, Article 1.

first accession negotiations in the 1960s, 'We don't know where we're going… [a]ll we know is that we're going there together.'[54]

This is not by accident, of course – Schuman and Monnet had created the perfect conditions for a series of functional and political 'spillovers' where the interconnectedness of the Internal Market and the very existence of a centralised governance structure would create pressure for ever-deeper integration.[55] Yet there is plenty of discontent: Whether in the form of national governments accusing the CJEU of '*mégalomanie maladive*'[56] or right-wing tabloids lampooning the undemocratic Brussels bureaucracy's obsession with regulating bendy bananas (a long-standing myth; more on which in Chapter 2), European integration has led to plenty of tensions.

(A) Three Themes

As we embark upon our exploration of EU law, there are three such fault lines, or themes, that will continue to crop up in the Great Debates. Each represents a tension inherent in the development of the new legal order – taken together, they go a long way towards explaining many of the apparent contradictions we will unearth.

Individuals vs Member States

The EU is the creation of sovereign states, acting as high contracting parties in international law. Yet, ultimately, it is the individual citizen who sits at the core of the European project. As explained in *Van Gen den Loos*, she enjoys a host of rights. Who should carry the corresponding obligations? As Treaty signatories, the Member States are obvious candidates, but what about private parties? Could – or rather, should – EU law impose burdens on parties in entirely private ('horizontal') disputes? We discuss horizontality of EU law in Chapter 6, following the debate in Chapter 5 on how the doctrines of direct effect, harmonious interpretation, and state liability (among others) – developed by the Court under the banner of securing the protection of individual rights – dig deep into the procedural space of the Member States.

Do they go too far in reshaping domestic legal orders? We return to the difficulty of balancing national regulatory prerogatives with individual rights in Chapters 9 and 10, where we find Member States keen on preserving their national preferences. The ensuing conflicts range from tensions between free movement rights and domestic immigration policy to the Internal Market's emphasis on consumer choice clashing with centuries-old laws on beer, pasta, and margarine cones.

---

[54] R Mayne, 'Seven Euro-heresies,' *London Review of Books* (London, 26 March 1992), https://perma.cc/8EZC-BXJ2.

[55] P Craig, 'Integration, democracy, and legitimacy' (n 10), p. 14 and sources cited therein.

[56] See Mancini (n 37), 'The making of a constitution for Europe', p. 595.

Enable vs Restrain

This is an age-old chestnut of constitutional law: governments need power in order to operate effectively, but its exercise must be carefully controlled and, where necessary, restrained. In the Union context, this tension takes on an additional dimension. Not only is there a question of the *horizontal* distribution of powers between, say, the Council and the Commission; even more important is the *vertical* relationship between Member States and the Union. As explained in Chapter 2, the Treaties provide a neat list of competences that entrust legislative power to the Union in a wide range of categories – in all other areas, the Member States alone are entitled to act. Yet in practice, such clear boundaries are difficult to uphold, especially when the objective is to establish an *integrated* market. Does this mean that EU law-making is overcentralised? Are there any ways of challenging 'Brussels'? If so, *who* is allowed to swing the sword and ask for EU law to be struck down – only the Member States, or individuals, too? We deal with these questions in Chapters 3 and 4, respectively, before examining the broader role of the interjudicial relationship between national courts and Luxembourg in Chapter 7. Is the CJEU a Supreme Court, or is its role more limited? If so, how?

Mondrian vs Pollock

As Cartabia and Ninatti so memorably suggest, the language of the Treaties can often resemble the clear lines and bold colours of Mondrian's compositions, whereas the reality is often much closer to the messy multiple layers of Pollock's drip paintings.[57] This observation was prompted by fundamental rights protection in the EU – we will encounter that 'crowded house'[58] of multiple, overlapping sources and judicial methods in Chapter 8. On reflection, however, it fits all of the Great Debates ahead. Intuitively, we may be tempted to blame this messiness on the CJEU's case law – and occasionally (though by no means always) this is right.

We hope that the debates in this book will add other possible explanations. Political compromise between 27 negotiating parties may well come at the cost of legal clarity. As Schuman predicted, European integration needs to proceed step-by-step. This process is laden with uncertainty, compromise, and tensions. Because it is an open-ended project, and because the Treaties are revised as this building work is carried out, EU law often appears messy and thus Pollockian. Even as we look toward the Union's future challenges, outlined in Chapter 11, several open-ended questions and dilemmas loom. The Union, and thus its legal regime, are in a constant state of development.

[57] M Cartabia and S Ninatti, 'Fundamental rights in the European Court of Justice and the European Court of Human Rights' in S Douglas-Scott and N Hatzis (eds), *Research Handbook on EU Law and Human Rights* (Edward Elgar 2017).

[58] P Cruz Villalón, 'Rights in Europe: The crowded house' (King's College London 2012, Working Paper in European Law 01/2012).

(B) The Ride Ahead

A French commentator once linked the behaviour of a certain Member State to that of a passenger who 'had boarded the plane without checking where it was bound for – and now [keeps] trying to divert it, or jump out in mid-air'.[59] We hope you will stay the course with us, remembering always that tensions do not necessarily have to be resolved – sometimes they *cannot* be. This is where the real fascination of EU law lies. Exploring the new legal order helps us return to many questions that have long been settled in domestic (constitutional) law. The EU provides a unique case study of an evolving legal order – and just over 60 years after the Treaty of Lisbon, there are still plenty of challenges ahead.

In the ensuing chapters, we cluster our discussion of EU law around these Great Debates, eschewing more traditional approaches that provide descriptions (often in historical order) of substantive and constitutional elements of EU law. By offering concise and lively analyses of core dilemmas and tensions, we hope to provide a different kind of introduction, emphasising the broader narratives upon which individual aspects and materials of EU law depend. Enjoy!

Further Reading

At the end of each chapter, we will suggest a few options for further readings that offer in-depth analysis of key arguments, different points of view, and/or provocative challenges to established orthodoxy. If you have additional suggestions for future editions, we would love to hear from you.

European Integration is not just fascinating to lawyers. A lot of political theory has sought to explain the processes we encountered in Debate 1, and considered different ways of understanding the EU's governance and construction. For an excellent introduction, try the essays in A Wiener, TA Börzel, and T Risse (eds), *European Integration Theory* (Oxford University Press 2018).

The CJEU tends to get the lion share of credit for shaping the contours of the new legal order – and rightly so. But what about academic perspectives? Mirroring the French public sector, the EU founded its own elite academic institutions (the College of Europe in Bruges and the European University Institute in Florence) to provide for the transnational education of civil servants and academics, respectively. See R Byberg, 'The History of the Integration Through Law Project: Creating the Academic Expression of a Constitutional Legal Vision for Europe' (2017) 18 German LJ 1531.

The relationship between nation states and democracy, on the one hand, and supranational governance, on the other, is a theme which we will explore throughout this volume (and in Chapter 3, Debate 3, in particular). For a first taste of these debates, try J Habermas, *The Crisis of the European Union: A Response* (Polity 2013). How can democratic political institutions operate beyond states?

[59] Mayne, 'Seven Euro-Heresies' (n 54) .

CHAPTER 2

Regulating Bananas

Conferral, Competence, and the Exercise of Union Powers

One of the most bizarre – and surprisingly persistent – myths about the EU is that it regulates the curvature of bananas.[1] That is simply not the case. There *are* minimum quality provisions to ensure that rotten or pest-infested fruit cannot be sold, but nothing to specify a particular degree of curvature.[2] Cucumbers are another matter altogether: until 2009, to qualify as 'extra' class quality, they were to 'be well shaped and practically straight (maximum height of the arc: 10 mm per 10 cm of length of the cucumber)'.[3]

Chances are that the finer points of phytosanitary regulation and EU food safety standards will not have made it onto your EU law syllabus.[4] And yet, it is worth taking some time to think about the broader tensions and anxieties that underpin these and other complaints of 'excessive meddling' by 'faceless Brussels Eurocrats'.[5] It is undoubtedly true that, since its inception as a European Economic Community in 1957, the Union's powers have grown significantly – spanning the gamut from agriculture to zoology. As a result, competence conferral, once 'the preserve of esoteric debates amongst specialist

[1] BBC News, 'Guide to the best Euromyths' (BBC News, 23 March 2007), https://perma.cc/9FAJ-6BW9.

[2] Commission Implementing Regulation (EU) No 1333/2011 of 19 December 2011 laying down marketing standards for bananas, rules on the verification of compliance with those marketing standards, and requirements for notifications in the banana sector [2011] OJ L336/23.

[3] Commission Regulation (EEC) No 1677/88 of 15 June 1988 includes quality standards for cucumbers [1988] OJ L 150/21; Commission Implementing Regulation (EU) No 543/2011 of 7 June 2011 describes detailed rules for the application of Council Regulation (EC) No 1234/2007 with respect to the fruit and vegetable sectors (including the processed fruit and vegetable sector) [2011] OJ L157/1.

[4] If you *are* interested, there is plenty of interesting material available at https://ec.europa.eu/info/food-farming-fisheries/food-safety-and-quality_en.

[5] For an entertaining list, see, e.g., S Cross, 'Hippoglossus hippoglossus and chips: Twice please love? Adventures in the underbelly of Euromyths' in R Keeble (ed.), *Communication Ethics Now* (Troubador Publishing 2008).

lawyers',[6] has become a major issue: where do the Union's powers come from? Who gets to exercise them, and how? What limits, if any, are there?

These are questions of fundamental constitutional importance that every legal order has to confront: government in all its branches needs to be empowered to act, but also restrained from abusing that power. In the context of the Union's 'new legal order', 'for the benefit of which the states have limited their sovereign rights, albeit within limited fields',[7] questions of empowerment and restraint take on a particular salience. The Union has no inherent claim to power or 'competence': it can only act where the Member States have delegated their powers to it.

This is the principle of conferral, which we explore in its *empowering dimension* in Debate 1. It is only through Treaty amendment that the Union can be granted additional powers. Conferral thus acts as the key enabler across a wide number of categories and areas. Even when looking at how Member States confer power to a central level, however, we already start to see their anxieties about retaining powers domestically – at least in certain circumstances. Recognising this tension, conferral is also designed to operate as a restraint: the Union cannot act outside its competences. Where powers have *not* been conferred, Member States alone are entitled to act.

While theoretically neat, this limitation causes significant difficulties in practice: in Debate 2, we encounter the tension between the principle of limited conferral and the reality of sweeping competences conferred on the Union. Whilst the ensuing debate about 'competence creep' is often framed in terms of legislation, we invite you to look at the full spectrum of possible Union 'action' (i.e. the exercise of conferred powers). How should the EU go about regulating the curvature of bananas, if it really wanted to do so? Through legislation? By bringing infringement proceedings against Member States who introduce their own banana laws? Or perhaps the question should be left to individual businesses and consumers to petition the CJEU for help in removing trade barriers?[8]

Debate 1

Conferral as *enabling* Union action

Unlike Member States, the EU has no inherent domain or power: it 'lacks what German scholars call *Kompetenz Kompetenz*, the ability to pull itself up legally by its own bootstraps'.[9] The solution to this puzzle is simple and elegant in principle. Union action is enabled through targeted transfers from the Member

[6] T Tridimas, 'Competence after Lisbon: The elusive search for bright lines' in D Ashiagbor, N Countouris, and I Lianos, *The European Union after the Treaty of Lisbon* (Cambridge University Press 2012), p. 47.

[7] Case 26-62 *NV Algemene Transport- en Expeditie Onderneming van Gend en Loos v Netherlands Inland Revenue Administration* [1963] ECR 2.

[8] As explored in Chapter 10, Debate 2.

[9] A Dashwood and others, *Wyatt and Dashwood's European Union Law*, 6th edn (Hart 2011), p. 99.

States: the principle of conferral. The number and scope of powers transferred has grown significantly over the decades, organised today into different categories (to determine, for example, when the Union is to act exclusively or in collaboration with the Member States) and areas. These, in turn, break down into specific legal bases or 'Treaty pegs' – detailed descriptions of individual competences on which all Union action must be based.

(A) Conferral

The Union's lack of inherent powers is clearly reflected in Article 1 TEU. The 'High Contracting Parties' (i.e. the Member States acting through their diplomatic and/or political representatives) establish a Union among themselves and, using the Treaties, 'confer competences to attain' their common objectives. This process is at the heart of the principle of conferral as an *enabler* of joint action in the common interest: the Union can only regulate bananas if, and to the extent to which, the power to do so is listed somewhere in the Treaties.

An important corollary of the principle of conferral is the absence of said *Kompetenz Kompetenz* – the power to determine the scope of competences in the first place. Put simply, the Union cannot legally extend or limit its own powers. Competence changes are the exclusive province of the 27 Member States. In the course of scrutinising the constitutionality of Germany's ratification of the Maastricht Treaty, the German Constitutional Court did not mince its words in spelling out the implications of this legal setup: the Union's common powers derive from the Member States, who are therefore the 'Masters of the Treaties'.[10]

The Union's powers thus come from the Member States. Any additions require explicit Treaty revision. Article 48 TEU sets out the relevant procedure, central to which is a so-called Convention 'composed of representatives of the national Parliaments, of the Heads of State or Government of the Member States, of the European Parliament and of the Commission'.[11] Any ensuing recommendations are then put to a 'conference of representatives of the governments of the Member States', who alone can determine 'by common accord the amendments to be made to the Treaties'. The pre-eminence of the Member States in this process is further underlined by the fact that, even if all governments agree on Treaty amendments, changes can only 'enter into force after being ratified by all the Member States in accordance with their respective constitutional requirements'.[12] Domestic ratification procedures can range from judicial and/or political scrutiny to public referenda, which can

[10] The Union is a 'Staatenverbund, dessen Gemeinschaftsgewalt sich von den Mitgliedstaaten ableitet' … 'Deutschland ist einer der "Herren der Verträge"': BVerfG, 12.10.1993 – 2 BvR 2134/92, 2 BvR 2159/92 (DE).

[11] TEU, Article 48(3).

[12] TEU, Article 48(4).

prove fatal. The Treaty establishing a Constitution for Europe remains unratified following high-profile defeats in both France and the Netherlands in the early summer of 2005.[13]

(B) From Agriculture to Zoology: Union Powers

The phoenix that rose out of these ashes was the Lisbon Treaty, bringing with it significant changes to competence arrangements – at least insofar as their organisation and presentation are concerned. For the first time, the Union's competences were explicitly split across several categories, with each made up of a number of areas that in turn point to specific competences.

Categories and Areas of Union Competence

Article 2 TFEU sets out the general scheme, characterised by exclusive Union competence, competence shared between the Union and the Member States, and a series of supporting and coordinating activities (omitted here):

1. When the Treaties confer on the Union exclusive competence in a specific area, only the Union may legislate and adopt legally binding acts, the Member States being able to do so themselves only if so empowered by the Union or for the implementation of Union acts.
2. When the Treaties confer on the Union a competence shared with the Member States in a specific area, the Union and the Member States may legislate and adopt legally binding acts in that area. The Member States shall exercise their competence to the extent that the Union has not exercised its competence. The Member States shall again exercise their competence to the extent that the Union has decided to cease exercising its competence.

The key distinction drawn concerns the relative distribution of powers. Where the Treaties confer *exclusive competence*, the Member States have ceded their power to the Union level. Article 3 TFEU sets out a relatively short list of areas where that is the case, including the customs union, competition rules within the Internal Market, the conservation of marine biological resources, and (for Member States whose currency is the euro) monetary policy.

In areas of *shared competence*, however, both Member States and the Union are free to legislate, subject to an important proviso of Union priority: Member States may only act to the extent that the Union has not.[14] For present purposes, this is the main category of competences we are interested in; it is here that most difficult constitutional questions arise, and where the vast majority of substantive competences can be found. Article 4(2) TFEU gives a sense of

[13] France (May 2005); Netherlands (June 2005).

[14] Remember this proviso when you read the case law. For example, the CJEU religiously repeats 'in the absence of [Union] rules' when it comes to the principle of National Procedural Autonomy: see, e.g., Case C-33/76 *Rewe-Zentralfinanz eG and Rewe-Zentral AG v Landwirtschaftskammer für das Saarland* [1976] ECR 1989 [5].

what is included: from the Internal Market, agriculture and fisheries to the environment, and the area of freedom, security, and justice.

The remaining areas of competence are more diffuse, including policy coordination in economic, employment, and social policy[15] and supporting, as well as coordinating, actions in fields ranging from industry and culture to education and sport.[16] Union action in these areas does not necessarily take the form of legislation, but it should not be underestimated. Policy coordination, for example, has led to the development of 'soft-law' mechanisms, which can be surprisingly hard-edged (as Portuguese pensioners and Greek trade unionists discovered after the 2008 debt crisis).[17] Support and coordination actions have also led to joyful programmes ranging from Erasmus+, the EU's student exchange and mobility programme,[18] to DiscoverEU, which provides tens of thousands of free Interrail passes to young Europeans on their 18th birthdays.[19]

(C) Member States as (Generous, Yet Anxious) Masters of the Treaties

Cooperation requires compromise – which means both gains and losses in specific battles. In the long run, things more than equal out, especially with scale: mutual cooperation leaves everyone better off. Think of 27 countries, each with a particular national hobby horse – whether it is an ancient law specifying the ingredients for beer or an aversion to workers' rights. In a world of powerful Union competences and qualified majority voting, each of them is set to lose out on occasion when defending these traditions: why should German consumers not be able to try a fine warm English ale, or British employees not enjoy a baseline of protection against a long-hours working culture?

This is why everyone has to be bound by the rules, as the Treaties make clear. The very article which states categorically that 'competences not conferred upon the Union in the Treaties remain with the Member States' also lays down an extensive version of the 'duty of sincere cooperation', including both an undertaking to take positive steps and to refrain from any obstacles to achieving the Treaties' goals.[20]

Put at its most succinct, a commitment to Union membership means the risk of losing one battle in 27, whilst winning the other 26.[21] Objectively, then,

[15] TFEU, Article 5.

[16] TFEU, Article 6.

[17] For a critical review, see, e.g., S Garben, 'The constitutional (im)balance between "the Market" and "the Social" in the European Union' (2017) 13(1) Eur Const L Rev 23.

[18] European Parliament and Council Regulation (EU) No 1288/2013 of 11 December 2013 establishing 'Erasmus+': the Union programme for education, training, youth and sport and repealing Decisions No 1719/2006/EC, No 1720/2006/EC and No 1298/2008/EC [2013] OJ L347/50.

[19] European Youth Portal, 'DiscoverEU', https://perma.cc/B7S4-LL8X.

[20] TEU, Article 4(2)–(3).

[21] Qualified majority skews the stats somewhat, but the overall point holds: European Council, 'Qualified majority', https://perma.cc/2D72-ANXZ.

the bargain is clear: commit to taking the occasional hit, whilst profiting overall. In practice, though, that is much easier said than done. Specific gains might be subtle, long-term, and hard to communicate – whereas losses can show up brutally and quickly, much to the joys of tabloid newspapers and Twitter warriors.

This is the fundamental bind Member State governments find themselves in when conferring powers on the Union. The overall benefits of membership are indisputable, yet even the occasional sacrifice risks local outrage in the short term. How can we square that circle? The Union must have significant powers in order to achieve the ambitious aims Member States have tasked it with – and yet, when push comes to shove, there will be at least one country protesting loudly. This leads to a major clash between law and politics: How does one grant vast powers and then narrowly circumscribe them?

Specific Competences: In Search of a Legal Basis

Merely identifying an *area* of competence is not enough to support Union action: 'The scope of and arrangements for exercising the Union's competences shall be determined by the provisions of the Treaties relating to each area.'[22] The broad headlines in Articles 3–6 TFEU need to be broken down into detailed provisions. To get a sense of what this means in practice, look at Part III of the TFEU. Under the heading of 'Union Policies and Internal Actions', we find more than 170 Treaty articles (i.e. nearly half of the TFEU), conferring powers from the Internal Market to administrative cooperation.[23]

When comparing this list of Union powers today with those conferred in the Treaty of Rome, the story is clear: from environmental protection to consumer law, the 'leitmotif of most of the periodic rounds of Treaty revision' has been competence growth.[24] The Member States, in other words, have clearly been generous. But the closer we look, the more we detect a healthy dose of anxiety mixed in.

Specific competences matter. No action can take place without a clearly identified legal basis. Some Treaty pegs are very straightforward: Article 100(2) TFEU, for example, simply provides that the Union legislature 'may lay down appropriate provisions for sea and air transport' in accordance with the ordinary legislative procedure. When the Commission put forward proposals to protect air passengers' rights in case of flight delays and cancellations, it did so on that legal basis.[25]

In other areas, however, the Treaty can be significantly more prescriptive, including specific goals to be achieved and prescribing details procedures and

[22] TFEU, Article 2(6).

[23] TFEU, Articles 21 and 197, respectively.

[24] S Weatherill, *Law and Values in the European Union* (Oxford University Press 2016), pp. 29–30.

[25] European Parliament and Council Regulation (EC) No 261/2004 of 11 February 2004 establishing common rules on compensation and assistance to passengers in the event of denied boarding and of cancellation or long delays of flights [2004] OJ L46/1.

instruments. This is usually the case where the stakes are high, from fighting the climate crisis to organising relationships between workers and their employers.

Take Article 4(2)(e) TFEU, which confers shared competence for the environment, as an example. 'The environment' is very broad indeed, so we need to turn to Title XX to learn about the details. Here, we find a list of objectives ('preserving, protecting and improving the quality of the environment'; 'protecting human health'; 'combating climate change'), different procedural routes to implement them, and a safeguard provisions for more stringent domestic protective measures (as long as they are compatible with the Treaties), as well as a special legislative procedure where fiscal measures are concerned.[26]

Significant political controversy, as well as major differences in pre-existing regulatory approaches, will often be reflected in highly specific drafting. Article 4(2)(b) TFEU confers another shared competence on the Union, this time covering 'social policy, for the aspects defined in this Treaty'. Take a moment to pause and read through Title X, paying particular attention to Article 153 TFEU: compared to transport policy, Union actions in the field of employment law come with a lot of strings attached.

Article 153(1) TFEU provides a list of very specific competences to tackle a wide range of labour market issues, such as health and safety, working conditions, dismissal protection, and the information and consultation of workers. Article 153(2) TFEU then sets out a list of measures that the Union institutions may adopt (such as coordination initiatives and directives) as well as providing further detail both in terms of substance and procedure. As regards the former, for example, directives can only set out 'minimum requirements for gradual implementation'. They also have to 'avoid imposing administrative, financial and legal constraints in a way which would hold back the creation and development of small and medium-sized undertakings'. As regards the latter, the Commission needs to consult the Economic and Social Committee and the Committee of the Regions, as well as paying attention to specific voting procedures in Council. A measure providing for dismissal protection, for example, requires unanimity, whereas directives providing for the information and consultation of workers can be adopted under qualified majority voting (QMV).

The detailed stipulations go on: there is an alternative legislative route, closely involving the social partners (representatives of management and labour), and an important provision, already familiar from environmental law, that Member States are free to 'maintain or introduce[e] more stringent protective measures' – as long as they are 'compatible with the Treaties', of course.[27] Article 153(5) TFEU, finally, specifically excludes some of the

---

[26] TFEU, Articles 191 and 193, respectively. This explains, for example, the EU's choice of emissions trading schemes over carbon taxes.

[27] In reality, that often translates to little freedom. See Case C-426/11 *Mark Alemo-Herron and ors v Parkwood Leisure Ltd* EU:C:2013:521; J Prassl, 'Freedom of contract as a general principle of EU law? Transfers of undertakings and the protection of employer rights in EU labour law' (2013) 42(4) ILJ 434, 444.

politically most controversial aspects of labour market regulation – including the setting of pay and the right to strike – from the scope of Article 153 TFEU.

***

Present space limitations prohibit a more extensive exploration of specific competences. Even from a quick survey, however, it has become clear that conferral is not merely a mechanism for enabling Union action – it is also central to anxieties about when the EU should *not* act at the expense of Member States' regulatory sovereignty.

Debate 2

Conferral as a *limit* on Union competence

The principle of conferral is designed to act *both* as an enabler and a constraint on the Union's powers. Article 5(2) TEU explains in some more detail how this limitation is to operate:

> Under the principle of conferral, the Union shall act only within the limits of the competences conferred upon it by the Member States in the Treaties to attain the objectives set out therein. Competences not conferred upon the Union in the Treaties remain with the Member States.[28]

When read in combination with the detailed contours of particular Treaty articles, such as the provisions on environmental law and employment law that we have just encountered, the system of conferral thus appears to draw a series of bright red lines: Can the EU legislate on the right to strike or minimum wage laws? No. According to the principle of conferral, it cannot stray beyond the limits of Article 153(5) TFEU.[29]

The reality is significantly more complicated. As Tridimas warns, given 'the complex constitutional model of the EU, the search for bright lines in competence partition is a somewhat Sisyphean task. … A lot depends on the interpretation of the specific provision of the TFEU which serves as the legal basis of EU measures, on the institutional practice, the attitude of the Member States and the response of the ECJ'.[30]

---

[28] See also TEU, Article 5(1), which explains that the 'limits of Union competences are governed by the principle of conferral. The use of Union competences is governed by the principles of subsidiarity and proportionality'. We will explore subsidiarity and proportionality as limits on the exercise of Union powers in the next chapter; for now, our focus is on the principle of conferral.

[29] Note that, in practice, it has attempted to regulate the right to strike – the so-called Monti II proposal (Proposal for a Council Regulation on the exercise of the right to take collective action within the context of the freedom of establishment and the freedom to provide services [2012] COM/2012/0130 final) – on the basis of TFEU, Article 352, and that consultation is ongoing on a Directive to ensure fair minimum wages (https://perma.cc/7LTT-NQSW).

[30] Tridimas, 'Competence after Lisbon' (n 6), p. 77.

This introduces a further dimension to the tension between enabling and constraining central powers: any drawing of red lines will quickly require an umpire to decide when they have been crossed. In the Union legal order, that task falls to the CJEU, which is mandated to ensure that 'in the interpretation and application of the Treaties the law is observed.'[31] It is a role that, at first glance, the Court takes seriously. Remember how the Union legislature has to point to the Treaty peg or 'legal basis' for every new measure proposed, and be prepared to justify its choices in the face of judicial scrutiny?[32] Getting it right, the Court insists, is a matter of 'constitutional significance'.[33]

That said, the central issue at stake in most legal basis disputes has tended to be the question of *which* power ought to be used for a particular measure, rather than establishing the underlying substantive limitations. Historically, this was driven by Community-internal power distribution, both in terms of voting arrangements ('The United Kingdom really will not like the Working Time Directive – can we use Health & Safety as the legal basis, and vote it through under QMV?'[34]) and inter-institutional debates ('Can we, the Member State governments in Council, get away with adopting this Regulation without letting the European Parliament scrutinise the deal?'[35]). Not all commentators seem to have been particularly fascinated by these essentially political games,[36] with one liking legal basis disputes to 'pettifogging 18th Century legal formalism run riot'.[37] Today, the Lisbon Treaty has removed (most of) the incentives for such trickery by adopting QMV for the vast majority of competences, as well as including the European Parliament in the ordinary legislative procedure.[38]

That, however, is not the end of the story: broader concerns about the Union's 'competence creep' continued to be voiced in the literature and political debates, particularly in the run-up to the failed Constitutional Treaty and its subsequent rebirth as the Treaty of Lisbon.[39] Rather than focusing on the ever-generous Masters of the Treaties, however, much of that debate was cast in terms of the role of the CJEU. The charge is relatively straightforward. Whereas the legal basis case law of the CJEU had over the years transformed 'from neg-

[31] TEU, Article 19(1).

[32] The key early decision is Case C-300/89 *European Commission v Council* [1991] ECR I-2867 (*Titanium Dioxide*). In judicial review proceedings, the CJEU will scrutinise both the aim of a measure and its substantive content [10].

[33] Opinion 2/00 of the Court on the Cartagena Protocol [2001] ECR I-9713 [5].

[34] Yes, with minor exceptions: Case C-84/94 *United Kingdom v Council* [1996] ECR I-5755.

[35] See, e.g., Case 5-73 *Balkan-Import-Export GmbH v Hauptzollamt Berlin-Packhof* [1973] ECR 1091.

[36] H Cullen and A Charlesworth, 'Diplomacy by other means: The use of legal basis litigation as a political strategy by the European Parliament and Member States' (1999) 36(6) CML Rev 1243.

[37] N March Hunnings, *The European Courts* (Cartermill International 1996), p. 152, as quoted in K Bradley, 'Powers and procedures in the EU Constitution: Legal bases and the court' in P Craig and G de Búrca (eds), *The Evolution of EU Law*, 2nd edn (Oxford University Press 2011).

[38] See TFEU, Article 289, discussed further in Chapter 3, Debate 1.

[39] S Weatherill, 'Competence creep and competence control' (2004) 23(1) YEL 1.

ligé to straitjacket'[40] when it comes to substantive limitations, *viz* the interpretation of the scope of specific powers referred, it appears to operate more like a free-floating summer tunic: 'the Court has held remarkably steady in attributing as *utile* an *effet* as possible to such provisions, presumably inspired by the dynamic character of the integration project reflected so eloquently in the preambles to the successive founding Treaties.'[41]

The breadth and depth of EU law's incursions into domestic law is rarely disputed.[42] But who is to blame for this competence 'creep'? An obsequious court, happy to nod through even the most egregiously broad readings of Treaty competence? Member State governments, engaged in a two-faced game of blaming 'Brussels' despite having voted for controversial measures?[43] Or is the search for any such 'blame' fundamentally misguided, given the Treaty's architecture of broad, functional competences designed to fuel a dynamic 'process of creating an ever closer union among the peoples of Europe'[44]?

(A) Red Lines ... or Gaping Holes?

Beginning with broad *legislative* powers, two Treaty articles in particular sit uneasily with the principle of conferral. Article 352 TFEU (sometimes referred to as the 'Flexibility' clause) and Article 114 TFEU (also known as the 'Harmonization' or 'Internal Market' clause) both confer potentially open-ended powers on the Union legislature, leading to difficult questions as to their proper boundaries and role in an overall regime of limited powers.

Attaining the Objectives of the Treaties

Article 352 TFEU is the broadest power found in the Treaties:

> If action by the Union should prove necessary, within the framework of the policies defined in the Treaties, to attain one of the objectives set out in the Treaties, and the Treaties have not provided the necessary powers, the Council, acting unanimously on a proposal from the Commission and after obtaining the consent of the European Parliament, shall adopt the appropriate measures.

Given the high-level objectives in Articles 2 and 3 TEU, from peace and the Internal Market to the sustainable development of the Earth and the eradication of poverty, the substantive field of this competence is potentially very broad indeed. Historically, the only potential break on its use was the unanimity requirement in Council. All Member State governments had to agree – which somewhat counterintuitively seems to have encouraged, rather than

[40] Bradley, 'Powers and procedures in the EU Constitution' (n 37), p. 89.
[41] Bradley, 'Powers and procedures in the EU Constitution', p. 107.
[42] However, cf M Bobek, 'EU law in national courts' in M Freedland and J Prassl (eds), *Viking, Laval and Beyond* (Hart 2014).
[43] Albeit in a slightly different context, see M Büchs, 'The open method of coordination as a "two-level game"' (2008) 36(1) Pol Polit 21.
[44] TEU, Article 1.

limited, its use. The article's predecessor provision was not infrequently used to push at the outer limits of (what was then) Community competence, for example in developing early environmental law.[45]

That is not to say that there are *no* limits: crucially, Article 352 TFEU cannot be used to outflank the Article 48 TEU Treaty revision procedure encountered in the last debate. It is not difficult to see the potential temptation for Member State governments keen to confer additional powers on the Union: full Treaty revision is likely to be met with intense political and/or legal scrutiny at home,[46] whereas Article 352 TFEU can be deployed in the relative obscurity of the Council's Europa building – with 'Brussels' conveniently taking the blame for any subsequent fallout.

Whilst the CJEU has generally been content to read the flexibility clause widely, however, a clear line is drawn at covert Treaty revision. In the early 1990s, the Community sought to accede to the European Convention of Human Rights, even though the Treaty did not provide any specific competence on point. Could the institutions rely on Article 352 TFEU instead? No. The provision was merely designed as a gap filler: given the principle of conferral, it could not 'serve as a basis for widening the scope of Community powers beyond … the provisions of the Treaty', especially where the 'effect would, in substance, be to amend the Treaty without following the procedure which it provides for that purpose'.[47]

In addition to this fundamental constitutional limit, the Lisbon Treaty introduced a number of additional procedural safeguards, including in particular a duty to alert national Parliaments to proposals based on Article 352 TFEU.[48] As a result, recourse to the flexibility clause as a legal basis has dwindled in practice; today, it is mostly limited to minor adjustment measures concerning, for example, the deposit of historical materials in the EU's archives or the electronic publication of the Union's official journal.[49] '[A]s a motor of

[45] A Dashwood, 'Article 308 EC as the outer limit of expressly conferred community competence' in C Barnard and O Odudu (eds), *The Outer Limits of European Union Law* (Hart 2009).

[46] See, e.g., the German Bundesverfassungsgericht's Lisbon judgment: BVerfG, 30.06.2009 – 2 BvE 2/08 (DE).

[47] Opinion 2/94 of the Court on the Accession by the Community to the European Convention for the Protection of Human Rights and Fundamental Freedoms [1996] ECR I-1759 [29]–[30]. The Member States *did* of course amend the Treaties and provide for explicit competence: TEU, Article 6(2). The CJEU returned to the question in Opinion 2/13 of the Court on the compatibility of the draft agreement with the EU and FEU Treaties EU:C:2014:2454, and accession still has not taken place. We discuss this extensively in Chapter 8, Debate 1: you might want to return to Opinion 2/94 in light of subsequent events and re-evaluate your analysis of the Court's reasoning.

[48] TFEU, Article 352(2)–(4). Individual Member States may also impose further domestic limits on their government's ability to support Article 352 proposals: see BVerfG Lisbon judgment (n 46).

[49] For an important exception, see Council Recommendation of 8 November 2019 on access to social protection for workers and the self-employed [2019] OJ C387/01. A full list is available at https://perma.cc/6R2M-VAXQ (we found 22 results, as opposed to more than 320 for Article 114 TFEU).

competence creep', Weatherill concludes, 'Article 352 has been drained of most of its poison.'[50]

Establishing the Internal Market

The competence conferred by Article 114 TFEU, on the other hand, continues to serve as a frequently deployed legal basis. It is, on paper at least, not unlimited in substantive scope. It is also much easier to use in practice, as qualified majority support is all that is required:

> Save where otherwise provided in the Treaties, the following provisions shall apply for the achievement of the objectives set out in Article 26.[51] The European Parliament and the Council shall, acting in accordance with the ordinary legislative procedure and after consulting the Economic and Social Committee, adopt the measures for the approximation of the provisions laid down by law, regulation or administrative action in Member States which have as their object the establishment and functioning of the Internal Market.

There follow a number of substantive and procedural specifications and safeguards: Article 114 TFEU cannot be used to legislate in the fields of employment law or free movement, for example, and measures 'concerning health, safety, environmental protection and consumer protection' need to 'take as a base a high level of protection'. Provision is also made for (limited) domestic derogations and expedited judicial review.[52] Overall, however, the picture is clear: Article 114 TFEU provides broad regulatory powers. These have been used to pass measures ranging from cybersecurity[53] and detailed production standards for beverages (including single-malt whisky, 'juniper-flavoured spirit drink[s] produced by flavouring ethyl alcohol of agricultural origin with juniper berries' (aka gin), and *glögg* (mulled wine),[54] to the gig economy[55] and COVID-19 vaccine testing.[56]

---

[50] Weatherill, *Law and Values* (n 24), p. 36.

[51] That is, 'establishing or ensuring the functioning of the Internal Market [... to] comprise an area without internal frontiers in which the free movement of goods, persons, services and capital is ensured'.

[52] TFEU, Article 114(2)–(10).

[53] European Parliament and Council Regulation (EU) 2019/881 of 17 April 2019 on ENISA (the European Union Agency for Cybersecurity) and on information and communications technology cybersecurity certification and repealing Regulation (EU) No 526/2013 (Cybersecurity Act) [2019] OJ L151/15.

[54] European Parliament and Council Regulation (EU) 2019/787 of 17 April 2019 on the definition, description, presentation, and labelling of spirit drinks, the use of the names of spirit drinks in the presentation and labelling of other foodstuffs, the protection of geographical indications for spirit drinks, the use of ethyl alcohol and distillates of agricultural origin in alcoholic beverages, and repealing Regulation (EC) No 110/2008 [2019] OJ L130/1. See Annexes I–III for a weird and wonderful romp through Europe's spirits.

[55] European Parliament and Council Regulation (EU) 2019/1150 of 20 June 2019 on promoting fairness and transparency for business users of online intermediation services [2019] OJ L186/57.

[56] European Parliament and Council Regulation (EU) 2020/1043 of 15 July 2020 on the conduct of clinical trials with and supply of medicinal products for human use containing or consisting of genetically modified organisms intended to treat or prevent coronavirus disease (COVID-19) [2020] OJ L231/12.

We will return to a detailed analysis of the scope of the Internal Market as defined in Article 26 TFEU in Chapter 9. Suffice it to say that its fundamental economic freedoms have consistently been interpreted in a generous fashion. Translated into the present context, does this mean that the Union legislature enjoys a 'general power to regulate the Internal Market' on the basis of Article 114 TFEU?[57] Not quite.

In *Tobacco Advertising I*, the German government set out to challenge a directive banning most forms of advertising for tobacco products, enacted under Article 114 TFEU's predecessor provision, Article 100a EC.[58] The Directive's real goal, it alleged, was not the promotion of the Internal Market, but the protection of public health: the measure therefore fell outside the scope of conferred competences and should be annulled accordingly.[59] AG Fennelly urged careful scrutiny. The Internal Market provisions were to be interpreted generously, and not limited to deregulation and liberalisation. At the same time, however, they could not become 'a general ... regulatory power', offering '*carte blanche* ... to harmonise any national rules that meet the eye'.[60]

The Court agreed. In order to rely on Article 114 TFEU, a

> measure ... must genuinely have as its object the improvement of the conditions for the establishment and functioning of the Internal Market. If a mere finding of disparities between national rules and of the abstract risk of obstacles to the exercise of fundamental freedoms or of distortions of competition liable to result therefrom were sufficient to justify the choice of Article 100a as a legal basis, judicial review of compliance with the proper legal basis might be rendered nugatory. The Court would then be prevented from ... ensuring that the law is observed in the interpretation and application of the Treaty.[61]

This is a crucial threshold: simply pointing to different rules in different Member States is not enough to give the Union regulatory competence. What is required instead is demonstrable impact on cross-frontier trade *viz* the genuine 'improvement of the conditions for the establishment and functioning of the Internal Market', including the prevention of 'future obstacles to trade' and the elimination of 'appreciable' distortions to competition.[62] On the facts of the case, the legislator was unable to show that the Directive had contributed to eliminating obstacles to free movement and removing distortions of competition. The measure was annulled accordingly.[63]

---

[57] Case C-376/98 *Germany v European Parliament and Council* [2000] ECR I-8419 (*Tobacco Advertisement I*) [83].

[58] European Parliament and Council Directive 98/43/EC of 6 July 1998 on the approximation of the laws, regulations and administrative provisions of the Member States relating to the advertising and sponsorship of tobacco products [1998] OJ L213/9.

[59] *Tobacco Advertisement I* (n 57), [13]–[34].

[60] *Tobacco Advertisement I*, Opinion of AG Fennelly [83]–[89].

[61] *Tobacco Advertisement I*, [84].

[62] *Tobacco Advertisement I*, [83], [86], [106].

[63] *Tobacco Advertisement I*, [96]–[116].

Where does this leave us? Commentators disagree. Is *Tobacco Advertising I*, the decision of 'a true constitutional court whose role is to police the fine boundaries between Union and Member State competence'?[64] Or does it provide 'little more than a "drafting guide" for a legislature which finds it all too easy to assert compliance' with the principle of conferral?[65] The empirical evidence suggests that, despite the sharp rebuke in *Tobacco Advertising I*, the Court is content to countenance a generous interpretation of the harmonisation clause. Germany's follow-up challenge to a hastily redrafted directive setting out marginally narrower bans on tobacco advertising was unsuccessful,[66] and subsequent cases have readily accepted arguments as to the future emergence of trade barriers.[67]

Is this competence creep at its worst? Who, if anyone, is to blame? In answering these questions, it is important to consider several elements of the broader background. First, what is at stake? *Tobacco Advertising*, it is fair to say, *was* a genuine constitutional challenge. Germany had *not* transferred the power to make public health regulations to the Union. The majority of other competence challenges, on the other hand, are not necessarily driven by such noble motives. Airline operators, for example, do not care about the finer points of the Union's balance of powers – they seek to protect their shareholders' profits from passenger rights pay-outs.[68]

Second, consider the fact that despite repeated protests, the Member States have never taken active steps to limit the broad legislative competence first introduced as Article 100a EEC in 1986. The Laeken Declaration on the Future of the European Union, which paved the way for the Convention on the Future of Europe and thus ultimately the Treaty of Lisbon, had explicitly highlighted the need 'to clarify, simplify and adjust the division of competence between the Union and the Member States in the light of the new challenges facing the Union', and gone as far as singling out the predecessor provisions of Articles 352 and 114 TFEU for special scrutiny.[69] Yet when the Draft Constitutional Treaty emerged from extensive Convention discussions some two years later, preciously little had changed: suggestions of a 'hard list' of Union competences or exclusive Member State domains had been ruled out as practically unworkable, as was the deletion of broad legislative powers.[70] This is

[64] Dashwood and others (n 9), *Wyatt and Dashwood's European Union Law*, p. 108.

[65] S Weatherill, 'The limits of legislative harmonization ten years after *Tobacco Advertising*: How the Court's case law has become a "drafting guide"' (2011) 12(2) German LJ 827, 828.

[66] Case C-380/03 *Germany v European Parliament and Council* [2006] ECR I-11573 (*Tobacco Advertisement II*).

[67] Case C-58/08 *The Queen on the Application of Vodafone and ors v Secretary of State for Business, Enterprise and Regulatory Reform* [2010] ECR I-4999.

[68] For details of this long-running saga, see J Prassl, 'The European Union and The Montreal Convention: A new analytical framework' (2013) 12(3) Issues Aviation L Pol'y 381.

[69] European Commission, 'Presidency conclusions: European Council meeting in Laeken 14 and 15 December 2001' [2001] DOC/01/18.

[70] Weatherill, 'Competence creep and competence control' (n 39), provides an incredibly helpful guide to the twists and turns of a saga which would otherwise risk 'submerging a bewildered reader in the sheer volume of material': 19ff.

not to say that nothing had changed. We have already encountered some of the modifications that ensued, including notably a much clearer distinction between different categories of Union competence, and the inclusion of additional procedural safeguards for Article 352 TFEU. Overall, however, 'the dominant concern was evidently to secure clarification of key organizing principles, not a radical setting aside of the essence of the current system [...] flawed much more in its presentation than its practice.'[71]

Most importantly, the fault might not lie with the Court, or any one actor in the system, but rather the overall design of *what* is conferred and *how* those powers have been developed in practice.[72] The Treaties are, depending on your preferred imagery, frameworks (*traités cadres*) or a skeleton, to the bones of which flesh has to be added.[73] Viewed thus, the strict instruction only to use the powers conferred quickly becomes meaningless where the powers in question include just about anything. This is not an accident – but (Member State) design.

(B) Competence Creep Revisited

So far, our focus has been on competence creep through legislative activity. A full appreciation of the phenomenon, however, should not be limited thus. The principle of conferral encompasses *all* Union action, and the Treaties do not merely confer powers on the Union institutions – in some sense, they confer powers on all of us, whether as citizens or traders.

In 'Competence Creep Revisited', Sacha Garben spells out the manifold areas in which competence creep could be said to occur beyond legislative powers: from the case law of the CJEU to international agreements, soft law, economic governance mechanisms, and parallel integration.[74] Technically speaking, these are fundamentally different mechanisms (and thus mostly beyond the scope of an introductory EU law course). Yet they all 'induce the approximation of national laws, regulations and/or administrative practices by reference to a common [European] norm'.[75]

The concern here is once more for Member State regulatory autonomy – which requires restraint on central powers, and sits in tension with the coherent development of a well-functioning and effective Union. For present purposes, we can illustrate this tension with reference to the Court's case law in two areas: EU citizenship and the free movement provisions. We will explore

[71] Weatherill, 'Competence creep and competence control', p. 21. This is evidently a very different story from the rules relating to the *exercise* of Union competences: see discussion on subsidiarity and the yellow card mechanism in the next chapter.

[72] P Craig, 'Competence and Member State Autonomy: Causality, Consequence and Legitimacy' in B de Witte and H Micklitz (eds), *The European Court of Justice and the Autonomy of Member States* (Intersentia 2011).

[73] Case C-411/05 *Félix Palacios de la Villa v Cortefiel Servicios SA* [2007] ECR I-8531, Opinion of AG Mazák [85].

[74] S Garben, 'Competence creep revisited' (2019) 57(2) JCMS 205, 206.

[75] Garben, 'Competence creep revisited', 207.

these topics in depth in subsequent chapters.[76] For now, let us look at their interaction with Member State regulatory powers in a number of highly sensitive domains: from immigration and sport to labour market regulation. Is there anything that is entirely exempt from EU law influence?

Citizenship

Article 20 TFEU establishes Union citizenship: 'Every person holding the nationality of a Member State shall be a citizen of the Union.' A wide range of rights come with this status: from voting and free movement, to a broad prohibition against 'discrimination on grounds of nationality'[77] – a powerful tool in the hand of individual litigants faced with Member State powers.

The CJEU has been generous in interpreting Article 20 TFEU, to put it mildly. In *Ruiz Zambrano*, Belgium sought to deport a Colombian family, at least one of whose children had been born during their time in Belgium and was therefore a European citizen.[78] The family could not point to any cross-border activity. This was, in technical terms, a so-called purely internal situation – and thus an area in which Member States were free to determine without Union interference. The relevant directive on citizens' (and their family members') rights was inapplicable.[79]

Yet the Court disagreed with Belgium's assertion that the situation therefore lay within domestic regulatory competence: 'Article 20 TFEU precludes national measures which have the effect of depriving citizens of the Union of the genuine enjoyment of the substance of the rights conferred by virtue of their status as citizens of the Union.'[80] Deporting the parents would have precisely that effect: the toddlers would have to come with them, thus no longer being able to enjoy the benefits of their Union citizenship. The absence of Union competence to regulate the specific question of third country migration was irrelevant. Belgian law could not be allowed to interfere with rights granted in the Treaties.

Obstacles to Free Movement

Similarly stark examples abound in the Internal Market context, where *negative* integration can go deep into Member State regulatory competence even when there has been no explicit conferral of competence on the Union in a particular field. In *Mary Carpenter*, the UK Home Secretary was stopped from deporting a Philippine national who had broken immigration rules because doing so

[76] Specifically, Chapters 9 and 10.

[77] TFEU, Article 18.

[78] European Parliament and Council Directive 2004/38/EC of 29 April 2004 on the right of citizens of the Union and their family members to move and reside freely within the territory of the Member States amending Regulation (EEC) No 1612/68 and repealing Directives 64/221/EEC, 68/360/EEC, 72/194/EEC, 73/148/EEC, 75/34/EEC, 75/35/EEC, 90/364/EEC, 90/365/EEC and 93/96/EEC [2004] OJ L158/77.

[79] Case C-34/09 *Gerardo Ruiz Zambrano v ONEM* [2011] ECR I-1177.

[80] *Ruiz Zambrano* [42].

would have violated her husband's free movement rights. Once the case was thus brought within the scope of EU law, the government's decision was subjected to full scrutiny, including the Union's fundamental rights apparatus.[81]

In *Bosman*, the Court struck down long-established rules on inter-club transfers, controlled by international football associations including FIFA and UEFA, usually requiring payment of significant transfer fees.[82] The fact that the Community had no competence in the field of sport was irrelevant – the question at hand concerned football players' free movement rights under Article 45 TFEU.[83] The case thus fell within the scope of EU law, requiring the Court carefully to scrutinise the transfer regime. The Court concluded that its operation could not be excluded from the scope of free movement law.[84] Competence concerns do not end here. The effects of such landmark decisions are not limited to an individual incursion in a particular case – they can trigger substantive involvement across the field. When it comes to sports law, for example, '*Bosman* changed everything'.[85]

Perhaps the starkest competence issues arise in areas where the Member States have not merely been silent in not conferring a particular power to the Union, but where they have spelled out explicit carve-outs. Remember how Article 153(5) TFEU excludes its application to 'the right of association, the right to strike or the right to impose lock-outs'? In *Viking Line*,[86] an international seafarer's union had organised industrial action against the eponymous ferry operator in response to a proposed 'reflagging' – the changing of a ship's registration to a lower-wage Member State, with a view to undermining workers' collective agreements. The strike was entirely lawful as a matter of Finnish law, but Viking Lines alleged a breach of its freedom of establishment under Article 49 TFEU. The strike was, after all, designed to stop the reflagging of the vessel Rosella from Finland to Estonia. The Court of Justice agreed that the strike action fell within the scope of EU law:

> even if, in the areas which fall outside the scope of [Union] competence, the Member States are still free, in principle, to lay down the conditions governing the existence and exercise of the rights in question, the fact remains that, when exercising that competence, the Member States must nevertheless comply with [EU] law.

---

[81] Case C-60/00 *Mary Carpenter v Secretary of State for the Home Department* [2002] ECR I-6279.

[82] Case C-415/93 *Union royale belge des sociétés de football association ASBL v Jean-Marc Bosman, Royal club liégeois SA v Jean-Marc Bosman and ors* and *UEFA v Jean-Marc Bosman* [1995] ECR I-4921.

[83] *Bosman* [78].

[84] *Bosman* [114].

[85] S Weatherill, 'Bosman changed everything: The rise of EC Sports Law' in MP Maduro and L Azoulai (eds), *The Past and Future of EU Law: The Classics of EU Law Revisited on the 50th Anniversary of the Rome Treaty* (Hart 2010), p. 481.

[86] Case C-438/05 *International Transport Workers' Federation and Finnish Seamen's Union v Viking Line ABP and OÜ Viking Line Eesti* [2007] ECR I-10779 (*Viking Line*).

The Article 153(5) TFEU exclusion was irrelevant and could not 'exclude collective action such as that at issue in the main proceedings from the application of Article [49 TFEU].'[87] The unions which had engaged in an entirely lawful strike under domestic law, operating in an area where the Member States had explicitly excluded harmonisation, nonetheless found themselves in the crosshairs of EU law – with disastrous consequences.[88]

***

These high-profile cases are but the tip of the iceberg. And yet, as Garben rightly concludes, all forms of competence creep identified are 'perfectly *legal*', for good reason: 'as policy areas are not watertight compartments but closely interrelated [...] such "spill-over" or "cross-cutting" may be inevitable for effective government.'[89] The real problem, then, is not so much a competence battle between the Union and its Member States, but rather the exercise of power by national executives (acting under the guise of the Union institutions), courts, and (we would add) individual citizens and traders – 'particularly to the extent that they displace ... the national and European legislator.'[90] Her prescription to remedy the situation is clear: We should stop tinkering with existing categories of competence, 'dispose of demarcation as a way to contain EU action and instead [...] openly recognise the inevitable broadness of the EU's powers while containing the exercise of these powers through democratising the legislative process'.[91]

(C) Regulating Bananas – Properly

Such democratisation could go a long way towards addressing questions of *legitimacy*. But there is a broader issue which we should briefly highlight in closing. In practice, unbalanced competence creep can lead to a breakdown of the carefully calibrated interaction between different methods of market integration, and thus remove even the most sensitive topics from the reach of *any* legislature – whether at the domestic or the European level.

We will return to different regulatory mechanisms in detail when looking at the Internal Market in Chapter 10, but the key concern can nonetheless be explained quickly. Imagine (hypothetically!) that each of the 27 Member States *has* decided to regulate banana curvature. Chances are that they have chosen different standards, making life more difficult for producers and ultimately more expensive for customers. There are, broadly speaking, two ways in which

[87] *Viking Line* [40]–[41]. We return to *Viking Line* and its extensive political and legislative aftermath in Chapter 3. And contrast this with the Court's earlier approach in Case C-67/96 *Albany International BV v Stichting Bedrijfspensioenfonds Textielindustrie* [1999] ECR I-5751, where matters of collective labour relations were found to fall outside the scope of the competition law provisions.

[88] K Apps, 'Damages claims against trade unions after *Viking* and *Laval*' (2009) 34(1) EL Rev 141.

[89] Garben, 'Competence creep revisited' (n 74), 213.

[90] Garben, 'Competence creep revisited', 214.

[91] S Garben, 'Confronting the competence conundrum: Democratising the European Union through an expansion of its legislative powers' (2015) 35(1) *OJLS* 55, 57.

this problem could be addressed within EU law.[92] Under a model of *negative integration*, traders would enlist the Court in challenging the different rules as a violation of their free movement rights – national rules on product standards constitute measures equivalent to quantitative restrictions, and are therefore caught by Article 34 TFEU. Unless the Member State in question could justify the rules (which, in practice, it rarely will), the CJEU would strike them down. The Internal Market, in other words, would have gone from having 27 rules on banana curvature to none – consumer choice (in theory) and market power (in practice) have replaced national regulation.

When it comes to the curvature of bananas, we might not think of that as particularly worrying. But what about potentially carcinogenic pesticides used to extend their shelf life? It is here that Article 114 TFEU and related legislative competences play an important role in ensuring *positive integration*: 27 different standards can be harmful, but so can the complete absence of rules. A Banana Safety Directive could square the circle, laying down a single regime applicable to fruit pesticides across all 27 national markets. National regulators would still get to have a say, as would trade organisations and consumer representatives: we are about to discover the intricacies of the Union's approach to polycentric standard setting.

Competence creep, particularly in the field of negative harmonisation,[93] can quickly break this model. Think back to the Court's decision in *Viking*, which put severe limits on the right to strike in cross-border scenarios. Through an expansive reading of the Freedom of Establishment, such industrial action had become *prima facie* illegal, with an obligation (impossible to discharge in practice) on the Trade Union to justify any interference with employers' economic freedoms as legitimate and proportionate. Despite a lack of explicit competence to legislate on the right to strike, the Court had with a single stroke *de facto* outlawed the exercise of a near-universally recognised fundamental right.[94]

As the Monti Report on the Future of the Internal Market realised, this quickly 'brought to the surface the strains to which the current regulatory framework for posting of workers is subject, in a context of divergent social and employment conditions among Member States and acute sensitivity about the perceived risks of social dumping and unfair competition.'[95] Yet there was little

---

[92] For a much more detailed account, see Chapter 17 in S Weatherill, *Cases & Materials on EU Law*, 12th edn (Oxford University Press 2016).

[93] But by no means exclusively: 'soft law' measures, particularly those insulated from judicial and/or political scrutiny, have similar effects. Garben, 'Competence creep revisited' (n 74), 216–18. For a specific case study in the context of the Greek bailouts, and their (arguably illegal) influence on EU law as implemented domestically, see N Countouris and others, *Report on Collective Dismissals: A Comparative and Contextual Analysis of the Law on Collective Redundancies in 13 European Countries* (ILO 2016).

[94] Including in the Union's own Charter of Fundamental Rights: CFR, Article 28.

[95] M Monti, 'A new strategy for the single market: At the service of Europe's economy and society' (European Commission, 9 May 2010), p. 68.

the Union legislature could do to address the problem and provide for a more nuanced approach to balancing fundamental human rights and fundamental economic freedoms. A proposed 'Monti II' regulation was resolutely opposed by a majority of Member States, employer representatives, and trade unions – albeit for diametrically opposed reasons – before the debate had even reached any legal basis challenge.[96]

Conclusion: Competence Creep as a Bug, or Feature?

Competence creep is a concern to be taken seriously. It can create real problems for the exercise of Union powers, albeit not necessarily the ones we encounter at first glance. Like the notion of the Union's democratic deficit (more on which in Chapter 3), competence creep is an easy slogan, but it is much less clear how the perceived problems should be solved.

In deciding where you stand on the debates we have encountered, remember always that political and legal choices surrounding conferral are marked by the tension between enabling and empowering the institutions, on the one hand, and restraining them and limiting the domains in which their regulatory power can be exercised, on the other. Member State governments explicitly recognised this in the Laeken declaration:

> [T]here is the question of how to ensure that a redefined division of competence does not lead to a creeping expansion of the competence of the Union or to encroachment upon the exclusive areas of competence of the Member States [...] How are we to ensure at the same time that the European dynamic does not come to a halt? In the future as well, the Union must continue to be able to react to fresh challenges and developments, and must be able to explore new policy areas.

The growth of the Union's powers did not take place by accident, and has rarely been challenged as genuinely excessive or inappropriate. In the run-up to the Brexit referendum, the UK government commissioned an extensive 'Review of the Balance of Competences between the UK and the EU', designed to create a 'clear sense of how [the UK's] national interests interact with the EU's roles' and which competences should be repatriated. Following two years' worth of hearings and enquiries, as well as 32 reports covering every conceivable area of Union competence, the result was surprising (to some at least): the balance of competences, the exercise concluded, was broadly right.[97]

None of this should be taken as a suggestion that the challenges raised by conferral in practice are not important matters for legal and constitutional

[96] Monti II proposal (n 29). Fully aware of the constraints of Article 153(5) TFEU, the Commission had picked Article 352 TFEU as the proposed legal basis.

[97] UK Government, 'Review of the balance of competences', https://www.gov.uk/government/collections/review-of-the-balance-of-competences.

debates: plenty of unease remains, notably with domestic judiciaries.[98] At the same time, however, think back to Schumann and Monnet's grand plans in the previous Chapter. Perhaps competence creep is not a bug, but a feature of European integration.

Further reading

Steve Weatherill traces the first decade after *Tobacco Advertising No 1* and concludes that the constitutionally important limits laid down in the landmark case have not lived up to their promise: 'The Limits of Legislative Harmonization Ten Years after Tobacco Advertising: How the Court's Case Law Has become a "Drafting Guide"' (2011) 12(2) German LJ 827. Do you agree?

Perhaps the answer to the 'competence conundrum' which we have encountered is not further tinkering, *Laeken*-style, but a radical rethink of the Union's legislative power setup? This interesting thought is developed by Sacha Garben in 'Confronting the Competence Conundrum: Democratising the European Union through an Expansion of its Legislative Powers' (2015) 35(1) OJLS 55.

For a full and intriguing account of the difficulties encountered in the legislative response to *Viking and Laval*, see 'The life of a death foretold: The proposal for a Monti II regulation' in M Freedland and J Prassl, *EU Law in the Member States: Viking, Laval and Beyond* (Hart 2015) – written frankly and anonymously by the Regulation's 'Adoptive Parents'. On the saga itself, see ACL Davies, 'One Step Forward, Two Steps Back? The *Viking* and *Laval* Cases in the ECJ' (2008) 37(2) ILJ 126.

[98] See, e.g., the BVerfG in *Manfred Brunner and ors v European Union Treaty (Cases 2 BvR 2134/92 & 2159/92)* [1994] I CMLR 57, and the debates in Chapter 6.

CHAPTER 3

Inside the Sausage Factory
EU Law-Making, Political and Legal Safeguards, and Democracy

Laws, Bismarck suggested, are like sausages: best not watch their production too closely.[1] EU food regulation may have changed his mind – today, the process is pretty sanitary, if also considerably more complex.[2] In consequence, peddlers of Euro-myths tend to be particularly fond of the Union's regulation of various foodstuffs. The common story is that 'Brussels' is forcing Member States to give up their beloved foods – be it prawn cocktail crisps or 'Bombay mix' – through excessive regulation.[3] The pervasive caricatures of EU food regulation are telling. Food encodes a range of cultural meanings: what we are prepared to consume reflects our 'social identifies, and ... membership of social groups'.[4] It is not surprising that national politicians are tempted to take up arms, pledging to defend their country's 'eating habits' against 'Brussels' meddling'.[5]

But are we really being force-fed an unhealthy diet of EU law by the 'Eurocrats', in a process that is top-down and undemocratic? Union rules can be complex and elaborate, for sure – the EU's chemicals regulation runs to over 849 pages.[6] However, there is good reason for this: scientific and technological progress raise intricate regulatory questions, and the Member States do

[1] Sausage producers feel unfairly tainted by this association: R Pear, 'If only laws were like sausages' (*The New York Times*, 4 December 2010), https://perma.cc/ZV3M-UX6Q.

[2] An overview of measures aimed at streamlining food hygiene regulation is available at https://ec.europa.eu/food/safety/biosafety/food_hygiene_en.

[3] K Lyons, 'The 10 best Euro myths – From custard creams to condoms' (*The Guardian*, 23 June 2016), https://perma.cc/RQK4-3CFY.

[4] A Murcott, 'Symposium on "food habits and culture in the UK": The cultural significance of food and eating' (1982) 41 Proc Nutr Soc 203, 203–04.

[5] Lyons, 'The 10 best Euro myths' (n 3).

[6] European Parliament and Council Regulation (EC) No 1907/2006 of 18 December 2006 concerning the Registration, Evaluation, Authorisation and Restriction of Chemicals (REACH), establishing a European Chemicals Agency, amending Directive 1999/45/EC and repealing Council Regulation (EEC) No 793/93 and Commission Regulation (EC) No 1488/94 as well as Council Directive 76/769/EEC and Commission Directives 91/155/EEC, 93/67/EEC, 93/105/EC and 2000/21/EC [2006] OJ L396/1.

not always trust each other to pursue agreed policy objectives faithfully.[7] Perhaps, then, the 'Brussalo'[8] coming after Member States' regulatory sovereignty is just as fictional a monstrous creature as Donaldson and Scheffler's Gruffalo.

We consider this question by examining, in Debate 1, the EU law-making process. Who, ultimately, gets to decide on the regulatory proposals to be debated by legislators, and which actors are entrusted with law-making powers? Is power, in this regard, truly (or overly) centralised? We then assess, in Debate 2, the different avenues available to those seeking to challenge 'Brussels', including both political and legal restraints on the Union's law-making powers. Debate 3 explores the allegation, not infrequently levelled, that the Union suffers from a democratic deficit. Should we insist on more democratic accountability, analogous to standards imposed on the nation-state?

Debate 1

Is EU law-making overly centralised?

Rupert Murdoch, the American media mogul, is no fan of the EU. The explanation, he once quipped, is simple: 'When I go into Downing Street [the seat of the UK government] they do what I say; when I go to Brussels they take no notice'.[9] His answer tells us a great deal about national politics, but also about the nature of the Brussels polity. Complexity can act as a safeguard against outsized political influence: there are simply too many pressure points in the EU legislative process for a single actor to insist on a particular outcome. This limits the risk of powerful individuals or interests exercising undue influence on policymakers.[10] But does it also mean that EU law-making is overcentralised?

There is a tendency to speak of EU law-making as something that happens 'over there' – in Brussels, a city 'seen as a distant, unfamiliar, even threatening place, populated by antagonistic strangers with different interests and goals'.[11] The *Leave* campaign's slogan to 'take back control from Brussels' in the 2016 Brexit referendum speaks precisely to this sense of alienation from EU

[7] K Bradley, 'Legislating in the European Union' in C Barnard and S Peers (eds), *European Union Law*, 3rd edn (Oxford University Press 2020).

[8] A Scheffler, 'There's no such thing as a Brusselo!' (*The Guardian*, 23 June 2016), https://perma.cc/46BZ-H7K9.

[9] As cited in A Hilton, 'Stay or go – The lack of solid facts means it's all a leap of faith' (*Evening Standard*, London, 25 February 2016).

[10] This is not to say that EU decision-making is free from lobbying. See, e.g., D Coen and J Richardson, *Lobbying the European Union: Institutions, Actors and Issues* (Oxford University Press 2009), and the following note, in this debate, on the Commission's impact assessments.

[11] D Kenealy and F Hayes-Renshaw, 'How policies are made' in D Kenealy, J Peterson, and R Corbett (eds), *The European Union: How Does It Work?*, 5th edn (Oxford University Press 2018), p. 124.

law-making, as does Eurosceptic populism elsewhere in Europe.[12] Yet, we know from the previous chapter that the EU is founded on the principle of conferral, meaning that it can only act insofar as the Member States have delegated their powers to it. Why then does the myth of 'Brussels dictates' persist?

The short answer is that the Union institutions provide a convenient scapegoat for national actors, even when they have been fully involved in the decision-making process. Should a particular policy outcome prove to be unpopular, national politicians can simply blame it on 'faceless Eurocrats'. If a measure turns out to be popular, on the other hand, national governments will be quick to take the credit.[13] 'Rip-off card charges will be consigned to history, after Ministers act to end these unfair fees for millions of people across the country', a UK government press release proudly proclaimed in July 2017 – conveniently ignoring the fact that they had had no choice but to do so under the EU's Payment Services Directive.[14] The political gamble is based on an assumption that EU law and the processes underpinning it are misunderstood. But how *does* the EU law-making machinery actually work?

(A) EU Legal Acts: From Cradle to Adulthood

At first glance, the life of an EU act appears fairly simple: it starts as a legislative proposal initiated by the Commission; the European Parliament and the Council co-decide on it; and finally, the Member States implement it as and when required. This is the so-called ordinary legislative procedure – the default legislative method that produces regulations, directives, and decisions.[15] When it comes to particularly sensitive policy areas, such as fiscal matters or competition law, a special legislative procedure applies instead: here, the Council is the sole legislator and the European Parliament is merely consulted.[16] So far, so 'Mondrianesque' – clear and straightforward.[17]

Yet upon closer examination, EU law-making is more like a Pollock painting – complex and all over the place. To start with, legislative power can be delegated to the Commission for the adoption of delegated and implementing measures, which, because of their departure from the legislative procedures described previously, are called 'non-legislative acts'. Delegated acts are adopted by the Commission in consultation with national experts.[18] Although the Commission (and in exceptional cases, the Council) also takes the lead on

[12] R Csehi and E Zgut, '"We won't let Brussels dictate us": Eurosceptic populism in Hungary and Poland' (2021) 22 Eur Polit Soc 53.
[13] Kenealy and Hayes-Renshaw, 'How policies are made' (n 11).
[14] UK Government, 'Rip-off card charges to be outlawed,' https://www.gov.uk/government/news/rip-off-card-charges-to-be-outlawed.
[15] TFEU, Articles 289 and 294.
[16] TFEU, Article 289(2).
[17] See Chapter 1, Debate 2.
[18] TFEU, Article 290.

implementing acts, the process is subject to the complex Neo-Comitology Regulation,[19] which grants committees of Member State government representatives extensive co-decision powers.[20] The reason for delegation is to ease the burden on legislators and allow for the quick revision of existing legislation. The obvious downside is a lack of transparency, especially in the workings of the committees.

Additionally, specialised agencies have gained considerable significance in the EU decision-making process. There are more than 30 agencies under the auspices of the Commission,[21] covering a wide range of fields, from environmental statistics to veterinary pharmacology, and specialist roles, from the gathering and dissemination of information to product authorisation.[22] Although the agencies are accountable for their financial management to the Court of Auditors, and the European Parliament receives their reports and holds hearings, the lack of transparency and accountability of agencies continues to raise eyebrows.[23]

There are also miscellaneous organisations, such as the European Standardisation Organisations (ESOs), which do not fall under the umbrella of any EU institution but which are mandated by the Commission to, for example, define and test various product standards that are then endorsed in legislative and nonlegislative acts. Standard setting is an important business (consider, for example, the A4 requirement for sheets of paper) but the relationship between the independent ESOs and the EU institutions, in terms of law-making, is far from straightforward. On what basis may the Commission delegate standardisation to private bodies? And what are the legal implications for national standardisation bodies keen on conflicting standards?[24]

Clearly, the broad notion of EU law encompasses many different legislative and non-legislative processes, involving different actors and questions of accountability and transparency. To consider each and every decision-making process goes beyond the ambitions of this book. We will, however, return to these various acts in the next debate when considering ways in which they can be challenged through political and legal means. For now, we focus instead on the ordinary legislative procedure and ask: who is this 'Brussels' that decides on EU laws?

---

[19] European Parliament and Council Regulation (EU) No 182/2011 of 16 February 2011 laying down the rules and general principles concerning mechanisms for control by Member States of the Commission's exercise of implementing powers [2011] OJ L55/13.
[20] TFEU, Article 291.
[21] An overview is available at https://europa.eu/european-union/about-eu/agencies_en.
[22] M Shapiro, 'Independent agencies' in P Craig and G de Búrca (eds), The *Evolution of EU Law*, 2nd edn (Oxford University Press 2011), p. 111.
[23] Shapiro, 'Independent agencies', p. 117.
[24] Case C-613/14 *James Elliott Construction Limited v Irish Asphalt Limited* EU:C:2016:821 [43].

(B) Initiating Legislation: Starting the Production Line

The basic rule is that 'Union legislative acts may only be adopted on the basis of a Commission proposal, except where the Treaties provide otherwise'.[25] This grants the Commission a powerful agenda-setting role. But does it mean that EU laws are 'dictated by Brussels' – that is, a single EU institution? What processes are in place to ensure that different stakeholders' views are taken into account in making polycentric decisions?

At the outset of a new legislative project, the Commission undertakes extensive impact assessments (which can easily run to 200 pages or more[26]) to estimate, *ex ante,* the anticipated effects of its regulatory proposals in terms of economic, social, and environmental implications. This involves engaging with relevant stakeholders and considering the costs, benefits, and risks of proposals, as well as exploring alternative policy avenues.[27] It also creates a space for lobbyists to influence and shape the regulatory agenda. When the Commission began in 2009 to revise the 2001 Tobacco Product Directive, the process took 5 years, with Philip Morris International alone employing more than 160 lobbyists to subvert the Directive.[28] Brussels has been crowned the 'lobbying capital of Europe'.[29] Stroll down the Rue de la Loi and marvel at the range of outfits: from a 'European Cockpit Association' to the 'Toy Industries of Europe'.[30]

But it is not just lobbyists that get involved. A broad range of actors are consulted in the process, from academic specialists and social partners to citizens.[31] The Commission's recent proposal for a European Climate Law, for example, draws on nearly 1000 contributions from citizens,[32] and the fact that 'Europe's citizens have continued to call for stronger climate action'[33] was

[25] TEU, Article 17(2). In limited circumstances, EU legislative acts can be initiated at the request of a group of Member States or the CJEU or pursuant to a recommendation by the European Central Bank: TFEU, Article 289(4).

[26] See, e.g., European Commission, 'Commission staff working document: Impact assessment accompanying the Proposal for a Directive of the European Parliament and of the Council on transparent and predictable working conditions in the European Union' [2017] SWD/2017/478 final.

[27] J Torriti and R Löfstedt, 'The first five years of the EU Impact Assessment system: A risk economics perspective on gaps between rationale and practice' (2012) 15(2) J Risk Res 169.

[28] S Peeters and others, 'The revision of the 2014 European tobacco products directive: An analysis of the tobacco industry's attempts to "break the health silo"' (2015) 25(1) Tob Control 108.

[29] O Hoedeman, 'The world of EU lobbying in Brussels' (*HesaMag*, Brussels, Autumn-Winter 2018), https://perma.cc/5G4F-TUEW.

[30] An overview of EU lobbyists is available at https://www.integritywatch.eu/organizations.

[31] See e.g. in the context of social policy TFEU, Article 154.

[32] European Commission, 'European climate law', https://perma.cc/G2GW-LKVX.

[33] European Commission, 'Commission staff working document: Impact assessment accompanying the Communication from the Commission to the European Parliament, the Council, the European Economic and Social Committee and the Committee of the Regions on steeping up Europe's 2030 climate ambition' [2020] SWD/2020/176 final, 3.

presented as a major driver behind legislative action. That said, the Commission is not *legally* bound to follow any particular stakeholder's view: the primary purpose of the impact assessment process is to help ensure that proposed legislation is fit for purpose and acceptable to a broad coalition of policymakers, who will need to be aware of affected interests and possible implementation obstacles.[34]

One important Lisbon innovation, finally, is that citizens' initiatives can call on the Commission to initiate legislation.[35] This procedure seeks to strengthen citizens' participation in EU law-making by allowing them, upon collecting one million signatures, to request that the Commission consider particular legislative action. At the time of writing, almost 100 registration requests have been issued, including calls to provide housing for all, stop starvation, and stop plastic pollution in the sea.[36] Only a handful have managed to obtain the required number of signatures and so far the Commission has answered four. In one of its responses – to the request to respect the dignity and integrity of human embryos – it explained that it would not take further action as the European Parliament and the Council had already established a framework on point.[37] With regard to the remaining calls, existing directives were amended and revised so as to reflect the demands of the initiatives. There is also proposed legislation to enhance the transparency of certain decision-making procedures.[38] The citizens' initiative can be seen as a watered-down system of citizen participation, as it does not compel the Commission to act.[39] Its value, however, lies elsewhere – enabling a dialogue, even if not always successful, between citizens and the law-initiating EU institution.

The Commission, then, *does* enjoy vast agenda-setting power. But this power is not exercised in a vacuum. From stakeholder consultation to citizens' initiatives, there are plenty of avenues to ensure that a wide variety of voices are heard in the process.

---

[34] Impact assessments have been used as evidence before the CJEU in showing the suitability of a particular regulatory option adopted. For example, the market stability reserve added to the management of the EU emissions trading scheme was challenged and the impact assessments relied on in this regard by all actors in Case C-5/16 *Poland v European Parliament and Council* EU:C:2018:483.

[35] TEU, Article 11.

[36] Available online at https://europa.eu/citizens-initiative/home_en.

[37] European Commission, 'Communication from the Commission on the European Citizens' initiative "One of Us"' [2014] COM/2014/355 final.

[38] European Citizens' Initiative, 'Water and sanitation are a human right! Water is a public good, not a commodity!', https://perma.cc/PAW7-6KRC; European Citizens' Initiative, 'Ban glyphosate and protect people and the environment from toxic pesticides', https://perma.cc/N8JR-Z8KM.

[39] A Karatzia, 'The European Citizens' Initiative and the EU institutional balance: On realism and the possibilities of affecting lawmaking' (2017) 54(1) CML Rev 177.

(C) Decision-making: Polycentricity in Action

Once the Commission submits a proposal to the European Parliament and the Council, the two institutions must jointly adopt it in order to create binding EU law. There is a maximum of three rounds of readings, and a Conciliation Committee consisting of representatives from the Council and the Parliament is tasked with ensuring that acts are passed.[40] Without dwelling on the various stages of the decision-making process, a couple of points are important to note about the different institutions involved and the ever-shifting balance of power between them.

Although the European Parliament and the Council are the only bodies with decision-making authority, their decisions on Commission proposals are influenced by a variety of other actors. For example, the Economic and Social Committee (that is, economic and social actors from each of the Member States) and the European Committee of the Regions (representatives of EU-wide regional and local governments) are consulted on policy areas within their remit.[41] Whilst not binding, these recommendations are influential, especially as the institutions receive them early on in the decision-making process.[42]

National Parliaments also play an important role, at least where proposed legislation does not fall within the Union's exclusive competence. As part of an 'early warning system',[43] they are supposed to ensure that, in its legislative proposals, the Commission respects the principle of subsidiarity and makes decisions 'as closely as possible to citizens'. We will return to a more detailed account of this mechanism in the next debate. For now, note that it allows for input from national parliaments at the early stages of the EU legislative procedure.[44]

The Commission maintains an active role in decision-making through the practice of trilogues – informal meetings between representatives from the European Parliament, the Council, and the Commission aimed at facilitating debate and reaching compromise where required. These meetings have proven effective and are a key reason why most legislative acts are adopted at first reading.[45] The fact that they are carried out behind closed doors and precede the Conciliation Committee, however, has raised concerns about transparency and accountability.

[40] TFEU, Article 294.

[41] Remember also the special legislative procedure in the field of employment and social law as discussed in the previous chapter.

[42] C Hönnige and D Panke, 'The Committee of the Regions and the European Economic and Social Committee: How influential are consultative Committees in the European Union?' (2013) 51(3) JCMS 452, 467.

[43] Protocol No 2 on the application of the principles of subsidiarity and proportionality [2008] OJ C115/206.

[44] See European Commission, 'Subsidiarity control mechanism', https://perma.cc/C74B-F746.

[45] Bradley (n 7), 'Legislating in the European Union', p. 120.

In the end, any proposal's fate comes down to voting in the Council and the European Parliament. The latter votes in plenary sessions by simple majority, while the Council acts by qualified majority voting (QMV) unless otherwise stated in the Treaty. This means that 55 per cent of the members of the Council, 'comprising at least fifteen of them and representing Member States comprising at least 65% of the population of the Union',[46] need to be in favour. QMV ensures that decisions can be taken effectively in a large Union of diverse interests. On the flipside, even where a considerable number of Member States are against a legislative proposal, it can still pass and become legally binding.

(D) Implementation: It Ain't Over 'Till It's Over

Adoption by the EU institutions is not necessarily the end of the story. Most EU law has elements that require implementation before becoming legally effective. This holds foremost for directives, but sometimes regulations, too, need to be transposed into domestic legal orders. In the case of directives, the Member States are typically given two years from publication in the Official Journal to ensure implementation, although this can vary: the Water Framework Directive is a noteworthy outlier, with an implementation period of 15 years.[47]

There is an average delay of 8.4 months in Member States implementing EU acts.[48] But even when acts are implemented, uniformity is far from guaranteed. Unavoidably, the many different languages in which EU law appears may lead to different understandings and conceptualisations at the domestic levels.[49] Differences in domestic regulatory approaches are another important factor. Take, for example, the regulation establishing common rules on compensation in the event of flight cancellation or delays.[50] Implementation differed widely between Member States: from facilitating tort or contract law claims before ordinary civil courts, to establishing specialised administrative proceedings.[51]

This is why the principle of direct effect – the conferral of EU rights (provided they are sufficiently clear and precise) directly onto individuals, without

[46] TEU, Article 16(4).

[47] European Parliament and Council Directive 2000/60/EC of 23 October 2000 establishing a framework for Community action in the field of water policy [2000] OJ L327/1.

[48] The Commission runs a scoreboard on Member States' implementation practices, but note that this is with regard to Internal Market law only. The single-market scoreboard is available at https://ec.europa.eu/internal_market/scoreboard/performance_by_member_state/se/index_en.htm.

[49] See, e.g., M Derlén, *Multilingual Interpretation of European Union Law* (Wolters Kluwer 2009).

[50] European Parliament and Council Regulation (EC) No 261/2004 of 11 February 2004 establishing common rules on compensation and assistance to passengers in the event of denied boarding and of cancellation or long delays of flights [2004] OJ L46/1.

[51] See M Bobek and J Adams-Prassl (eds), *Air Passenger Rights: Ten Years On* (Bloomsbury 2015).

the need for implementation – is so important in EU law. It makes EU law real for individuals independently of Member States' (in)action. We will return to direct effect in Chapter 5. For now, let us examine the final step in making EU rights a reality: enforcement action.

(E) Enforcement: The Last Resort

As a final resort, the Commission, in its capacity as 'guardian of the Treaties', may take infringement actions against Member States failing to implement EU law, or implementing it incorrectly.[52] To this end, in addition to implementation reports prepared by the Member States, it relies on reports about possible breaches from citizens, businesses, and other stakeholders. For example, the UK's persistent failure to implement the Bathing Water Directive,[53] which aimed to safeguard public health and protect the aquatic environment from pollution, was brought to the Commission's attention via a postcard from concerned holidaymakers. Even when information about possible infringements surfaces, however, judicial action does not necessarily ensue, as the Commission's resources to pursue breaches before the CJEU are limited.

What happens when the CJEU finds an infringement, but a Member State refuses to comply with the judgment? Not much, prior to the Maastricht Treaty. Since 1992, however, the CJEU has been able to impose financial sanctions on recalcitrant Member States. Article 260(1) TFEU provides that a Member State found in breach of EU law by the CJEU must take necessary measures to implement the judgment. Further shirking may lead to penalties, ranging from daily fines to lump sums punishing continuing infringement. The Lisbon Treaty further beefed up this mechanism, adding an additional limb: Article 260(3) TFEU deals with a distinct breach of the duty to transpose involving the failure to notify the Commission of measures to transpose a directive.[54] In practice, however, Article 260 TFEU is rarely invoked. When it is employed, it tends to be for rather spectacular breaches. In *Commission v Ireland*, for example, the Member State had failed to comply with EU waste law for more than 19 years. Ireland was ordered to pay a penalty of €12,000 for each day of delay in complying with the judgment, in addition to a lump sum of €2 million.[55]

***

Understanding EU law-making is not for the fainthearted or impatient. It is a complicated process, and a lengthy one: it takes 18 months on average for an

---

[52] TEU, Article 17(1).

[53] Council Directive 76/160/EEC of 8 December 1975 concerning the quality of bathing water [1976] OJ L31/1.

[54] S Bogojević and N Petit, 'Deterring the state versus the firm: Soft and hard deterrence regimes in EU law' (2016) 23(1) Colum J Eur L 55.

[55] Case C-374/11 *European Commission v Ireland* EU:C:2012:827.

EU law to reach maturity.[56] This is sometimes followed by an implementation period and, if the law remains unimplemented, enforcement actions further prolong the realisation of Union rights.[57] Yet it is a price worth paying. In a Union of 27 different Member States, policy formation needs to take account of a complex set of competing considerations, from technical and scientific questions to local political sensitivities. The Union's law-making process goes a long way towards recognising and accommodating the challenges of polycentric standard setting. But chances are that someone, somewhere will not be satisfied with the result. What happens then?

Debate 2

Is there any way of challenging 'Brussels'?

In manufacturing sausages, end-of-line testing is vital in securing both the quality of the product and stability of the overall production process. The same applies to law: without processes to test the legality of EU acts, the entire EU enterprise would be questionable. The Treaties provide a number of safeguards to that end, including both political and legal avenues for challenging the exercise of Union competences.

(A) Political Safeguards

Political safeguards allow for extrajudicial challenges during the legislative process. Both Member State governments and national parliaments are able to protest against a particular Union measure with a view to stopping a draft proposal from turning into binding law, including through (limited) veto powers in Council and by showing proposed measures a 'yellow card'.

Council Veto: Digging in the Heels
In the early days of European integration, an act would be adopted only if backed by all Member States. This quickly proved too prohibitive a restraint. In 1965, General de Gaulle's government halted all EU action when it refused to take a seat (hence the episode's name, *chaise vide*) in the Council until the French Republic had its way on the financial regulation of the common agricultural policy.[58] The voting rules have since been revised, but resistance from the Member States is still an important factor, even under

---

[56] That is for acts adopted at first reading; the figure rises to approximately 39 months for those adopted at second reading. See M McGuinness and others, 'Activity report: Developments and trends of the ordinary legislative procedure – 8th Parliamentary Term' (European Parliament, November 2019), p. 4.

[57] This explains why delegated and implementing measures are needed for quick updates and revisions of EU law, particularly in fast-moving technical areas.

[58] C Paolo, 'De Gaulle, the "empty chair crisis" and the European Movement' (2015) 7(2) Perspect Fed 163.

QMV. The Commission's repeated attempts to secure a directive on access to environmental justice,[59] for example, have been opposed and halted by the Member States.[60]

Certain policy fields, such as taxation and the Union's finances, continue to require unanimity in Council through the so-called special legislative procedure (the European Parliament is merely consulted).[61] There are many examples of Member States failing to reach agreement on EU acts in these sectors. Following the 1992 Earth Summit in Rio, which saw more than 100 heads of state agree on the urgent need to tackle environmental problems, including climate change, the Commission put forward a directive proposal for a carbon tax,[62] which was rejected by the Council on two separate occasions.[63] More recently, Hungarian and Polish Prime Ministers Viktor Orban and Mateusz Morawiecki repeatedly threatened to veto the EU's recovery deal aimed at helping coronavirus-ridden European economies, as other Member States insisted on including a clause making such aid contingent on recipient countries respecting the rule of law.[64] In Chapter 11, we will return to rule of law conditionality in relation to EU funds. The point here is that legislative procedures demanding Council unanimity ultimately permit Member States to engage in political arm-twisting: see, for example, the recent resistance from the Cypriot government on coordinated measures to sanction Belarus in response to state repression and intimidation of peaceful demonstrations in the wake of the 2020 presidential elections.[65]

The most dramatic measure available is Article 50 TEU, which may be triggered when a Member State no longer wishes to remain a member of the Union. This Treaty provision entered into force with the Lisbon Treaty and was drafted, ironically, by Lord Kerr, a former UK ambassador to the EU. The conditions for leaving, as set out under Article 50(1) TEU, seem simple enough: 'Any Member State may decide to withdraw from the Union in

---

[59] Proposal for a Directive of the European Parliament and of the Council on access to justice in environmental matters [2003] COM/2003/0624 final.

[60] A legislative overview of the legislative attempts and ultimate failure is available at https://eur-lex.europa.eu/procedure/EN/2003_246.

[61] TFEU, Article 289 (2).

[62] Proposal for a Council Directive introducing a tax on carbon dioxide emissions and energy [1992] COM/92/226 final.

[63] Amended Proposal for a Council Directive for a tax on carbon dioxide emissions and energy [1995] COM/95/172 final.

[64] M de la Baume, H von der Burchard, and DM Herszenhorn, 'Poland joins Hungary in threatening to block EU's budget and coronavirus recovery package' (*Politico,* 18 September 2020), https://perma.cc/FM36-AXAR.

[65] European Council and Council of the European Union, 'EU relations with Belarus', https://perma.cc/58UE-SGQG; J Rankin, 'EU imposes sanctions on Belarus officials but not on Lukashenko' (*The Guardian,* Brussels, 2 October 2020), https://perma.cc/5TDZ-K3FR.

accordance with its own constitutional requirements'. The reality, of course, is another matter altogether, as the ongoing reverberations of Brexit show.[66]

The Yellow Card System

The Lisbon Treaty also introduced more subtle political safeguards into the law-making process. Protocol 2 assigns national parliaments a novel role of scrutinising legislative proposals for compliance with the principle of subsidiarity. Including national parliaments in EU law-making was a response to allegations of a democratic deficit, to which we will turn in the final debate. As national parliaments ultimately enjoy the highest degree of democratic legitimacy, their involvement was seen as an important element of the Union's law-making process.[67]

The procedure is relatively straightforward.[68] Upon receiving a legislative proposal, national parliaments can express any objection to the draft and explain why it fails to comply with the principle of subsidiarity within eight weeks. If one-third or more of national parliaments submit such 'reasoned opinions', the Commission must review its draft and choose whether to maintain, amend, or withdraw its proposal. Borrowing a term from football, this procedure is called the 'yellow card' system. Should more than half of the national parliaments issue reasoned opinions, then a vote in the Council (via QMV) and the European Parliament (by majority vote) can immediately kill off the proposal. This rule was proposed by the Netherlands and was named the 'orange card' procedure, after that country's football team colour.[69]

The role of national parliaments, and the extent to which they enjoy sufficient powers to act as forceful safeguards in EU law-making, remain disputed. The track record thus far suggests that their influence is limited. No orange cards and only three yellow cards have been issued to date.[70] The first was issued in 2012 in connection with the so-called Monti II legislative proposal by the Commission, which sought to clarify the interplay of economic and social free movement provisions following the CJEU rulings in *Viking* and *Laval* (a major debate in itself!). The Commission withdrew this proposal, without addressing subsidiarity in particular: inadequate political support was cited as the main reason.[71] The second yellow card followed a year later and concerned

[66] See *R(Miller) v The Prime Minister* [2019] UKSC 41. See also the two-stepped analysis in P Craig, 'Brexit: A drama in six acts' (2016) 41(4) EL Rev 447, and P Craig, 'Brexit, A drama: The interregnum' (2017) 36 YEL 3.

[67] K Granat, 'National parliaments as political safeguards of federalism' in D Jančić (ed.), *National Parliaments after the Lisbon Treaty and the Euro Crisis: Resilience or Resignation?* (Oxford University Press 2017), p. 264.

[68] A dedicated platform provides a clear record of interparliamentary exchanges online: http://www.ipex.eu/IPEXL-WEB/home/home.do.

[69] R Corbett, 'Democracy in the European Union' in D Kenealy, J Peterson, and R Corbett (eds), *The European Union: How Does It Work?*, 5th edn (Oxford University Press 2018), p. 153.

[70] For an overview, see J Öberg, 'National parliaments and political control of EU competences' (2018) 24(4) Eur Pub L 695.

[71] European Commission, 'Report from the Commission: Annual Report 2012 on subsidiarity and proportionality' [2013] COM/2013/566 final.

the proposal for a Council regulation on the establishment of the European Public Prosecutor's Office. The Commission denied infringing the subsidiarity principle, offered reasoning to this effect, and maintained the proposal. The Regulation was later adopted and the Office was set up in 2017. So far, however, only 22 Member States have chosen to participate in its work.[72] A third yellow card was issued by 14 national parliaments against the Commission's review of the 1996 Posted Workers' Directive in 2016, but the Commission once more decided not to withdraw its proposal despite those complaints.[73]

The fact that national parliaments can exercise safeguarding powers only in relation to subsidiarity has been criticised. Some have suggested that the scope of their review should extend to surveying compliance with the principle of proportionality, and perhaps further yet.[74] The idea to entrust national parliaments with a veto power, however, was rejected by Member State governments during the Lisbon Treaty negotiations. Whilst open to involving the national parliaments in EU decision-making, the 'Masters of the Treaties' clearly did not favour tipping the balance too much in their own parliaments' favour.

(B) Legal Safeguards

In addition to these political restraint mechanisms, legal safeguards are in place to allow the CJEU to review the legality of EU acts. There are two avenues for review: the preliminary reference procedure and annulment actions.[75] We discuss who can bring such actions, and how, in the next chapter. For now, let us examine what can be challenged and on which grounds.

What Can Be Challenged?

The substantive scope of judicial review in EU law is generous, both in terms of institutions covered and acts that can be reviewed:

> The Court of Justice of the European Union shall review the legality of legislative acts, of acts of the Council, of the Commission and of the European Central Bank, other than recommendations and opinions, and of acts of the European Parliament and of the European Council intended to produce legal effects vis-à-vis third parties. It shall also review the legality of acts of bodies, offices or agencies of the Union intended to produce legal effects vis-à-vis third parties.[76]

---

[72] See European Commission, 'European public prosecutor's office', https://perma.cc/SJK8-KK8M.

[73] European Commission, 'Communication from the Commission to the European Parliament, the Council and the National Parliaments on the proposal for a Directive amending the Posting of Workers Directive, with regard to the principle of subsidiarity, in accordance with Protocol No 2' [2016] COM/2016/505 final.

[74] D Jančić, 'The game of cards: National Parliaments in the EU and the future of the early warning mechanism and the political dialogue' (2015) 52(4) CML Rev 939.

[75] TFEU, Articles 267 and 263, respectively.

[76] TFEU, Article 263(1).

All major EU institutions are subject to judicial review – with the exception of the CJEU, which does the reviewing – as is any other body, office, or agency 'of the Union', provided that its acts have legal effect. But how far does this legal safeguard extend?

One clear limitation is that primary Treaty law is not reviewable – even if, in *Pringle*, the Court examined whether a certain amendment to the Treaty had been validly adopted.[77] Legislative acts, including regulations, directives, and decisions, are most obviously subject to review. Non-legislative acts, such as delegated and implementing acts with legal effect, similarly fall within the ambit of the Court's scrutiny, as does any EU institution's delegation of law-making power to another agency, insofar as the ensuing acts carry legal effect.[78] This means that the European Chemicals Authority's authorisation practices are reviewable,[79] as are voluntary standards developed by ESOs and adopted by the Commission.[80] The Court has even been willing to review broad policy instruments, such as Commission communications intended to have 'legal effects of [their] own'.[81]

On What Grounds?

Four grounds of review are listed in the Treaties: (i) lack of competence; (ii) infringement of an essential procedural requirement; (iii) infringement of the Treaties or of any rule of law relating to their application; and (iv) misuse of powers.[82]

These are clearly very broad. We have seen in the previous chapter that the basic principle of EU law is one of conferral: the EU cannot legislate if the Member States have not empowered it to do so in the Treaties. This means that EU acts risk annulment if enacted beyond the Union's competence,[83] if there has been excessive delegation of power to an agency or institution,[84] or when the institution implementing an EU act has gone beyond the powers listed in the implementing act.[85] The Court, however, allows broad and purposive interpretation of the EU's powers to achieve Treaty objectives, for example in permitting regulatory action in the Internal Market to have a 'spill-over effect' into other areas.[86] This does not mean that the legislator has a *carte blanche*

---

[77] Case C-370/12 *Thomas Pringle v Government of Ireland and ors* EU:C:2012:756.

[78] Case C-57/95 *France v European Commission* [1997] ECR I-1627.

[79] See, e.g., Case T-185/17 *PlasticsEurope v European Chemicals Agency* EU:T:2019:492.

[80] *James Elliott* (n 24).

[81] *France v European Commission* (n 78) [23].

[82] TFEU, Article 263(2).

[83] C-376/98 *Germany v European Parliament and Council* [2000] ECR I-8419.

[84] Case 9/56 *Meroni & Co., Industrie Metallurgiche, SpA v High Authority of the European Coal and Steel Community* EU:C:1958:7.

[85] Case 22/88 *Industrie- en Handelsonderneming Vreugdenhil BV and Gijs van der Kolk – Douane Expediteur BV v Minister van Landbouw en Visserij* [1989] ECR 2049.

[86] See, e.g., Case C-380/03 *Germany v European Parliament and Council* [2006] ECR I-11573 (*Tobacco Advertising II*).

under internal market provisions. Overall, however, competence is not a particularly high hurdle for the institutions to jump.

Annulment for infringing an essential procedural requirement is similarly straightforward, covering situations where an EU institution has not complied with the legislative protocol pertaining to the enactment of a particular act. This includes ignoring the European Parliament in the legislative procedure,[87] or failing to provide adequate reasons for adopting an act.[88]

Misuse of power is the narrowest of the four grounds and is rarely relied on for review, undoubtedly because the required standard of proof is difficult to meet.[89] The application would need to show that the institutions had intended to use powers for a purpose other than what the conferred competence permits. Among the rare cases in which this claim has been successfully invoked are challenges to the internal recruitment procedures of EU institutions.[90]

The most frequently employed ground of review is the broadest one – that is, infringement of the Treaties or any rule of law relating to their application. The Court has often relied on this provision to develop general principles, which we discuss in Chapter 8. In *Kadi*, for example, the Court powerfully declared that respect for human rights was a condition for the lawfulness of EU acts, and proceeded to annul a regulation that failed to do so.[91] Similarly, Articles 7 and 8 CFR (respect for private and family life, and protection of personal data) were invoked successfully in *Digital Rights Ireland* to annul a directive.[92] Judicial review under this heading is not limited to human rights protection: in *Pfizer*, the Court relied on the precautionary principle found in the Treaties to justify a Commission decision to ban the export of beef from the UK in the wake of mad cow disease.[93]

***

Much of the debate on legal safeguards tends to focus on subsidiarity (or rather, its weakness) as a ground for review.[94] But is this the fault of the Court or the wording of Article 5(3) TEU? Upon closer inspection, it appears that the latter is largely to blame here. Once the EU legislator identifies a competence, it is easy to argue that 'because of the dimensions of the intended action,

---

[87] Case C-138/79 *SA Roquette Frères v Council* [1980] ECR 3333.

[88] Case 18/57 *Firma J. Nold KG v High Authority of the European Coal and Steel Community* EU:C:1957:11.

[89] A Albors-Llorens, 'Judicial protection before the Court of Justice of the European Union' in C Barnard and S Peers (eds), *European Union Law*, 3rd edn (Oxford University Press 2020), p. 311.

[90] For a rare success, see Case 105/75 *Franco Giuffrida v Council* [1976] ECR 1395.

[91] Joined Cases C-402/05 P and C-415/05 P *Yassin Abdullah Kadi and Al Barakaat International Foundation v Council and European Commission* [2008] ECR I-6351.

[92] Joined Cases C-293/12 and C-594/12 *Digital Rights Ireland Ltd v Minister for Communications and ors* [2014] ECR I-238.

[93] Case T-13/99 *Pfizer Animal Health SA v Council* [2002] ECR II-3305.

[94] G Davies, 'Subsidiarity: The wrong idea, in the wrong place, at the wrong time' (2006) 43(1) CML Rev 63.

[it is] best achieved at Union level'.[95] When the legislator relies on Article 114 TFEU, for example, there is 'considerable overlap' between the reasoning which it is required to provide under that provision and Article 5(3) TEU. As soon as competence is established, then, the principle of subsidiarity is easily satisfied. This is why subsidiarity is considered ill-suited to be a legal safeguard, although the Court has explained that its subsidiarity checks include compliance with the procedural safeguards provided for by the subsidiarity protocol, as well as the substantive conditions set out in Article 5(3) TEU.[96]

Proportionality is often thought more fit to serve as a legal safeguard, especially as it allows the Court to review whether the relevant EU act intrudes too far into a Member State's values in relation to the objectives sought by the Union.[97] Proportionality requires that the EU measure be suitable, as well as necessary for the desired outcome, and not place an excessive burden on those subject to it. When the Court is asked to review policy choices, however, it tends to offer the legislator broad discretion 'where its action involves political, economic and social choices and where it is called on to undertake complex assessments and evaluations'.[98] In other words, the Court is careful not to let judicial safeguards trump political processes.

That said, it is bolder when reviewing potential infringements of individual rights. In *ABNA*, for example, the Court found that requirements under EU acts, such as the need to identify animal feed ingredient percentage in order to detect contamination, needlessly infringed the economic interests of manufacturers. As such, these requirements were disproportionate and had to be annulled.[99] Note that a proportionality test is applied to both EU acts and acts of the Member States. The two tests differ, however, and the Court is far more restrictive in its application of proportionality with regard to national measures.[100]

Debate 3

Is EU law-making undemocratic?

The complex law-making apparatus we have encountered thus far is not universally appreciated. One particular concern raised in certain quarters is that the Union suffers from a democratic deficit – an allegation that has sparked more

[95] Case C-233/94 *Germany v European Parliament and Council* [1997] ECR I-2405 [26].

[96] Case C-547/14 *Philip Morris Brands SARL and ors v Secretary of State for Health* EU:C:2016:325 [216]–[217].

[97] ibid.

[98] Case C-127/07 *Société Arcelor Atlantique et Lorraine and ors v Premier minister and ors* [2008] ECR I-9895 [57], and later in Case C-5/16 *Poland v European Parliament and Council* EU:C:2018:483 [112].

[99] Case C-453/03 *The Queen on the application of ABNA Ltd and ors v Secretary of State for Health and Food Standards Agency* [2005] ECR I-10423.

[100] W Sauter, 'Proportionality in EU law: A balancing act?' (2013) 15 CYELS 439.

general legitimacy concerns about the EU as a legal enterprise.[101] At the same time, however, it is not necessarily clear which aspect of democracy the EU should be tested against. Is the reason for concern the fact that democracy requires a 'demos', which Europe lacks?[102] Or is it rather that the EU's institutions are largely unresponsive to democratic pressures?

In addressing these questions, we first need to work out an appropriate counterfactual. As the CJEU consistently reminds us, the Union is neither a nation state nor a federal entity,[103] so why should it be measured against state paradigms? Might international organisations not be better comparators? If so, which ones? The EU, after all, purports to be a *sui generis* legal order. Rather than try to duplicate domestic or international governance structures at the European level, perhaps the more pertinent question focuses on the restraints in place to ensure the legitimacy of EU law. Let us explore these questions in turn.

(A) Unpacking the Democratic Deficit

The notion of a 'democratic deficit' is unhelpfully vague. Traditionally, it stood for concerns targeted at the transfer of legislative powers from national parliaments to the Council.[104] Remember that the Member States, in agreeing on the Rome Treaty, had entrusted the European Parliament with but the smallest role in the legislative procedure – the right to be consulted where specific Treaty articles provided for it. Over the years, this role developed, although it was not until the Maastricht Treaty that the European Parliament became a co-legislator.

This coincided with the creation of Union citizenship, and thus arguably a European 'demos'.[105] Does this mean that we should no longer worry about democratic deficit critiques? After all, citizens have enjoyed universal suffrage since 1979, directly electing Members of the European Parliament (MEPs). Concerns, however, did not necessarily disappear, with the debate shifting instead to the distance between the European Parliament and its voters, and a broader lack of democratic accountability on the part of the remaining EU institutions involved in EU decision-making.

---

[101] Much ink has been spilt on this topic. See, e.g., S Garcia (ed.), *European Identity and the Search for Legitimacy* (Pinter 1993); JHH Weiler, *The Constitution of Europe* (Cambridge University Press 1999); P Eleftheriadis, *A Union of Peoples* (Oxford University Press 2020), ch. 10.

[102] See, e.g., S Hix, *What's Wrong with the European Union and How to Fix It* (Polity 2008).

[103] Opinion 2/13 of the Court on the compatibility of the draft agreement with the EU and FEU Treaties EU:C:2014:2454 [49].

[104] Corbett, 'Democracy in the European Union' (n 69), p. 148.

[105] For an overview of the history of the European Parliament, see European University Institute, *Building Parliament – 50 Years of European Parliament History: 1958–2008* (European Communities 2009), https://op.europa.eu/en/publication-detail/-/publication/67991291-12ef-45d5-a7a9-85bb5c4c3ff7. For discussion about the position of citizens in the EU legal order with a strange executive presence, see K Nicolaïdis, 'European democracy and its crisis' (2013) 51(2) JCMS 351.

With regard to the European Parliament, the argument is that, even though it is directly elected, these elections are not visible in the way that citizens are used to at the national level. Historic turnout to EP elections was low, although it has risen steadily more recently.[106] Similar problems exist at the national level, but voters' loss of appetite for participating at the EU level has been linked to a lack of trust in the European Parliament to represents citizens' interests in EU law-making.[107] Indeed, the European Parliament is but one actor in the legislative procedure, and a change in its composition will not impact the set-up of the Council or the Commission (beyond that of approving its President). Elections could thus be thought to have limited effect on bringing about policy change, especially given that there is comparatively less competition for political leadership.[108] What is more, MEPs do not represent citizens equally, as the ratio of member to population is considerably lower in the smaller Member States – a point highlighted by the German Constitutional Court in arguing that the European Parliament could not be compared to national parliaments that represent a single people.[109]

Democratic deficit concerns are more potent when it comes to the other EU institutions because they are not directly elected and so are not subject to electoral accountability. For example, the fact that the Commission operates outside of democratic paradigms has been taken to mean that it is not compelled to respond to citizens' initiatives.[110] The Council has similarly been criticised for the lack of transparency in its legislative procedure – most notably by the European Ombudsman in 2017[111] – and for making decisions behind closed doors.

The situation continues to evolve. Commissioners are increasingly subject to national political debates,[112] and EUR-lex today provides an easily navigated website for EU law-making procedure where legislative proposals, impact assessment reports, and the various positions of the consulted and deciding committees and institutions for each EU act are presented.[113]

---

[106] Note, however, that in recent years the turnout has increased. For example, the turnout of voters in 2019 is available at https://europarl.europa.eu/election-results-2019/en/turnout.

[107] N Clark, 'Explaining low turnout in European elections: The role of issue salience and institutional perceptions in elections to the European Parliament' (2014) 36(4) J Eur Integr 339.

[108] A Follesdal and S Hix, 'Why there is a democratic deficit in the EU: A response to Majone and Moravcsik' (2006) 44(3) JCMS 533.

[109] BVerfG, 30.06.2009, 2 BvE 2/08 (Lisbon judgment) (DE).

[110] Karatzia, 'The European Citizens' Initiative and the EU institutional balance' (n 39) p. 195.

[111] Recommendation of the European Ombudsman in case OI/2/2017/TE on the Transparency of the Council legislative process [2018].

[112] N O'Leary and others, '"I did not break any law": Phil Hogan formally resigns as EU commissioner' (*The Irish Times,* Dublin, 26 August 2020), https://perma.cc/NL97-7TU5.

[113] European Commission, 'Annex to the Proposal for a Council Decision on the position to be taken, on behalf of the EU, in the Joint Council established under the Economic Partnership Agreement between the European Union and its Member States, of the one part, and the SADC EPA States, of the other part, as regards the adjustment of certain reference quantities contained in Annex IV of the EPA' [2020] COM/2020/633 final.

(B) To Whom Are EU Institutions Accountable?

In any event, a lack of regular scrutiny at the ballot box does not necessarily mean that key institutions – from the Council and the Commission to the CJEU itself – are not held accountable in different ways.

The composition of the Commission starts with selecting its President, which is a task for the European Parliament acting on the suggestion of the European Council.[114] It is then up to the President, together with the Council, to choose candidates for her team from a pool proposed by the Member States. In all, 27 are chosen to make up the College of Commissioners, each responsible for a particular policy area.[115] Although both the European Council and the Council have a say in deciding the composition of the Commission, the latter is responsible to the European Parliament. This is not a toothless safeguard: in 1999, the Santer Commission was forced to resign after evidence of fraud, mismanagement, and nepotism emerged.[116]

The Council,[117] on the other hand, is not politically accountable to any one body at the Union level. Individually, however, each of its members is accountable through national elections, governments, and parliaments. Moreover, Council members' voting power is proportional to the size of their representative countries and, in this way, they act as citizens' representatives.[118]

As for the EU courts, it is the task of the Member States to pick judges and advocates general from a pool of candidates 'whose independence is beyond doubt', based on the qualifications required for 'appointment to the highest judicial offices in their respective countries'.[119] Since the Lisbon Treaty came into force, the Member States are obliged, under Article 255 TFEU, to consult an expert panel tasked with delivering either a favourable or an unfavourable reasoned opinion on the suitability of candidates. The Panel, in part proposed by the European Parliament, and comprising former justices of EU courts and national judiciaries, performs a rigorous filtering of candidates, not infrequently rejecting unsuitable candidates.[120]

Even if directly democratically elected bodies are scarce in EU law-making procedures, the remaining institutions, including the CJEU, are either formed through indirect democratic means, or are accountable to democratic bodies

[114] See TEU, Articles 14(1) and 17(7).

[115] European Commission, 'The Commissioners', https://perma.cc/YR9H-RBJ2.

[116] Committee of Independent Experts, 'First report on the allegations regarding fraud, mismanagement and nepotism in the European Commission' (European Parliament, 15 March 1999), https://perma.cc/X576-P2UB.

[117] TEU, Article 16.

[118] Corbett, 'Democracy in the European Union' (n 69), p. 151.

[119] TFEU, Article 253.

[120] T Dumborvsky, B Petkova, and M van der Sluis, 'Judicial appointments: the Article 255 TFEU advisory panel and selection procedures in the Member States' (2014) 51(2) CML Rev 455.

either at the national or at the EU level.[121] In any event, is democracy really the only benchmark against which to test the legitimacy of EU law-making?

***

The democratic deficit argument has led to several suggestions about how to make EU law-making *more* democratic by reforming its institutions. One such suggestion is to grant the European Parliament the right to take legislative initiatives and extend the ordinary legislative procedure to all policy fields.[122] The idea is to diminish, in this way, the influence of the Commission, as well as the Council.

Another line of response has questioned whether it is useful to compare EU law-making with some ideal type of plebiscitary or parliamentary democracy, as opposed to national democracies as they actually operate across the world.[123] In any case, to take the nation-state as a suitable analogue to EU governance is to assume that the EU is a state, which it is clearly not.[124] After all, democratic deficits are found at the national legislative levels, too: from unelected chambers in national parliaments to the ecclesiastical law of the Evangelische Kirche which we will encounter in Chapter 6.[125]

Conclusion: An Endowment for Democracy

Law-making is not the snazziest topic in EU law. Studying it requires keeping track of the various institutions: what they do, how they vote (if relevant), and their relationship to each other. It is easy to feel disconnected from the institutions. Yet understanding how they function, and on which premises, is essential to understanding the EU's legal architecture.

More recently, the Union has become keener to meet accusations of democratic deficits head-on: there is even a dedicated website to explain the arguments, as well as a list of ways in which they are countered.[126] The Member States also addressed the problem by stipulating in the Treaties that the Union is committed to democratic principles, specifically that the 'functioning of the Union shall be founded on representative democracy'.[127] The role of citizens in EU governance is obviously important, especially given the Union's task of creating an 'ever closer'

[121] Space limitations preclude a detailed engagement with delegated law-making, as well as the decision-making powers of various agencies.
[122] See, e.g., J Haberman, 'Democracy in Europe: Why the development of the EU into a transnational democracy is necessary and how it is possible' (2015) 21(4) Eur LJ 546.
[123] A Moravcsik, 'In defence of the "democratic deficit": Reassessing legitimacy in the European Union' (2002) 40(4) JCMS 603, 606.
[124] A point developed further by A Menon and S Weatherill, 'Democratic politics in a globalised world: Supranationalism and Legitimacy in the European Union' (2007) LSE Law, Society and Economy Working Paper 13/2007.
[125] Case C-414/16 *Vera Egenberger v Evangelisches Werk für Diakonie und Entwicklung eV* EU:C:2018:257.
[126] EUR-Lex, 'Glossary of summaries: Democratic deficit', https://perma.cc/6EKE-PC5J.
[127] TEU, Articles 9-12.

union. At the same time, we should not forget the multiple alternative safeguards in place, whether political or legal, ensuring that EU acts live up to fundamental rights, the rule of law, and the Treaties' overarching objectives.

Further Reading

Does broad participation lead to better law-making? EU environmental governance provides a useful case study: see M Lee, *EU Environmental Law, Governance and Decision-Making* (Hart Publishing 2014). In light of Lee's findings, how appropriate is the direct involvement of citizens in EU law-making? Consider this question in light of calls under the citizens' initiative.

Pick a legislative act and follow its implementation process online at https://eur-lex.europa.eu/collection/legislative-procedures.html. What considerations does the Commission take into account in its impact assessment? What are the respective positions of the European Parliament and the Council, as well as (in relevant instances) the Economic and Social Committee and the European Committee of the Regions, with regard to the enactment of your chosen EU act? What does this say about polycentricity in EU law-making?

Cheneval and Nicolaïdis offer the theory of 'demoicracy' to better explain the EU legal order as one where the connection between a single 'demos' and democratic political authority is more flexible, and contains both national and European dimensions without any one unit being a threat to the other (see F Cheneval and K Nicolaïdis, 'The Social Construction Of Democracy in the European Union' (2017) 16 Eur J Political Theory 235). How fitting do you find the description of the EU institutional set-up as a 'multilateral democracy'? How useful is it to think of the EU in terms of democratic governance?

Political scientists have described annulment actions as legal instruments that are typically used for political reasons, and which yield significant political consequences on policy content, political procedures, and the EU's constitutional order. See C Adam and others, *Taking the EU to Court: Annulment Proceedings and Multilevel Judicial Conflict* (Palgrave Macmillan 2020). What political consequences, do you think, have followed the annulment actions we have mentioned in this chapter?

CHAPTER 4

Ferraris vs Bicycles

Challenging EU Action: A Complete System of Remedies?

In Chapter 2, we began to explore an important tension that underpins the EU's constitutional framework: the Union needs to be enabled to act, but it also needs to be held to account. In the previous chapter, we saw how judicial review is a crucial feature in a system of conferred competences, complementing political control. This accountability is a fundamental feature of the rule of law, as the Court of Justice explicitly recognised in a much-cited passage from its judgment in *Les Verts v Parliament*.[1] The Union, it emphasised, is

> based on the rule of law, inasmuch as neither its Member States nor its institutions can avoid a review of the question whether the measures adopted by them are in conformity with the basic constitutional charter, the Treaty.

We will encounter the scrutiny of Member State action in detail in Chapters 5 and 6. In this chapter, we focus on the judicial review of Union action.

This raises an important question of terminology. Throughout this book, we repeatedly encounter the notion of *remedies* – the law's response to wrongdoing, which comes in a wide range of shapes and forms from financial penalties to annulment. In this chapter, we are specifically interested in a subset of remedies: the judicial review of the legality of Union action – whether legislation or other acts of the institutions, such as decisions by the Commission to fine a company for price-fixing. This is distinct from the remedies we explore in subsequent chapters, which are focused on vindicating rights conferred by EU law vis-à-vis Member States and private parties.[2]

Ultimately, these are all building blocks in the effective judicial protection guaranteed by Article 47 of the Charter of Fundamental Rights (CFR). For purposes of this chapter, however, our focus is firmly on the judicial review of Union action. This leads to one more important preliminary note. The CJEU today

[1] Case 294/83 *Parti écologiste "Les Verts" v European Parliament* [1986] ECR 1339 [23].

[2] Whether through infringement proceedings (TFEU, Articles 258–260) or on the basis of domestic claims enabled by EU law's direct effect; this 'dual vigilance' is explored in Chapter 5, Debate 1.

consists of the General Court (known as the Court of First Instance until the Treaty of Lisbon) and, above it in the judicial hierarchy, the Court of Justice.[3] For practical purposes, the difference is broadly speaking as follows: requests for preliminary rulings go straight to CJEU, whereas the General Court hears annulment actions brought by individuals. Jurisdiction over Member State challenges to Union actions and interinstitutional disputes is dependent on the precise nature of the impugned measure.[4]

Debate 1 explores the most peculiar aspect of judicial review in the EU: who gets to challenge Union action, and how? In particular, can its institutions be held accountable both at the European level and domestically? The answer lies in a combination of direct actions, brought by Member States and Union institutions under Article 263 TFEU, and indirect actions, brought by individuals and corporations via the Article 267 TFEU preliminary reference procedure. Debate 2 then turns to an important complication in this relatively straightforward picture: under what circumstances can individuals enjoy *direct* access to the CJEU? Drawing these two issues together, in Debate 3, we turn to an overarching question, which has yet to be settled: Does the EU provide a complete system of remedies? Or is it in reality 'a Ferrari with its doors locked shut'? As AG Sharpston so memorably warned, '[a]n intensive system of [judicial] review is of little practical help if the system itself is totally inaccessible'.[5]

Debate 1

Who gets to challenge EU action – and how?

The majority of Member States approach relations between domestic and international law on a so-called dualist basis, leaving the latter as a matter for international actors (i.e. sovereign states represented by their governments and international institutions) settling their disputes before international courts. Domestic legal matters are dealt with by the public law and judicial review regime of each Member State. The two systems coexist independently, like oil floating on water. EU law, on the other hand, operates on both levels. EU law is not just binding on Member States; it also confers rights – and potentially imposes obligations – on private individuals.

---

[3] Article 19(1) TEU also provides for 'specialised courts', although none exist today. A special Civil Service Tribunal, introduced in 2004, proved to be relatively short-lived and was absorbed into the General Court in 2016.

[4] Protocol (No 3) on the Statute of the Court of Justice of the European Union (Consolidated Version) [2016] OJ C202/210, art 51. Direct claims brought by individuals had been heard by the Court of First Instance since 1994.

[5] Case C-115/09 *Bund für Umwelt und Naturschutz Deutschland* v *Bezirksregierung Arnsberg* [2011] ECR I-3673, Opinion of AG Sharpston [77]. Strictly speaking, her remark concerned the German system of administrative law, but as we will see, the metaphor translates surprisingly well into the EU context.

In developing a complete system of judicial review of Union action, it is therefore necessary to establish two channels of judicial review. In addition to traditional models of public international law, in which the Member States (and Union institutions) can hold the Union to account, the Treaty also envisages an avenue for citizens who wish to challenge EU acts. In *Les Verts*, the Court explained how the system was designed to achieve this:

> In particular, in Articles [263 TFEU] and [277 TFEU], on the one hand, and in Article [267 TFEU], on the other, the Treaty established a complete system of legal remedies and procedures designed to permit the Court of Justice to review the legality of measures adopted by the institutions. Natural and legal persons are thus protected against the application to them of general measures which they cannot contest directly before the Court by reason of the special conditions of admissibility laid down in [Article 263 TFEU]. ... Where implementation is a matter for the national authorities, such persons may plead the invalidity of general measures before the national courts and cause the latter to request the Court of Justice for a preliminary ruling.[6]

This is the basic framework for multilevel Union accountability. Article 263 TFEU provides for review of the legality of Union acts at the international plain,[7] whereas Article 267 TFEU allows for review proceedings to be launched before domestic courts by citizens, non-governmental organisations (NGOs) and corporations.

(A) Judicial Review at the Union Level

The primary avenue for judicial review at the Union level is set out in Article 263 TFEU, which provides a comprehensive overview of direct actions. Read it carefully to understand its design and return to it frequently whilst thinking through subsequent debates.

> The Court of Justice of the European Union shall review the legality of legislative acts, of acts of the Council, of the Commission and of the European Central Bank, ... and of acts of the European Parliament and of the European Council intended to produce legal effects vis-à-vis third parties. It shall also review the legality of acts of bodies, offices or agencies of the Union intended to produce legal effects vis-à-vis third parties.
>
> It shall for this purpose have jurisdiction in actions brought by a Member State, the European Parliament, the Council or the Commission on grounds

[6] *Les Verts* (n 1) [23].

[7] Other articles, including Articles 265 TFEU (challenges to Union *inaction*) and 277 TFEU (the illegality exception), complement this picture. For details regarding their operation and how they slot into the 'complete system of remedies', see, e.g., A Albors-Llorens, 'Judicial protection before the Court of Justice of the European Union' in C Barnard and S Peers (eds), *European Union Law*, 3rd edn (Oxford University Press 2020), ch. 10.3.3 and 10.3.4, respectively.

of lack of competence, infringement of an essential procedural requirement, infringement of the Treaties or of any rule of law relating to their application, or misuse of powers.

The Court shall have jurisdiction under the same conditions in actions brought by the Court of Auditors, by the European Central Bank and by the Committee of the Regions for the purpose of protecting their prerogatives.

The proceedings provided for in this Article shall be instituted within two months of the publication of the measure, or of its notification to the plaintiff, or, in the absence thereof, of the day on which it came to the knowledge of the latter, as the case may be.

Article 263 in Action

The envisaged review system is reasonably self-explanatory. We have already noted the broad scope of Article 263(1) TFEU in the previous chapter: it covers both legislative and executive action. With the explicit exception of recommendations and opinions, the Court can review any Union act 'intended to produce legal effects vis-à-vis third parties' (i.e. any legally binding act). Reviewable action also includes the 'acts of bodies, offices or agencies of the Union', such as the European Central Bank's rulemaking for the Eurozone.[8]

The direct annulment procedure is primarily designed for use by Member States, the European Parliament, the Council, and the Commission, as the wording of Article 263(2) TFEU makes clear: these parties (sometimes referred to as 'privileged applicants') are listed in the same breath as the grounds of review. A second group of Union institutions ('semi-privileged applicants', if you will) enjoy somewhat more limited access: the Court of Auditors, the European Central Bank, and the Committee of the Regions can only bring actions 'for the purpose of protecting their prerogatives'.[9]

The substantive grounds of review are generous, encompassing 'lack of competence, infringement of an essential procedural requirement, infringement of the Treaties or of any rule of law relating to their application, or misuse of powers'. We have already encountered several amongst them in the previous two chapters (lack of competence, in particular, is the crucial counterpart to the principle of conferral debated in Chapter 2) and will continue to come across further examples, notably in Chapter 8. 'Infringement of the Treaties' today includes the Charter of Fundamental Rights, whereas 'any rule of law relating to [the] application' of the Treaties has been interpreted by the CJEU to include the full range of general principles of EU law – from proportionality and legitimate expectations to non-discrimination.[10] Taken together, the grounds thus cover 'almost all conceivable cases of illegality'.[11] In combination

---

[8] Case T-496/11 *United Kingdom v European Central Bank* EU:T:2015:133.

[9] TFEU, Article 263(3).

[10] See Chapter 8, Debate 2.

[11] A Toth, *The Oxford Encyclopaedia of European Community Law*, vol I (Oxford University Press 1990), p. 282, as cited in A Arnull, 'Judicial review in the European Union' in D Chalmers and A Arnull (eds), *The Oxford Handbook of European Union Law* (Oxford University Press 2015), p. 377.

with the wide range of reviewable acts, this makes judicial review appear surprisingly powerful: the Union's rule of law 'Ferrari', not least when compared with domestic administrative law provisions in many Member States.

The time limit to bring annulment actions is set at two months from the publication or notification of a measure (or, failing either of these, the date of the claimant's actual knowledge of the measure). This limit is strictly enforced: a party who has failed to bring their claim in time cannot then try to engineer a claim via the preliminary reference procedure in an attempt to outflank Article 263(6) TFEU.[12]

Remedies and Interim Relief

Article 264 TFEU provides that if an annulment 'action is well founded, the Court of Justice of the European Union shall declare the act concerned to be void'. The Court is left some flexibility, however. First, a measure does not necessarily need to be struck down in its entirety: it is not uncommon for the Court to limit annulment to particular offending provisions, leaving the remainder of the act 'blue-pencilled' and in force.[13]

Second, the Court may delay annulment to allow the EU institutions to remedy the defects identified.[14] Whichever option is chosen, the 'institution, body, office or entity whose act has been declared void or whose failure to act has been declared contrary to the Treaties shall be required to take the necessary measures to comply with the judgment'.[15] Whilst an annulment action is pending, the measure in question is not suspended automatically.[16] The Court may, however, 'prescribe any necessary interim measures'.[17]

Third, applicants who have suffered loss as a result of an illegal measure can seek financial recourse against the Union.[18] Article 340 TFEU merely decrees that in cases 'of non-contractual liability, the Union shall ... make good any damage caused by its institutions or by its servants in the performance of their

[12] Case C-188/92 *TWD Textilwerke Deggendorf GmbH v Germany* [1994] ECR I-833. This does not apply if there was genuine doubt as to the availability of an Article 263 TFEU action: Case C-408/95 *Eurotunnel SA and ors v SeaFrance* [1997] ECR I-6315.

[13] See, e.g., different provisions of the Working Time Directive in Case C-84/94 *United Kingdom v Council* [1996] ECR I-5755.

[14] Joined Cases C-402/05 P and C-415/05 P *Yassin Abdullah Kadi and Al Barakaat International Foundation v Council and European Commission* [2008] ECR I-6351.

[15] TFEU, Article 266.

[16] TFEU, Article 278.

[17] TFEU, Article 279. These measures were thrown into the limelight in recent proceedings brought by AG Sharpston against the Member States and the CJEU as part of proceedings concerning the expiry of her mandate following Brexit. The General Court's injunction (Case T-550/20 R *Eleanor Sharpston v Council and Representatives of the Governments of the Member States*) EU:T:2020:475 against the appointment of her Greek successor was annulled on application to the CJEU (Case C-423/20 P(R) *Council v Eleanor Sharpston* EU:C:2020:700; Case C-424/20 P(R) *Representatives of the Governments of the Member States v Eleanor Sharpston* EU:C:2020:705). AG Rantos was duly installed 30 minutes later.

[18] TFEU, Article 268.

duties', leaving the details to be spelled out by the Court. Whilst the initial approach saw claimants for damages faced with the significant hurdle of proving 'flagrant violations',[19] in *Bergaderm*,[20] the liability requirements were aligned with the regime for *Francovich* damages actions against Member States as set out in *Brasserie du Pêcheur* (explored in detail in the next chapter).[21]

(B) Judicial Review for Individuals

The default route for individual claimants seeking judicial review of Union action is found in Article 267 TFEU:

> The Court of Justice of the European Union shall have jurisdiction to give preliminary rulings concerning: (a) the interpretation of the Treaties; (b) the validity and interpretation of acts of the institutions, bodies, offices or agencies of the Union…
>
> Where any such question is raised in a case pending before a court or tribunal of a Member State against whose decisions there is no judicial remedy under national law, that court or tribunal shall bring the matter before the Court.

We will return to the detailed operation of this so-called preliminary reference procedure, and its central role in establishing the new legal order, in Chapter 7. For now, our interest is limited to its role in judicial review proceedings against Union action. The basic idea is relatively straightforward: if a point of EU law arises in the course of domestic litigation, the judge can (or, in certain circumstances, must) ask the CJEU for assistance in interpreting the relevant provisions. She then applies that preliminary ruling to the facts of the case. Time limits, remedies, and other procedural questions are dealt with in accordance with domestic law, subject only to the principles of equivalence and effectiveness.[22]

Article 267 in Action

Article 267(1)(b) TFEU can thus be used as an indirect vehicle for judicial review of 'the validity … of acts'. When an airline is sued for compensation following flight delays, for example, it could focus its defence not on the relevant facts, but rather on a claim that the EU's Air Passenger Rights Regulation is the result of illegal and/or disproportionate Union action.[23] This raises two issues:

[19] Case 5/71 *Aktien-Zuckerfabrik Schöppenstedt v Council* [1971] ECR 975 [11]. This is not to say that there was not the rare case of success: see, e.g., Joined Cases C-104/89 and C-37/90 *J.M. Mulder and ors v Council and European Commission* [2000] ECR I-203.

[20] Case C-352/98 P *Laboratoires Pharmaceutiques Bergaderm SA and Jean-Jacques Goupil v European Commission* [2000] ECR I-5291.

[21] Joined Cases C-46/93 *Brasserie du Pêcheur SA v Germany* and C-48/93 *The Queen v Secretary of State for Transport, ex p Factortame Ltd and ors* [1996] ECR I-1029.

[22] See Chapter 5, Debate 2.

[23] As attempted (nearly) *ad infinitum*: see J Malinowsky, 'Regulation 261: Three major issues in the case law of the Court of Justice' in M Bobek and J Prassl, *EU Law in the Member States: Air Passenger Rights, Ten Years On* (Hart 2016).

the need for a domestic 'hook' on which to base the challenge, and the (limited) role of the national court.

The party seeking to bring an indirect review action must first identify a 'hook' on which to hang their claim in domestic law. In most scenarios, this will be relatively straightforward because the majority of Union measures will require some form of domestic implementation – from legislation giving effect to a directive, to executive action as specified by a Commission decision.[24] The notion of an implementing measure has been interpreted generously, including the mere 'intention and/or obligation' of a Member State government 'to transpose a directive into national law.' Indirect judicial review, the Court asserted in *ex parte BAT*, is 'not conditional upon … implementing measures adopted pursuant to national law … it is sufficient if the national court is called upon to hear a genuine dispute in which the … validity of [EU law] is raised indirectly'.[25] Another (albeit rather risky) way of triggering domestic proceedings involves deliberately breaching the law, with a view to then pleading the invalidity of its underlying Union act as a defence.[26]

Once seised, it is up to domestic court to hear the parties in line with national procedures and establish all relevant facts. If the indirect challenge to Union action is manifestly unfounded, it may even dismiss the case.[27] Declarations of invalidity, on the other hand, are the exclusive domain of the CJEU. The point was not uncontroversial: the drafting committee of the Rome Treaty had decided not to spell out competence division on point.[28] As a result, the issue looked likely to raise 'one of the thorniest that the Court has ever had to tackle'.[29] When faced with the choice between a 'literal interpretation of the text and the workability of the system',[30] the Court unequivocally opted for the latter: '[d]ivergences between courts in the Member States as to the validity of Community acts would be liable to place in jeopardy the very unity of the Community legal order and detract from the fundamental requirement of legal certainty.'[31]

---

[24] As was the case in Case 314/85 *Foto-Frost v Hauptzollamt Lübeck-Ost* [1987] ECR 4199.

[25] Case C-491/01 *The Queen v Secretary of State for Health, ex p British American Tobacco (Investments) Ltd and Imperial Tobacco Ltd* [2002] ECR I-11453 [2], [40]. Note that this route may no longer be available to litigants after Brexit: civilian legal systems tend not to allow free-standing declaratory actions; however, such a refusal could itself be challenged as a violation of an applicant's rights to effective judicial protection under Article 47 CFR.

[26] See, e.g., Case C-189/95 *Criminal proceedings against Harry Franzén* [1997] ECR I-5909 (challenge to domestic law), and the host of cases where airlines refuse to pay passenger compensation discussed in Malinowsky, 'Regulation 261' (n 23).

[27] *Foto-Frost* (n 24) [14].

[28] D Edwards, '*CILFIT* and *Foto-Frost* in their historical and procedural context' in MP Maduro and L Azoulai (eds), *The Past and Future of EU Law: The Classics of EU Law Revisited on the 50th Anniversary of the Rome Treaty* (Hart 2010), pp. 173, 180.

[29] *Foto-Frost* (n 24), Opinion of AG Manici [4].

[30] Edwards (n 28), '*CILFIT* and *Foto-Frost* in their historical and procedural context', pp. 180, 182.

[31] *Foto-Frost* (n 24) [15].

As the official guidance for domestic judges explains, therefore, when a national court 'has doubts about the validity of [a Union] act, [it] must ... refer the matter to the Court, stating the reasons for which it considers that the act is invalid'.[32] These reasons must be drawn from Article 263(2) TFEU. Because Article 267 TFEU does not spell out distinct grounds of review, the extensive list we have already encountered applies in parallel.

Remedies and Interim Relief

If an indirect challenge to a Union measure is well founded, the consequences set out in the previous section will ensue, with any required follow-up (such as the annulment of implementing measures) left to the national court.

Although domestic courts cannot declare EU law invalid, they may in certain (limited) circumstances suspend its operation or offer other interim measures.[33] The criteria for such relief were set out in *Atlanta*: it can only be granted if the national court 'entertains serious doubts' as to the validity of EU law and has made a reference on point; there is 'urgency' in the sense of 'serious and irreparable damage' to the applicant; and due account has been taken of the Union interest, as well as any precedent regarding both the substance of the challenge and the form of relief sought.[34]

***

The picture thus appears to be pretty straightforward. The CJEU alone can rule on the validity of EU law, even though judicial review proceedings can reach it in two distinct ways. Member States and Union institutions can bring their claims directly, on the international plain, under Article 263 TFEU. Private individuals, NGOs, small- and medium-sized enterprises, and large multinational corporations are able (in principle, at least) to bring their claims through national courts via the Article 267 TFEU preliminary reference procedure.

Debate 2

Should individuals enjoy direct access to Luxembourg?

So far, so neat. But matters are not quite as simple. A significant complication arises where EU law is not mediated through Member State action. A classic illustration of this scenario includes decisions taken by the Commission. Think of a company fined for breach of competition law or a researcher who has applied for funding from the European Research Council: the decisions in question will be addressed directly to them, with the Union bureaucracy itself

---

[32] Recommendations of the Court of Justice of the European Union to national courts and tribunals in relation to the initiation of preliminary ruling proceedings [2018] OJ C257/01, para 7.

[33] Joined Cases C-143/88 *Zuckerfabrik Suderdithmarschen AG v Hauptzollamt Itzehoe* and C-92/89 *Zuckerfabrik Soest GmbH v Hauptzollamt Paderborn* [1991] ECR I-415.

[34] Case C-465/93 *Atlanta Fruchthandelsgesellschaft mbH and ors v Bundesamt für Ernährung und Forstwirtschaft* [1995] ECR I-3761 [51].

in charge of any administrative follow-up. In the scheme we have explored thus far, this would appear to leave a gap, because there is no domestic 'hook' for judicial review litigation under Article 267 TFEU. In *Les Verts*, the Court of Justice addressed this scenario:

> Where the Community institutions are responsible for the administrative implementation of [EU law], natural or legal persons may bring a direct action before the Court against implementing measures which are addressed to them or which are of direct and individual concern to them.[35]

(A) Standing for Natural and Legal Persons

The legal basis for such challenges is Article 263(4) TFEU, which in its pre-Lisbon form provided that:

> Any natural or legal person may, under the conditions laid down in the first and second paragraphs, institute proceedings against an act addressed to that person or which is of direct and individual concern to them.

This is 'revolutionary'.[36] Individuals who are the addressees of a Union act get the key to the Ferrari[37] and can litigate directly at the international plain. When the EU Intellectual Property Office declared invalid a patent designed to impersonate a famous footballer, for example, the tricky fraudster was able (unsuccessfully) to argue directly before the General Court that his desire for exclusive control over the sign 'Neymar' was sheer coincidence.[38]

Decisions addressed to a specific person, then, pose few conceptual difficulties. Article 263(4) TFEU is not limited thus, however. Could it also be used to bring direct challenges against measures of general application (i.e. not ones addressed to the litigant)? Here, matters get more difficult. Until the Lisbon reforms, a joyride in the shiny Luxembourg Ferrari was only possible for 'non-privileged applicants' if they could show both 'direct' and 'individual' concern.

Direct Concern

The case law on direct concern is relatively straightforward.[39] In essence, the applicant must demonstrate 'a ***direct causal link*** between the contested

[35] *Les Verts* (n 1) [23].

[36] Arnull, 'Judicial review in the European Union' (n 11), p. 385.

[37] Indeed, such acts tend to come with an explicit reference to Article 263 TFEU printed on them.

[38] Case T-795/17 *Carlos Moreira v EUIPO* EU:T:2019:329.

[39] We say 'relatively' because of emerging discussions surrounding standing rules for certain 'atypical non-privileged applicants' after the Lisbon Treaty reforms; see, e.g., Case C-352/19 P *Région de Bruxelles-Capitale v European Commission*, Opinion of AG Bobek EU:C:2020:588 [141]. See also the Opinion of AG Bobek, albeit in the context of Article 265 TFEU (failure to act), in Joined Cases C-596/15 P and C-597/15 P *Bionorica SE and Diapharm GmbH & Co. KG v European Commission* EU:C:2017:297.

EU act and the alteration in [her] legal situation.'[40] Key to this is the absence of any discretion on part of the national authorities: even though a Member State might issue import licences, for example, an importer will be able to show direct concern where the Commission alone can assess the underlying economic questions that determine whether licences will be granted.[41]

Individual Concern

In practice, the most difficult hurdle for private parties who are not addressees of an EU act will usually be the requirement to demonstrate individual concern. The Court's consistently narrow interpretation of this concept dates back to the 1960s. In *Plaumann*,[42] the German government had unsuccessfully requested Commission authorisation to lower tariffs on the import of fresh clementines by 25 per cent. When the eponymous importer sought to challenge this refusal, the Court of Justice declared the application inadmissible. Individual concern, it explained, was to be limited to scenarios where a Union act affects a party

> by reason of certain attributes which are peculiar to them or by reason of circumstances in which they are differentiated from all other persons and by virtue of these factors distinguishes them individually just as in the case of the person addressed.

Plaumann may well have suffered economic consequences as a result of the Commission's refusal, but it was merely engaged in 'a commercial activity which may at any time be practised by any person' – which was not 'such as to distinguish the applicant in relation to the contested decision as in the case of the addressee'.[43]

This test continues to be good law to this day. 'Individual concern in its *Plaumann* incarnation', Arnull notes, 'has been one of Union law's great survivors.'[44] It is not impossible to find the odd exception. In *Codorníu*, for example, vintners of fine Spanish sparkling wine succeeded in demonstrating individual concern when challenging a Council regulation which limited the *crémant* appellation to French and Luxembourgish bubbly. Their vineyards had trademarked *Gran Crémant de Codorniu* and sold it exclusively since 1924, which was enough to convince the Court that 'from the point of view of the contested provision' the vintners were differentiated from all other

---

[40] *Bruxelles-Capitale* (n 39) [48] (emphasis supplied).

[41] Joined Cases 41-44/70 *International Fruit Company and ors v European Commission* [1971] ECR 411 [25], [24].

[42] Case 25/62 R *Plaumann & Co. v European Commission* [1963] EU:C:1963:17.

[43] *Plaumann & Co.* p. 107.

[44] Arnull, 'Judicial review in the European Union' (n 11), p. 388.

traders.[45] Overall, however, the Court has consistently stuck to its narrow line, even where broader standing might intuitively be warranted.[46]

Against a backdrop of sustained academic criticism,[47] matters eventually came to a head in the early 2000s. AG Francis Jacobs led the charge in *UPA*.[48] In an opinion deserving of close reading, he set out a comprehensive critique of the narrow *Plaumann* approach: the Court of First Instance was the appropriate forum for determining the validity of Union acts,[49] and given the drawbacks of the Article 267 TFEU preliminary reference procedure, the indirect route to Luxembourg could hardly be characterised as a suitable alternative.[50] As a result, the Court's narrow reading of direct concern was 'incompatible with the principle of effective judicial protection'. The defect could only be cured by a new interpretation, centred on a measure's 'substantial adverse effect on [claimants'] interests'.[51]

The Court of First Instance enthusiastically embraced the proposed widening of standing in its decision in *Jégo-Quéré*, handed down shortly after the publication of AG Jacobs' opinion.[52] '[I]n order to ensure effective judicial protection', not least in the light of Articles 6 and 13 ECHR, as well as Article 47 CFR, the CFI proposed to extend individual concern to all situations where the impugned measure affects the claimant's 'legal position, in a manner which is both definite and immediate, by restricting [their] rights or by imposing obligations on [them]'.[53]

The Court of Justice, however, was distinctly unimpressed. The fact that individuals do not enjoy unfettered access to direct challenges against measures of general application could not call into question the fact that the Union was 'based on the rule of law'. The Treaty *had* 'established a complete system of legal remedies and procedures designed to ensure judicial review': the preliminary reference procedure under Article 267 TFEU provided a clear alternative

[45] Case C-309/89 *Codorníu SA v Council* [1994] ECR I-1853 [22].
[46] Case C-321/95 P *Stichting Greenpeace Council (Greenpeace International) v European Commission* [1998] ECR I-1651. This particular point may well be revisited imminently in light of the Aarhus Convention; see European Commission, 'Commission staff working document: Report on European Union implementation of the Aarhus Convention in the area of access to justice on environmental matters' [2019] SWD/2019/378 final, as discussed in S Bogojević, 'Human rights of minors and future generations: Global trends and EU environmental law particularities' (2020) 29(2) RECIEL 191.
[47] See, e.g., L Gormley, 'Judicial review: Advice for the deaf?' (2006) 29(4) Fordham Int LJ 655.
[48] Case C-50/00 P *Unión de Pequeños Agricultores v Council* [2002] ECR I-6677 (*UPA*). The facts are relatively straightforward: a farmers' association appealed against the CFI's declaration that it was not individually concerned by a Regulation amending rules for the olive oil markets.
[49] *UPA* [45]–[49].
[50] *UPA* [38]–[44].
[51] *UPA* [49], [60].
[52] Case T-177/01 *Jégo-Quéré & Cie SA v European Commission* [2002] ECR II-2365. The case concerned a challenge against a Regulation seeking to protect certain fish species by requiring larger net sizes, brought by a French fishing company operating in Irish waters.
[53] *Jégo-Quéré* [47], [51].

route to direct proceedings. If anything, it was therefore up to 'the Member States to establish a system of legal remedies and procedures which ensure respect for the right to effective judicial protection.' The principle of sincere cooperation required domestic courts to facilitate indirect validity challenges whenever possible. It may well be 'possible to envisage a [more generous direct] system of judicial review', but 'reform [of] the system [then] in force' was strictly a matter for the Member States as Masters of the Treaties.[54]

(B) Regulatory Acts: The Post-Lisbon Landscape

The Convention tasked with preparations for a Constitutional Treaty was quick to accept this invitation.[55] Instead of embracing the radical suggestion put forward by AG Jacobs, however, it adopted a more subtle approach in keeping with the two-tiered approach to judicial review explored in our opening debate. At the domestic level, Article 19(1) TEU embraced the Court's emphasis on Member State responsibility, stipulating that domestic courts 'shall provide remedies sufficient to ensure effective legal protection in the fields covered by Union law'. At the Union level, the Lisbon Treaty added an additional category to the Article 263(4) TFEU list of direct challenges available to individuals: henceforth, such actions would also lie against any 'regulatory act which is of direct concern to them and does not entail implementing measures'.

This formulation dispenses with the problems surrounding individual concern. But it opens up a whole host of questions instead:[56] what is a 'regulatory act'? And when does such an act 'not entail implementing measures'?

The definition of regulatory acts was fleshed out in two cases handed down in the autumn of 2011. In *Inuit*, a number of claimants sought to challenge a Union regulation which severely restricted trade in seal products.[57] After a detailed exploration, the General Court concluded that the new category was to encompass 'all acts of general application apart from legislative acts'.[58] As the Regulation under scrutiny had been adopted pursuant to a legislative procedure, the established test of direct and individual was therefore to be applied, leaving the applicants without standing.[59] The opposite conclusion was reached

---

[54] *UPA* (n 48) [38], [40]–[42], [45]. In a similar vein, the Court subsequently allowed the Commission's appeal against the CFI's decision in *Jégo-Quéré* (n 52): Case C-263/02 P *European Commission v Jégo-Quéré & Cie SA* [2004] ECR I-3425.

[55] For more on the Convention, see Chapter 7, Debate 1 and Chapter 2, Debate 1.

[56] Direct concern has in essence the same meaning as what we have already seen: Case T-18/10 *Inuit Tapiriit Kanatami and ors v European Parliament and Council* [2011] ECR II-5599 [71].

[57] European Parliament and Council Regulation (EC) No 1007/2009 of 16 September 2009 on trade in seal products [2009] OJ L286/36.

[58] *Inuit* (n 56) [56].

[59] *Inuit* [66], [94]. The GC's findings were upheld on appeal by the Grand Chamber of the Court of Justice: C-583/11 P *Inuit Tapiriit Kanatami and ors v European Parliament and ors* EU:C:2013:625.

on the facts of *Microban*, a challenge to Commission Decision 2010/169/EU, which had removed the antibacterial chemical triclosan from the Union's list of permitted plastic additives.[60] As the decision had been 'adopted by the Commission in the exercise of implementing powers and not in the exercise of legislative powers', and was furthermore 'of general application in that it applies to objectively determined situations and it produces legal effects with respect to categories of persons envisaged in general and in the abstract', it was to be considered a regulatory act.[61]

As the decision left no discretion to the Member States, the applicants were directly concerned by it,[62] thus only leaving the question of whether the act entailed any implementing measures. The removal of triclosan from the list of approved chemicals had not required Member States to adopt any further measures. Microban's claim for judicial review was therefore admissible.[63]

In principle, at least, this has made it possible to challenge administrative Union acts that were previously beyond the scope of judicial review.[64] At the same time, however, *Microban* should not be taken as a suggestion that the Lisbon amendments to Article 263(4) TFEU have opened the floodgates to direct judicial review for individual applicants. The fact that most Union acts require some form of Member State cooperation means that, in practice, claims frequently founder on the rock of implementing measures – from effecting state aid disbursements to reclaiming them.[65]

***

Insofar as access to the Ferrari of direct judicial review is concerned, the list of those with a key thus continues to be limited. Short of having an invitation personally addressed to you, chances are that the test of direct and individual concern will keep the doors firmly shut. The Lisbon reforms have admitted a few more members to the fancy car club. Overall, however, the list of those entitled to take Article 263(4) TFEU for a spin continues to be an exclusive one.

Debate 3

Can there be gaps in a complete system of remedies?

The constitutional importance of judicial review can hardly be understated, as is reflected by the Member States' commitment to effective judicial protection and access to justice across the Treaties and the Charter of Fundamental Rights.

---

[60] Case T-262/10 *Microban International Ltd and Microban (Europe) Ltd v European Commission* [2011] ECR II-7697.
[61] *Microban* [22]–[23], [25].
[62] *Microban* [29]–[30].
[63] *Microban* [39]. The applicants went on to succeed in substance: [69].
[64] Case C-274/12 P *Telefónica SA v European Commission* EU:C:2013:852 [28]–[29].
[65] Case T-238/14 *EGBA and RGA v European Commission* EU:T:2016:259 [40]–[41]; *Telefónica SA* [36].

And yet, we have clearly identified a number of 'gaps' in the system – scenarios where individuals or small traders might find themselves unable to challenge Union action with significant implications for them.

Was AG Jacobs right, after all? Should the Court approach a more liberal approach in interpreting the notions of individual and direct concern, as well as the more recent Lisbon innovations? Not necessarily. We should be careful not to conflate the rule of law with unlimited access to direct judicial review under Article 263 TFEU – or even unlimited judicial review, regardless of the route taken. Countervailing considerations range from legal certainty to resource allocation.

Translated into AG Sharpston's metaphor, even where everyone has the right to transport, this does *not* necessarily mean unlimited access to a Ferrari. A bike or a bus may well be a much more efficient way of getting around. There might even be situations where you should not have access to transport at all: mobility requirements apart, some short trips are best taken on foot.

(A) How Big Are the Holes in the Net?

Having some holes in a net does not necessarily make it less efficient: as we saw in *Jégo-Quéré*, it may well be environmentally desirable to limit catches to larger species. In evaluating AG Jacobs' claims, we must therefore begin by scrutinising the gaps identified and ask ourselves about the extent to which they continue to be problematic today, or might be addressed by alternative mechanisms.

Perhaps the most significant issue identified before Lisbon was the potential need to self-incriminate in order to bring judicial review proceedings. The Court seemed surprisingly unfazed by arguments about the ensuing incentives to break the law.[66] This is a serious gap, with considerable rule of law implications, but it is one that has largely been plugged by the Lisbon reforms. As the Court of Justice explained in *T & L Sugars*, the 'objective of that [reform] … as is apparent from its drafting history, was to ensure that individuals do not have to break the law in order to have access to a court'. In the absence of a domestic implementing measure, and therefore a hook into the 267 TFEU indirect review mechanism, this would otherwise mean that where 'a regulatory act directly affects the legal situation of a natural or legal person … that person could be denied effective judicial protection.' If the 'regulatory act entails implementing measures', however, 'litigants will be protected against the application to them of such an act by the ability to challenge the implementing measures which the act entails'.[67]

This brings us to the second gap identified by AG Jacobs: the potential shortfalls of the preliminary reference procedure when compared with direct

[66] For example, in allowing the Commission's appeal in *Jégo-Quéré* (n.52).

[67] Case C-456/13 P *T & L Sugars Ltd, Sidul Açúares, Unipessoal Lda v European Commission and ors* EU:C:2015:284 [29]–[30].

actions, despite the Court's repeated insistence that responsibility for any possible gaps ought to be borne by domestic courts. Arnull, a leading sceptic, is not impressed: 'Why', he asks, did the Court 'impose duties on national courts, of respect for the principle of effective judicial protection and consistent interpretation, which it was not prepared to assume itself?'[68]

AG Jacobs' charge sheet here is long, beginning with the fact that individuals do not enjoy a *right* to a preliminary reference request: the decision to request any such ruling under Article 267 TFEU is in the discretion of the national court.[69] Upon closer inspection, however, that argument turns out to be somewhat of a red herring. As national courts cannot declare Union acts invalid, once litigants have raised a genuine challenge,[70] the judge will have no choice but to refer the case to the CJEU.[71] The lack of an automatic right to a reference request may well constitute a genuine virtue of the system, as Member State courts act as an important filtering layer, sorting out obviously hopeless cases before they waste court and litigants' time and resources: 'the mere fact that a party contends that the dispute gives rise to a question concerning the validity of Community law does not mean that the court concerned is compelled'[72] to submit a preliminary ruling request.

Another concern raised by AG Jacobs is the supposed efficiency and cost savings of direct actions under Article 263 TFEU. These, however, are not empirically substantiated claims, and it is not difficult to see counterarguments.[73] It is not disputed that a request for a preliminary reference can add significant amounts of delay and cost to legal proceedings,[74] but such analyses rarely consider the counterfactual. Even a significantly enlarged General Court could never hope to match the work of courts and tribunals at all levels across the 27 Member States,[75] and conducting whole cases in Luxembourg comes with its own significant cost implications. Similar considerations apply to the General Court's expertise in EU proceedings (cases requiring detailed factual and procedural analysis could quickly clog up the General Court), and any

---

[68] Arnull, 'Judicial review in the European Union', p. 400 (n 11).

[69] *UPA* (n 48), Opinion of AG Jacobs [42].

[70] Case 283/81 *Srl CILFIT and Lanificio di Gavardo SpA v Ministry of Health* [1982] ECR 3415 (Chapter 7, Debate 1) does *not* apply to negative responses to questions of validity: Case C-461/03 *Gaston Schul Douane-expediteur BV v Minister van Landbouw, Natuur en Voedselkwaliteit* [2005] ECR I-10513.

[71] *Inuit* (n 56) [96].

[72] Case C-344/04 *The Queen on the Application of International Air Transport Association and European Low Fares Airline Association v Department for Transport* [2006] ECR I-403 [28].

[73] For an excellent account, see Arnull, 'Judicial review in the European Union' (n 11).

[74] To get a sense of these, see T de la Mare and C Donnelly, 'Preliminary rulings and EU legal integration: Evolution and stasis' in P Craig and G de Búrca (eds), *The Evolution of EU Law*, 2nd edn (Oxford University Press 2011), pp. 375–76.

[75] European Parliament and Council Regulation (EU, Euratom) 2015/2422 of 16 December 2015 amending Protocol No 3 on the Statute of the Court of Justice of the European Union [2015] OJ L341/14. We return to this point in the conclusion.

gains in legal certainty under the direct route (offset by the possibility of appeals to the CJEU).

Furthermore, not every litigant denied direct access to judicial review is confronted with a genuine gap. In *Greenpeace*, the Court pointed out that the environmental NGO had already sought to challenge the power station regime it objected to in domestic proceedings, and was really after a second bite of the cherry in bringing Article 263 TFEU proceedings after the domestic action had failed.[76] The Court's emphasis on domestic proceedings could also be seen as a positive attempt to distribute responsibility for judicial review in line with the principle of subsidiarity, 'reducing CJEU intervention and enabling judicial matters to be resolved closer to the citizens'. Under that analysis, the real emphasis for those seeking to foster access to justice should be on *national* rules – from standing to costs[77] – as the best way of 'catching the few cases that still slip through the net'.[78]

(B) Remaining Gaps: So What?

Does that leave us with any genuine gaps? Yes, it does. Individual litigants will struggle to challenge general legislative acts which do not entail any implementing measures, as their applications for annulment will be inadmissible under both Articles 263 and 267 TFEU. This can lead to understandable frustrations: Why should the Union's climate change goals, for example, be insulated against judicial scrutiny?[79]

Upon closer inspection, however, is this really a fundamental flaw in the Union's legal order? Not necessarily. The narrow reading of the Treaty may well be justified. Having considered the matter, the Member States have refused to make the sweeping changes suggested by AG Jacobs. Moreover, from a constitutional perspective, judicial review is but one of the important elements in vindicating the rule of law. Unlimited review of Union acts would come with its own problems.

As regards the narrow reading of standing rules, it is important to recall that the CJEU is not in principle averse to judicial review: 'provisions of the Treaty regarding the right of interested parties to bring an action must not be interpreted restrictively'.[80] Historically, the Court *has* been generous in interpreting the predecessor provision of Article 263 TFEU to fill gaps in the system – for

---

[76] *Greenpeace* (n 46) [32].

[77] S Bogojević, 'Judicial protection of individual applicants revisited: Access to justice through the prism of judicial subsidiarity' (2015) 34(1) YEL 5.

[78] S Enchelmaier, 'No-one slips through the net? Latest developments, and non-developments, in the European Court of Justice's Jurisprudence on Art. 230(4) EC' (2005) 24(1) YEL 173, 221. (The article is a case note on *Jégo-Quéré* – get it?)

[79] Bogojević, 'Human rights of minors and future generations' (n 46).

[80] *Plaumann* (n 42) [107].

example, in allowing annulment actions to be brought by (and against[81]) the European Parliament.[82]

Why did this generosity not extend to direct and individual concern? Remember just how unusual it is for individuals to litigate directly in international law. Article 263 TFEU is designed first and foremost for use by the 'privileged applicants' listed in Article 263(2) TFEU alongside the substantive review grounds. The wording of Article 263(4) TFEU is key: it is deliberately narrow, designed as a 'pressure valve' for the rare situations where an individual has come into direct contact with Union institutions. Understood thus, the requirement of 'direct and individual concern' is merely an alternative formulation ('just as in the case'[83]) to cover scenarios where a decision has been disguised as a measure of general applicability.[84]

More fundamentally, unlimited judicial review is not necessarily a desirable feature of any legal system. 'In the majority of the Member States, the right of individuals to bring direct proceedings for the annulment of a measure of general application is limited in various ways' – from standing rules to a complete lack of a general right to judicial review of legislative acts.[85]

Writing extra-judicially, the President of the Court of Justice, Koen Lenaerts, once noted the 'impossibility of attempting to imagine the course of European law without *Les Verts*. The five crucial sentences of paragraph 23 have made an indelible imprint on the European judicial landscape.' This, he explained, was for two reasons. First, the recognition of the 'constitutional functions accorded to the Court of Justice that embody the mainstay of its activities through the present day' – a claim we will investigate in detail in Chapter 7. Second, because 'the complete and coherent system of judicial protection espoused [there] continues to provide the benchmark for the ... Union'.[86]

Not everyone is convinced by this. Was the Court's *dictum*, Alemanno asks, 'a statement of fact, a prediction or a wish?' – not least given the fact that, by the time of *UPA*, 'the rhetoric of completeness generated by *Les Verts* ha[d] lost ... its argumentative force by failing to persuade the Court itself'?[87]

Perhaps, however, we should not be quite so fast in equating the existence of a 'complete system' with the ability to bring judicial review against *every* Union act. The EU's commitment to the constitutional ideals underpinning *Les Verts* (access to justice and the rule of law) does *not* necessarily point to

[81] *Les Verts* (n 1).

[82] Case C-70/88 *European Parliament v Council* [1991] ECR I-4529 (*Chernobyl*).

[83] *Plaumann* (n 42) [107].

[84] Arnull, 'Judicial review in the European Union' (n 11), p. 385.

[85] *Jégo-Quéré* (n 54) [24].

[86] K Lenaerts, 'The basic constitutional charter of a community based on the rule of law' in MP Maduro and L Azoulai (eds), *The Past and Future of EU Law: The Classics of EU Law Revisited on the 50th Anniversary of the Rome Treaty* (Hart 2010), p. 315.

[87] A Alemanno, 'What has been, and what could be, thirty years after *Les Verts/European Parliament*' in MP Maduro and L Azoulai (eds), *The Past and Future of EU Law: The Classics of EU Law Revisited on the 50th Anniversary of the Rome Treaty* (Hart 2010), pp. 324, 332.

unlimited judicial review. Indeed, too easy access to annulment proceedings could in itself jeopardise both the rule of law (by creating constant uncertainty about the legal status of measures) and access to justice (if the Court became flooded with claims, leading to a substantial increase in delays).[88]

Other factors will also mitigate against judicial review. Some legal theorists, for example, have voiced concerns about the implications of overturning democratically mandated norms.[89] These concerns do not necessarily map precisely onto the Union's legal order,[90] but there might be closely related reasons for embracing caution when it comes to judicial scrutiny. As explained in the previous chapter, EU legislative acts will often represent careful polycentric bargains, struck between competing interests over the course of extensive consultations and negotiations between the Commission, the Council, and the European as well as national parliaments.[91] There will be winners and losers, but that does not necessarily entitle the latter to an automatic right to air their grievances before a Court. When Vodaphone challenges the Roaming Regulation, or Ryanair questions the legality of the Passenger Rights regime, their primary motivation is not to uphold the rule of law, but to maximise shareholder profits.

Where does this leave us? (Re-)consider the different gaps we have identified, and ask yourself how the considerations just outlined match up against them. The current approach may well fail to recognise the high degree of heterogeneity which characterises judicial review proceedings, for example: Union acts which have run the whole gamut of the ordinary legislative procedure are very distinct from administrative decisions concerning the classification of particular chemicals; as are multinational corporations and large NGOs with professional litigation departments when compared with small businesses or local authorities. Abandoning the simplistic conflation of a complete system of remedies with unlimited direct or indirect access to the CJEU is an important first step in building a more subtle framework for the judicial review of Union acts.

This was recognised in the Grand Chamber's judgment in *Inuit*. Having confirmed the General Court's interpretation of regulatory acts, the Court took the opportunity to return to *Les Verts* and review the overall system of judicial review of Union actions.[92] The pattern of argumentation is reassuringly familiar: a Union based on the rule of law, to which end there is a complete system of remedies, providing multiple levels of review as appropriate for different litigants (i.e. in the case of nearly all applications brought by individuals, the domestic courts via Article 267 TFEU). Article 47 of the Charter was not

[88] As has happened in the case of the ECHR: F de Londras and K Dzehtsiarou, *Great Debates on the European Convention on Human Rights* (Palgrave 2018).

[89] J Waldron, 'The core of the case against judicial review' (2006) 115(6) Yale LJ 1346.

[90] Arnull, 'Judicial review in the European Union' (n 11), section III.

[91] See Chapter 2, Debate 2.

[92] C-583/11P *Inuit* (n 59), [89]–[106] provides a clear and concise overview of the Court's approach to most of the debates in this chapter.

intended to change the narrow standing rules under Article 263 TFEU and, as Article 19(1) TEU confirms, whilst Member States are not under a general duty to create new remedies, they may well be obliged to do so if there are no ways of challenging Union acts other than to break the law.

The casual reader might be lulled into a sense of complacency at this stage. But just as Haydn's Surprise Symphony jolts its audience with a surprise stroke of the kettledrum after the most *piano* of openings,[93] so the Court of Justice's final paragraphs surprise with a subtle, yet tectonic, shift in approach. When faced with the concern that (certain) legislative actions may be rendered 'virtually immune to judicial review', the Court notes that Article 47 CFR does 'not require that an individual should have an unconditional entitlement to' direct annulment actions.[94] Nor does it require the Member States to furnish a solution in all scenarios, in a major change of tack: neither Article 47 CFR nor Article 19(1) TEU 'require that an individual should be entitled to bring actions against such acts, as their primary subject matter, before the national courts or tribunals.'[95]

Conclusion: Ferraris, Bicycles, and the 'Art of Traffic Control'

The shiny blue and yellow Ferrari of Union-level judicial review is thus likely to remain firmly locked for most applicants, and even domestic bicycle services might not always be available. This is entirely justified in certain cases, whilst causing serious hardship in others. What may well be required to square that circle is a careful recalibration in the relationship between different modes of transport (and avenues of judicial review), not least by recognising that 'non-privileged' applicants do not constitute a homogeneous group. Sometimes, different road users faced with a similar commute nonetheless require different modes of transportation.

This call for more sophisticated traffic management is reflected in a recent Opinion of AG Bobek, in which he joins a long line of Advocates General concerned with 'the overly restrictive tendency in interpreting and applying [standing] rules, especially 10 years after the Treaty of Lisbon, which was supposed to alleviate at least some of those concerns.'[96] As opposed to some predecessors, however, he does not go on to suggest 'that the categories of direct and individual concern should be radically reinterpreted and the gates suddenly opened'.[97] Instead, he explains that certain cases – whether those brought by 'atypical non-privileged applicants', such as regions or states constituting the Member States, or others raising 'complex, regulatory and technical issues' – might best be served by a full hearing directly before the General Court, rather than, say, tempting the

[93] J Haydn, Symphony No. 94 in G Major ('The Surprise Symphony') H. 1/94.
[94] *Inuit* (n 59) [105].
[95] *Inuit* [106].
[96] *Bruxelles-Capitale* (n 39) [138].
[97] *Bruxelles-Capitale* [137].

Brussels Capital Region '(naturally, entirely hypothetically) [to instruct] some of its employees to go out and vandalise a few shops in Brussels'.

Neither the radical extension of standing nor a continuation of the narrow dogma we have encountered are likely to achieve this goal. The only 'short- and mid-term viable alternative is to channel, via a more reasonable interpretation of the criteria of the fourth paragraph of Article 263 TFEU with regard to at least some non-privileged applicants, … those types of cases before the General Court'.[98]

Further Reading

A different perspective to the one developed in this chapter is suggested by Albertina Alborns-Llorens, who proposes that the CJEU may be becoming 'more progressive in the assessment of the substance of [judicial review] claims than in issues of admissibility': 'Edging towards closer scrutiny? The Court of Justice and its review of the compatibility of general measures with the protection of economic rights and freedoms' in A Arnull and others (eds), *A Constitutional Order of States? Essays in EU Law in Honour of Alan Dashwood* (Hart 2011). What do you make of her claim, especially in light of Chapters 2 and 3?

Not everyone agrees with *Foto-Frost*. Dorota Leczykiewicz, for example, argues that Member State Courts should be able to strike down EU law in certain situations: 'Effective Judicial Protection of Human Rights after Lisbon: Should National Courts Be Empowered to Review EU Secondary Law?' (2010) 35(3) EL Rev 326.

The emphasis on the role of national courts does not just come in the context of judicial review of *Union* measures, but also when it comes to reviewing the compatibility of *national* measures with EU law – see the debates in Chapters 5 and 6. This raises an interesting *comparative* question as between the two regimes: are the parallel paths developing in a coherent fashion? Yes, absolutely, according to Koen Lenaerts: 'The Rule of Law and the Coherence of the Judicial System of the European Union' (2007) 44 CML Rev 1625. Arnull is not convinced, however. Why is domestic law meant to evolve, when the CJEU is steadfastly sticking to *Plaumann*?: 'The Principle of Effective Judicial Protection in EU Law: An Unruly Horse?' (2007) 44 CML Rev 1763.

[98] *Bruxelles-Capitale* [146], [147].

CHAPTER 5

Claws for Paper Tigers

Harmonious Interpretation, Direct Effect, Damages, and the Quest for National Procedural Autonomy

Rights without remedies are meaningless. What use is the promise of pay equality to women forced to retire long before their male colleagues,[1] or the prohibition of religious discrimination to workers who receive less holiday pay because they do not worship in a specific church?[2] EU law provides plenty of rights for individuals – but what happens when a Member State has no equal pay legislation in place, or when it has failed to implement anti-discrimination law properly? There is a real danger that rights end up as 'paper tigers, fierce in appearance but missing in tooth and claw.'[3]

Sharpening the claws and teeth of (paper) tigers is tricky! In the first Debate, we explore a number of different techniques to ensure that citizens' rights enjoy *effet utile*[4] (i.e. that they can readily be enforced in practice). The tool kit includes a duty on all courts to interpret national law in line with EU rules; the doctrine of direct effect, which we first encountered in Chapter 1; and monetary compensation (damages) for loss suffered as a result of Member State breaches. We then need to think about the interaction of these different avenues. Is it preferable to bend national law into shape, rely directly on an EU right, or hope for damages? What about rights which are not easily quantifiable, such as clean air and workplace representation?[5]

There is also the risky business of introducing a new predator into well-established, complex ecosystems: a delicate balance must be struck to ensure the co-existence of species.[6] In principle at least, each Member State enjoys autonomy in deciding on national procedures for enforcing EU law rights.

[1] Case 43-75 *Gabrielle Defrenne v SABENA* [1976] ECR I-455.

[2] Case C-193/17 *Cresco Investigation GmbH v Markus Achatzi* EU:C:2019:43.

[3] B Hepple, *Social and Labour Rights in a Global Context* (Cambridge University Press 2003), p. 238.

[4] Or 'effective judicial protection'.

[5] On workplace representation, see Case C-176/12 *Association de médiation sociale v Union locale des syndicats CGT and ors* EU:C:2014:2 (*AMS*).

[6] For more on biological invasions, see RM Pringle and others, 'Predator-induced collapse of niche structure and species coexistence' (2019) 570 Nature 58.

When it comes to ensuring compliance with judgments, for example, courts in different Member States have an array of different techniques available to them: from the power to hold a party in contempt of court[7] to imposing periodic payments,[8] or even to adopt and determine directly the content of particular decisions.[9] Too much procedural autonomy, on the other hand, could threaten the vindication of Union rights. The principle of effectiveness seeks to strike the balance, but how far should it go in reshaping domestic legal orders?

Debate 1

Making rights effective?

EU law recognises plenty of individual rights in the Treaties, the Charter of Fundamental Rights, and even secondary legislation. Citizens enjoy the right to be consulted before a new powerplant is built,[10] air passengers are entitled to compensation if their flights are delayed,[11] and workers are eligible for compensation when their employer becomes insolvent.[12] These look great on paper, but how do they become *real*?

EU law can take effect in national legal orders in a number of ways. Take the right to equal pay for male and female workers for equal work found in Article 157 TFEU, and imagine that your employer has underpaid you on the basis of your sex. There are three principal avenues for seeking redress. First, the ***duty of harmonious interpretation*** requires national employment tribunals to interpret the relevant domestic wage laws in line with EU law. A provision on 'just wages' for the work you have carried out, for example, would have to be read to include 'pay equality': your claim would be based on national law, which has been bent into shape to match EU rules.

This approach is distinct from ***direct effect***, which substitutes EU law for conflicting national law. If domestic employment law simply leaves remuneration to contractual agreements, then the relevant provision would be thrown out ('disapplied') and replaced by EU rules on equal pay: your claim would be based directly on EU law. If neither of these avenues is available, then you

[7] CPR 81 (Applications and Proceedings in Relation to Contempt of Court) (UK).

[8] Code de justice administrative: Livre IX: L'exécution des decisions (FR).

[9] Codice del Processo Amministrativo, Decreto Legislativo n 104/2010, Libro quarto, Titolo I, art 112-115: Giudizio di ottemperanza (IT).

[10] European Parliament and Council Directive 2011/92/EU of 13 December 2011 on the assessment of the effects of certain public and private projects on the environment [2011] OJ L26/1.

[11] European Parliament and Council Regulation (EC) No 261/2004 of 11 February 2004 establishing common rules on compensation and assistance to passengers in the event of denied boarding and of cancellation or long delays of flights [2004] OJ L46/1.

[12] European Parliament and Council Directive 2008/94/EC of 22 October 2008 on the protection of employees in the event of the insolvency of their employer [2008] OJ L283/36.

might alternatively be able to seek *damages* from the Member State to compensate for your loss.

Which of these avenues works best will depend on the specific context of a case. Remember also that a delicate balance needs to be struck between the interests of citizens and Member States – treading a careful line between giving effect to individual EU rights on the one hand, and preserving national legal autonomy on the other. Whilst there is a growing body of EU legislation that provides for remedies at the national level,[13] we need to take a close look at the remedies jurisprudence of the CJEU to understand how different enforcement mechanisms have been developed under the banner of effectiveness.

(A) Harmonious Interpretation: Bend It Like Beckham?

The obligation of harmonious interpretation has many names. You will see it referred to as 'indirect effect', 'the duty of conform', and/or 'purposive-' or 'consistent' interpretation. All these labels refer to the duty of all national bodies to interpret *all* national law in conformity with *all* EU law 'as far as possible'.[14] But just how far does that take us?

The duty of harmonious interpretation was first articulated in *Von Colson*.[15] It requires

> all the authorities of Member States including, for matters within their jurisdiction, the courts [...] to interpret their national law in the light of the wording and the purpose of [EU law].

This was later explained to apply regardless of 'whether the [national] provisions in question *were adopted before or after the directive*',[16] and to apply not only to the national law implementing a particular directive but to the national system '*as a whole*'.[17] Going back to our example of the right to equal pay, this means that a national judge is under the duty to interpret *all* types of national law – whether it is a constitution which long predates EU membership, or recent national provisions implementing EU law – in light of any primary or secondary EU law on equal pay relied upon by the litigants. Clearly, harmonious interpretation takes you far – potentially cutting all the way through your domestic legal order!

[13] FG Wilman, 'The end of the absence? The growing body of EU legislation on private enforcement and the main remedies it provides for' (2016) 53(4) CML Rev 887.

[14] Case C-106/89 *Marleasing SA v La Comercial Internacional de Alimentacion SA* [1990] ECR I-4135 [8].

[15] Case 14/83 *Sabine Von Colson and Elisabeth Kamann v Land Nordrhein-Westfalen* [1984] ECR 1891 [26].

[16] *Marleasing* (n 14) [8] [emphasis added].

[17] Joined Cases C-397/01 to C-403/01 *Bernhard Pfeiffer and ors v Deutsches Rotes Kreuz, Kreisverband Waldshut eV* [2004] ECR I-8835 [115] [emphasis added].

The CJEU justifies the wide scope of harmonious interpretation[18] with the need to ensure the 'full effectiveness' of EU law. National courts are to operate under the presumption that, in adopting EU law, the Member States 'had the intention of fulfilling entirely the obligations arising' from the Treaties.[19] That presumption is anchored in the principle of sincere cooperation, found today in Article 4(3) TEU: the Union and the Member States 'shall, in full mutual respect, assist each other in carrying out tasks which flow from the Treaties'. Indeed, as the Court subsequently asserted, harmonious interpretation is 'inherent in the system of the Treaty'.[20]

However, there is tension here. Harmonious interpretation is a sound compromise, ensuring respect for domestic structures whilst also vindicating individuals' rights. But it also puts a lot of pressure on domestic judges to revise *any* national law that fails to conform. Has the Court of Justice bent the duty of harmonious interpretation like Beckham? That is, does the duty change direction mid-air, from one of *interpreting* national law in light of EU law to that of *rewriting* it, all in the name of effectiveness but causing a much deeper disruption to national legal orders?

When Does Harmonised Interpretation Kick In?

In mapping the nature and scope of harmonised interpretation, imagine that you want to assert your right to parental leave, which is clearly provided by a directive[21] but not yet transposed into national law. At what point does the duty of harmonised interpretation kick in?

The Court of Justice decided in *Adeneler* that 'where a directive is transposed belatedly, the general obligation owed by national courts to interpret domestic law in conformity with the directive exists only once the period for its transposition has expired.'[22] However, national authorities are also to refrain, during that transitional period, from taking measures liable seriously to compromise the rights prescribed by EU law.[23] This means that without proper transposition into national law, you cannot rely on the directive – but neither can a Member State legislate to strip you of your prospective rights.

What happens when the directive is implemented but omits key provisions – for example, when it includes the right to *take* parental leave, but not the right to flexible working arrangements following your return to the workplace?[24] Here, the duty is more forceful, as it calls for *all* national law to be interpreted

---

[18] Note that harmonious interpretation is not unique to the EU, and that Member States have employed it in, for example, interpreting international obligations in a national legal setting.

[19] *Pfeiffer* (n 17) [112].

[20] *Pfeiffer* [114].

[21] See, e.g., European Parliament and Council Directive 2019/1158/EU of 20 June 2019 on work-life balance for parents and carers [2019] OJ L188/79.

[22] Case C-212/04 *Konstantinos Adeneler and ors v ELOG* [2006] ECR I-6057 [115].

[23] Case C-129/96 *Inter-Environnement Wallonie ASBL v Région wallonne* [1997] ECR I-7411 [45].

[24] See, e.g., Directive 2019/1158/EU (n 21), Article 1.

in conformity with EU rules, so that that the right to flexible working arrangements will be read into national employment law.

Harmonious interpretation thus provides a highly effective avenue to secure rights for individuals – not by replacing national law with EU provisions, but through the duty on courts to ensure that national rules are made to conform 'as far as possible' to EU standards. At the same time as remedying breaches of individual rights, however, harmonious interpretation also runs the risk of creating uncertainties and legal unpredictability. A balance needs to be struck.

Are There Any Limits?

The duty of harmonious interpretation is circumscribed in a number of ways. First, it is limited by several general principles, including legal certainty and nonretroactivity. This meant, in *Kolpinghuis Nijmegen*,[25] that Dutch authorities could not rely on an as-yet unimplemented EU directive defining 'mineral water' in taking criminal action against a cheeky café owner attempting to sell fizzy tap water as 'mineral water'. The Court of Justice ruled that given 'the principles of legal certainty and non-retroactivity [...] a directive cannot, of itself and independently of a national law adopted by a Member State for its implementation' lead to aggravated criminal liability on an individual.[26] On similar grounds, EU law could not be relied upon in criminal proceedings for false accounting against Silvio Berlusconi, a former Italian Prime Minister: an unimplemented directive could not have 'the effect of determining or increasing the liability in criminal law of accused persons'.[27]

Another significant limitation on harmonious interpretation is *interpretatio contra legem* – that is, the prohibition of going against national law's clear and explicit meaning. This was demonstrated in *Impact*,[28] where conformity with EU law could only be achieved by allowing retroactive interpretation of national implementing measures. As this had been explicitly denied in the domestic context, the national court could not insist on EU law conformity.

So there *are* limits to the judicial modification of national rules to fit EU law. But they are tightly circumscribed – not least because the *contra legem* exception is limited to rules legitimately laid down by national *legislation*. In *Ajos*,[29] the Court of Justice ordered a national court to change its established case law 'where necessary', insofar as past cases relied on an interpretation of national law incompatible with EU law.

***

Harmonious interpretation is a discreet yet effective remedy. The seemingly straightforward duty on *all* national bodies to interpret, 'as far as possible', all

---

[25] Case 80/86 *Criminal proceedings against Kolpinghuis Nijmegen BV* [1987] ECR 3969.
[26] *Kolpinghuis Nijmegen* [13].
[27] Case C-387/02 *Criminal proceedings against Silvio Berlusconi and ors* [2005] ECR I-3565 [77].
[28] Case C-268/06 *Impact v Minister for Agriculture and Food and ors* [2008] ECR I-2483.
[29] Case C-441/14 *Dansk Industri v Estate of Karsten Eigil Rasmussen* EU:C:2016:278 [33].

national law in conformity with EU law allows the latter to seep deep into national legal orders. But certain limitations exist: the implementation period must have passed, and national courts cannot rule *contra legem* or in conflict with general principles.

However, 'as far as possible' is a vague qualification. In its weakest form, it invites the invocation of EU law in matters that could safely be decided on the basis of national legal sources. In its strongest sense, it requires that national law be bent into conformity, even at the cost of legal certainty.[30] It is this uncertainty, and an inability to tackle explicitly conflicting national law, that are its weakest feature as a remedy – or a price worth paying, as these very limitations go a long way towards preserving judicial autonomy in domestic courts.

(B) Direct Effect: The 'Silent Right' of Individuals

Direct effect is the defining feature of EU law. As we saw in Chapter 1, it sets the EU apart from other international legal systems and sits at the core of the 'new legal order' marked by dual vigilance, with both states and individuals able to insist on the enforcement of transnational rights. The preliminary ruling in *Van Gen den Loos* truly 'revolutionised European law':[31]

> Independently of the legislation of Member States, [EU] law ... not only imposes obligations on individuals but is also intended to confer upon them rights which become part of their legal heritage.[32]

This was a powerful judgment on multiple levels. By deciding that EU law would not need any further domestic translation, the Court cured the 'infant disease'[33] of the Treaty of Rome and guaranteed the uniform application of EU law across the Member States. Even more importantly, *Van Gend en Loos* created a plethora of 'silent rights' for individuals, emerging as correlatives to Member State obligations: not only did the Treaty's ban on import duties prohibit Dutch revenue authorities from levying such taxes, but it also gave a small family-owned logistics business the right to object to their imposition on a tanker load of ureaformaldehyde.[34]

Direct effect, in other words, positions private parties at the centre of the new legal order, empowering individuals to insist on their rights before national

---

[30] M Bobek, 'The effects of EU law in the national legal systems' in C Barnard and S Peers (eds), *European Union Law*, 3rd edn (Oxford University Press 2020), p. 170.

[31] M Rasmussen, 'Revolutionizing European law: A history of the *Van Gend en Loos* judgment' (2014) 12(1) Intl J Const L 136.

[32] Case 26/62 *NV Algemene Transport- en Expeditie Onderneming van Gend en Loos v Netherlands Inland Revenue Administration* [1963] ECR 1, p. 12.

[33] P Pescatore, 'The doctrine of "direct effect": An infant disease of community law' (1983) 8 EL Rev 155.

[34] C Hilson, 'Substantive environmental rights in the EU: Doomed to disappoint?' in S Bogojević and R Rayfuse (eds), *Environmental Rights in Europe and Beyond* (Hart 2018), pp. 87, 92.

authorities. Again, however, this does not come without tensions: the doctrine also strips Member States of any discretion in formulating EU laws to fit their national legal orders. Given how potentially potent a remedy it represents, it is unsurprising that major battles ensued between national governments and courts, on the one hand, and the Court of Justice, on the other, in defining the precise contours and scope of direct effect.[35]

Clarity and Precision

The EU Treaties contain several hundred provisions in addition to the Charter and secondary legislation. Many are fluffy, high-level aspirations and political commitments, rather than hard-hitting legal standards.[36] How, then, do we decide which provisions create individual rights and thereby have direct effect? *Van Gend en Loos* concerned the question of whether individuals could rely on what was then Article 12 EEC, which abolished customs duties:

> Member States shall refrain from introducing between themselves any new customs duties on import or exports or any charges having equivalent effect, and from increasing those which they already apply in their trade with each other.

This provision is clearly addressed to the Member States. There is no mention of empowering individuals to appeal to the law. Yet the Court was not perturbed: the provision had direct effect as it

> contains a clear and unconditional prohibition which is not a positive but a negative obligation [and which] is not qualified by any reservation on the part of the states which would make its implementation conditional upon a positive legislative measure enacted under national law.[37]

In practice, these criteria have been interpreted generously and slowly become blurred, to include provisions that require implementation,[38] or which allow Member State derogation.[39]

Even more importantly, the doctrine of direct effect has not been limited to Treaty provisions. The Court has found that – in principle at least – nearly all sources of EU law can be directly effective. This includes the Charter,[40] regulations,[41] decisions,[42] and general principles,[43] as well as directives.

---

[35] We return to this question extensively in Chapter 6, and Chapter 7, Debate 1.

[36] Remember, e.g., TEU, Articles 2 and 3.

[37] *van Gend en Loos* (n 32), p. 13.

[38] See Case 13/68 *SpA Salgoil v Italian Ministry of Foreign Trade* [1968] ECR 453.

[39] See Case 2/74 *Jean Reyners v Belgium* [1974] ECR 631; Case 41/74 *Yvonne Van Duyn v Home Office* [1974] ECR 1337.

[40] See Case C-617/10 *Åklagaren v Hans Åkerberg Fransson* [2013] ECR I-9011; Joined Cases C-293/12 and C-594/12 *Digital Rights Ireland Ltd v Minister for Communications and ors* [2014] ECR I-238.

[41] See Case 39/72 *European Commission v Italy* [1973] ECR 101.

[42] Case C-80/06 *Carp Snc di L. Moleri e V. Corsi v Ecorad Srl* [2007] ECR I-4473.

[43] Case C-144/04 *Werner Mangold v Rüdiger Helm* [2005] ECR I-9981.

The Curious Case of Directives

The notion that directives might enjoy direct effect is puzzling at first glance. As the Treaty explains, they are legal instruments binding only 'as to the result to be achieved': the form and method of implementation is left to Member States.[44] Ascribing direct effect to directives thus runs the risk of encroaching on Member States' regulatory autonomy and triggers plenty of resistance.

The Court defends its position with reference to an even more important consideration: effectiveness. Remember dual vigilance, outlined in Chapter 1? EU law is at its most effective when individuals can enforce it before their national authorities – hence the inclusion of a preliminary reference procedure in the Treaty of Rome. In the alternative, Member States could simply avoid compliance with their Treaty obligations by failing to implement a directive, or doing so incorrectly.[45]

There is an important undercurrent in this reasoning. Pierre Pescatore, a long-time Member of the Court, explains that in introducing direct effect, technicalities were less important than the implicit political message. Behind debates surrounding '*invocabilité*' – the ability to invoke a provision before national courts – lurked the real prize: the conferral of rights on individuals.[46]

Take environmental law as an example. Under the Air Quality Directive, Member States are obliged to improve ambient air quality, and 'shall draw up action plans' where limit values or alert threshold are exceeded.[47] How do we measure whether this is unconditional and sufficiently precise? The CJEU provides limited guidance. It does not dwell on the definition, stressing instead that

> it is incompatible with the binding effect which [Article 288 TFEU] ascribes to a directive to exclude, in principle, the possibility of the obligation imposed by that directive being relied on by persons concerned. That consideration applies particularly in respect of a directive which is intended to control and reduce atmospheric pollution and which is designed, therefore, to protect public health.[48]

The deleterious consequences of poor air quality for human health justify investing the provision with direct effect, establishing air quality as an enforceable individual right. Direct effect does not merely provide a shield against conflicting national laws: it empowers individuals to enforce their rights.

Insofar as directives are concerned, however, two important limitations should be noted. First, as the Court held in *Ratti*, direct effect will only kick in once the

[44] See TFEU, Article 288.

[45] See *Van Duyn* (n 39); Case 148/78 *Criminal proceedings against Tullio Ratti* [1979] ECR 1629.

[46] Pescatore, 'The doctrine of "direct effect"' (n 33).

[47] Council Directive 96/62/EC of 27 September 1996 on ambient air quality assessment and management [1996] OJ L296/55, Article 7(3) – the precursor to European Parliament and Council Directive 2008/50/EC of 21 May 2008 [2008] OJ L152/1 on ambient air quality and cleaner air for Europe, Article 24.

[48] Case C-237/07 *Dieter Janecek v Freistaat Bayern* [2008] ECR I-6221 [37].

implementation period has come to an end: 'Until that date is reached the Member States remain free in that field'.[49] Ratti, who had relied on an unimplemented directive before the expiry of the transitional period, could therefore not rely on EU law to shield himself from criminal prosecution, even though the national law on which the charges against him were based conflicted with a directive.

Second, the direct effect of directives cannot be invoked in horizontal cases (i.e. in litigation between private parties).[50] This limitation has given rise to much controversy, so much so that we have dedicated the entirety of the next chapter to the ensuing debates. For now, consider how these limitations show the CJEU as careful to respect Member States' discretionary powers in deciding how to implement EU law, whilst remaining ever watchful to ensure the effective judicial protection of individuals' rights.

(C) Damages: 'A Lovers' Triangle'[51]

The final remedial card up the EU's sleeve is damages. Individuals may obtain compensation for losses incurred as a result of a Member State's breach of EU law. The principle's origins can be traced back to another landmark judgment: *Francovich*.[52]

The case arose out of Italy's persistent failure to implement a directive designed to protect workers in the event of employer insolvency.[53] This had already been the subject of an infringement action by the Commission: to no avail.[54] As a result, when Andrea Francovich's employer became insolvent, he and his colleagues did not enjoy the protection granted to workers elsewhere in Europe. In response to this lack of judicial protection, the Court recognised a new *jus commune*, common to all Member States and the Union,[55] by concluding that

> it is a principle of [Union] law that the Member States are obliged to make good loss and damage caused to individuals by breaches of [Union] law for which they can be held responsible.[56]

Thus was created a specific remedy not previously on offer in all Member States. Imagine the controversy: *Francovich* cut deep into Member States'

[49] *Ratti* (n 45) [44].
[50] *AMS* (n 5).
[51] A term coined by A Biondi, 'In praise of *Francovich*' in MP Maduro and L Azoulai (eds), *The Past and Future of EU Law: The Classics of EU Law Revisited on the 50th Anniversary of the Rome Treaty* (Hart 2010), p. 413.
[52] Joined Cases C-6/90 and C-9/90 *Andrea Francovich and ors v Italy* [1991] ECR I-5357.
[53] Directive 2008/94/EC (n 12).
[54] Shortly after the judgment in *Francovich*, the Maastricht Treaty introduced what is today Article 260 TFEU, providing for fines to be imposed on Member States for failing to implement CJEU judgments.
[55] R Caranta, 'Judicial protection against Member States: A new *Jus Commune* takes shape' (1995) 32(3) CML Rev 703.
[56] *Francovich* (n 52) [37].

freedom to define appropriate remedies, running the risk of muddling – even 'infecting'[57] – national liability systems.

The CJEU's rationale in establishing state liability for EU law breaches is grounded in Article 4(3) TEU – the principle of sincere cooperation, which we continue to encounter throughout this chapter – and motivated by the need to secure the 'full effectiveness' of Union rules. Damages provide a safety net for individuals harmed by Member State failure to comply with EU law, including (but not limited to) situations where they are unable to rely on directly effective provisions.

This creates potentially awkward tensions akin, as Biondi suggests, to 'a lovers' triangle'.[58] Member States are traditionally left alone in deciding the terms of their (remedial) relationship with citizens. When left empty-handed, however, individuals understandably seek solace in a new lover: the EU. As a result, the CJEU is faced with dual loyalties – not wanting to intrude on the first lover's territory, perhaps, but also keen to protect individuals.

One area where this plays out most clearly are the conditions for state liability: where the threshold is set tells us a lot about the doctrine's underlying purpose. Should we compensate all individuals suffering loss where EU law has been breached? Or is the purpose to punish and deter rulebreakers? And who should be made to pay – only governments, or all private parties?

Conditions for State Liability

In *Francovich*, the Court of Justice had outlined liability conditions for non-implementation of directives.[59] In subsequent case law, and notably in *Brasserie de Pêcheur*, the Court explained that state liability covers not only directives but any 'sufficiently serious' breach of EU law.[60] The test, as it still stands today, comprises three (cumulative) criteria:

1. The rule infringed must be intended to confer rights upon individuals;
2. The breach must be sufficiently serious; and
3. There must be a direct causal link between the breach and the damage sustained.

The CJEU provides limited guidance as to when each condition is met. Indeed, in principle at least, this is a decision left to national courts.[61] This may seem peculiar considering that, in *Brasserie de Pêcheur*, the Court of Justice

---

[57] C Harlow, '*Francovich* and the problem of the disobedient state' (1996) 2(3) Eur LJ 199.

[58] Biondi, 'In praise of *Francovich*' (n 51).

[59] The test is three-fold: specific individual rights must have been conferred; the contents of those rights need to be identifiable; and there must be a causal link between the breach of the state's obligation and the loss and damage suffered by the injured party.

[60] Joined Cases C-46/93 *Brasserie du Pêcheur SA v Germany* and C-48/93 *The Queen v Secretary of State for Transport, ex p Factortame Ltd and ors* [1996] ECR I-1029 *(Factortame III)*.

[61] Though national conceptions of fault are not necessarily a condition of liability: Case C-571/16 *Nikolay Kantarev v Balgaraska Narodna Banka* EU:C:2018:807.

explained that state liability is matched by the liability of EU institutions as outlined in Article 340 TFEU. However, the CJEU is careful not to step too far into the territory of the Member States and so allows considerable leeway for national authorities – the 'first lover' – to apply the liability test to the facts of any given case.

This is arguably evidenced by the way that the key criterion – 'sufficiently serious' – is applied.[62] The basic rule is that the more discretion a Member State enjoys in implementing a particular EU law, the less likely a sufficiently serious breach will be found. Take *British Telecom* as an example. Failure correctly to implement a public procurement directive was found not to be sufficiently serious on the basis that its provisions were unclear and imprecise, that the EU institutions had provided no guidance on their interpretation, and that the Member State acted in good faith and in keeping within the wording and aims of the directive.[63] Whether the final condition – proving a causal link – is met in the case at hand is similarly frequently left to the national courts to decide.[64]

Giving broad leeway to the Member States in this way recognises the importance of national procedural autonomy. At the same time, however, it also runs the risk of creating legal uncertainty and inconsistency as to how and when state liability is a viable remedial option for individuals. The nod to individual rights, outlined in the first criterion, is nonetheless significant. The CJEU takes a purposive and wide approach in defining provisions 'intended to confer' rights, up to and including provisions which do not possess direct effect. This means that state liability works as a remedy in some – but not all – situations where direct effect fails. Ultimately, the criteria for state liability reflect the pushes and pulls of the lover's triangle in both offering broad protection for individual rights and seeking to maintain a respectful relationship with the Member States.

Broad State Liability vs Narrow Private Enforcement

In bringing damages claims, what exactly counts as 'the state'? The CJEU provides a broad definition that covers all emanations of public power, including administrative, legislative, and judicial actions. The latter was established in *Köbler*,[65] where the Court of Justice explained that as decisions by national courts of final appeal cannot normally be corrected, excluding them from state

[62] The full list of factors is set out in *Brasserie du Pêcheur* (n 60) [55]–[57].

[63] Case C-392/93 *The Queen v H. M. Treasury, ex p British Telecommunications plc* [1996] ECR I-1631. As a contrast, see Case C-452/06 *The Queen v Licensing Authority of the Department of Health, ex p Synthon BV* [2008] ECR I-7681, where the failure to recognise products allowed on the market of other Member States was 'sufficiently serious', as that was a duty obvious from mutual recognition, even if the disputed directive was similarly complex and difficult to interpret.

[64] Cf. Case C-420/11 *Jutta Leth v Austria, Land Niederösterreich* EU:C:2013:166 and Case C-557/12 *Kone AG and ors v ÖBB-Infrastruktur AG* EU:C:2014:1317, where specific guidance was outlined.

[65] Case C-224/01 *Gerhard Köbler v Austria* [2003] ECR I-10239.

liability would deprive individuals of the possibility to 'obtain legal protection of their rights'.[66] What makes a court count as the final adjudicating instance is left to national legal systems.[67] In *Traghetti del Mediterraneo*, however, the Court of Justice made clear that EU law prohibits national legislation that limits such liability by, for example, narrowing these down to cases of 'intentional fault and serious misconduct on the part of the court'.[68]

That said, *Köbler* liability is likely to be established only in the most exceptional of cases. It is triggered only where a national court has *manifestly* infringed applicable EU law – for instance, by disregarding well-established case law.[69] It is nevertheless potentially powerful in securing remedial action for individuals, even in the face of considerations of judicial independence.

'The state', then, is broadly construed. But what about private enforcement? Does *Francovich*-type liability extend that far? In *Courage v Crehan*, the Court of Justice ruled that in the enforcement of competition law rules, actions for damages may be pursued against private parties. As with state liability, the Court invoked the importance of securing 'the full effectiveness' of the Treaty's competition provisions but added that these are significant in 'discourag[ing] agreements or practices [...] which are liable to restrict or distort competition'.[70] The Court thus explicitly recognised that the purpose of damages is not only to compensate those suffering loss as a result of a Treaty breach, but also to punish and deter rulebreakers – at least in the context of competition law, which, as per the wording in Article 101(2) TFEU, has horizontal application.[71]

It is unclear whether the Court's move to include private enforcement could be extended beyond competition law to Treaty provisions on, for example, free movement.[72] There are multiple reasons to be cautious, given the differences between approaches to private enforcement and the availability of certain defences to private parties. The EU institutions seem to agree, and have stressed the specificity of competition law in this regard by enacting Directive 2014/104, which sets out certain common standards in national proceedings on damages in the context of competition law.[73]

---

[66] *Köbler* [34].

[67] Case C-168/15 *Milena Tomášová v Slovakia* EU:C:2016:602.

[68] Case C-173/03 *Traghetti del Mediterraneo SpA v Italy* [2006] ECR I-5177 [46].

[69] *Tomášová* (n 67).

[70] Case C-453/99 *Courage Ltd v Bernard Crehan* [2001] ECR I-6297 [27].

[71] For the argument that the ECJ and the Commission rely on 'hard deterrence' in competition law, compared to soft deterrence in state liability, see S Bogojević and N Petit, 'Deterring the state versus the firm: Soft and hard deterrence regimes in EU law' (2016) 23(1) Colum J Eur L 55.

[72] Some domestic courts have found that it can: K Apps, 'Damages claims against trade unions after *Viking* and *Laval*' (2009) 34(1) EL Rev 141.

[73] European Parliament and Council Directive 2014/104/EU of 26 November 2014 on certain rules governing actions for damages under national law for infringements of the competition law provisions of the Member States and of the EU [2014] OJ L349/1.

Much Ado About Nothing?

Francovich is a landmark case, but does it matter in practice? The low success rate of state liability actions before national courts raises the question of whether private enforcement of EU law through state liability is simply a myth.[74] To some extent, modest success rates can be explained by the hurdles of the liability test. Liability actions also consume a great deal of time and money. Indeed, *Francovich* itself was the result of more than six years of courtroom battles in Italy and Luxembourg. Yet it left Andrea Francovich with no compensation, as the action had been initiated too late.[75]

Damages, then, are not necessarily a quick-stop-shop. Nor can every breach readily be remedied by financial compensation. Take *AMS*[76] as an example. How can we estimate the value lost to employees when French law repeatedly imposed hurdles to setting up works councils? Even when losses are quantifiable – as is the case with wages – the amount of compensation is not as easily determined. In some jurisdictions, like Sweden, wages are set not by contract but through collective bargaining. Should this make a difference to the EU? Or should it legislate on compensation sector by sector? Such legislation would also need implementation, as exemplified in *Francovich*. And what would happen, were a Member State then to ignore its obligations to the EU, leaving citizens out of pocket? We would be right back to the dilemmas of the lovers' triangle.

(D) A Hierarchy of Remedies?

We started the journey through the EU's remedial portfolio by outlining the different impact of various doctrines. Harmonious interpretation demands that the relevant national provisions be interpreted 'as far as possible' in line with EU law, making this remedy softer than direct effect, which substitutes EU law for conflicting national law. Damages, in turn, do not vindicate individuals' rights but compensate for their losses. Clearly, the impact varies between the remedial options. But is there a particular rule for when each is applicable?

Smith[77] offers some guidance. The case concerned litigation between private parties following a road crash, triggering a liability exclusion under national law that was incompatible with the relevant EU directive. The ruling instructs the national court first to interpret relevant national law in conformity with the EU directive. Only where *contra legem* interpretation would otherwise be required (as it was thought to be on the facts of *Smith*) should the national court abandon harmonious interpretation and turn to direct effect instead.

[74] T Lock, 'Is private enforcement of EU law through state liability a myth? An assessment 20 years after *Francovich*' (2012) 49(5) CML Rev 1675. Similarly, *Köbler*-type of offences have had limited success, see Z Varga, 'Why is the *Köbler* principle not applied in practice?' (2016) 23(6) Maastricht J Eur Comp L 984.

[75] *Francovich* (n 52).

[76] *AMS* (n 5).

[77] Case C-122/17 *David Smith v Patrick Meade and ors* EU:C:2018:631.

This system still leaves potential gaps, however. Remember especially that directives cannot be invoked to override domestic law in disputes between private parties,[78] leaving damages as the only potential remedy.

Debate 2

Should EU law respect national procedural autonomy?

The preceding debate shows that remedies in EU law are largely driven by the CJEU's jurisprudence. This reflects the political reluctance on the part of Member States as represented in the Council to legislate in this area, as well as the practical difficulty of doing so. Imagine constructing homogenous procedural rules to cover issues as diverse as limitation periods for bringing proceedings,[79] litigation costs,[80] access to justice,[81] *res judicata*,[82] and proceedings on interim measures;[83] as well as determining the finality of national judicial and administrative decisions,[84] national courts' obligations to raise issues of EU law on their own motion,[85] or the legal institutions permitted to hear complaints about equality matters and disapply national laws that run counter to EU law.[86] Yet the CJEU has ruled on each and every item in this procedural mix, seeking to uphold the principle of effectiveness. The result is a rich case law that, nonetheless, fails to provide consistent clarity. Even if the CJEU is adamant about the effectiveness of EU law, to what extent is it willing and able to intrude on and strike down national procedural choices?

In its early case law, the CJEU showed considerable reluctance in this regard. It underlined that the Treaty was not intended to create new remedies, and that, as such, remedies for any violation of EU law were dependent on existing national procedures:

> In the absence of [Union] rules on this subject, it is for the domestic legal system of each Member State [...] to determine the procedural conditions governing

---

[78] Other options – such as reliance on general principles and the Charter – might be available: we return to this point in Chapter 6.

[79] Case C-255/00 *Grundig Italiana SpA v Ministero delle Finanze* [2002] ECR I-8003.

[80] Case C-279/09 *DEB mbH v Germany* [2010] ECR I-13849.

[81] Case C-664/15 *Protect Natur-. Arten- und Landschaftsschutz. Umweltorganisation v Bezirkshauptmannschaft Gmünd* EU:C:2017:987.

[82] Case C-234/17 *XC and ors v Generalprokuratur* EU:C:2018:853; C-421/14 *Banco Primus SA v Jesús Gutiérrez García* EU:C:2017:60.

[83] Joined Cases C-143/88 *Zuckerfabrik Suderdithmarschen AG v Hauptzollamt Itzehoe* and C-92/89 *Zuckerfabrik Soest GmbH v Hauptzollamt Paderborn* [1991] ECR I-415.

[84] Case C-2/08 *Amministrazione dell'Economia e delle Finanze, Agenzia delle Entrate v Fallimento Olimpiclub Srl* [2009] ECR I-7501.

[85] Case C-168/05 *Elisa María Mostaza Claro v Centro Móvil Milenium SL* [2006] ECR I-10421; Case C-40/08 *Asturcom Telecomunicaciones SL v Cristina Rodríguez Nogueira* [2009] ECR I-9579.

[86] Case C-378/17 *The Minister for Justice and Equality and The Commissioner of the Garda Síochána v Workplace Relations Commission* EU:C:2018:979.

> actions at law intended to ensure the protection of the rights which citizens have from the direct effect of [Union] law.[87]

This approach, echoed today in Article 19(1) TEU,[88] is known as the doctrine of 'national procedural autonomy': EU law lays down substantive rights, whilst national legal systems are entrusted with their realisation in accordance with existing domestic procedures. National procedural autonomy was never unlimited, however. As the Court explained in *Comet*, it is subject to the twin requirements of equivalence and effectiveness.[89]

The former is relatively straightforward: procedural rules must apply without distinction between EU and national law.[90] Where there is no national equivalent to EU provisions, comparisons will be drawn with 'similar' claims.[91] The principle of equivalence thus recognises that national courts are better placed to consider the purpose and essential characteristics of domestic rules, and to make sure that these do not discriminate against EU law enforcement.

The principle of effectiveness, on the other hand, is significantly more powerful – and potentially intrusive. As we have seen, over the years it has enabled the Court to demand specific remedies (damages), the exclusion of national rules contrary to EU law (direct effect), and the conformity of all national law – including procedures – to EU law (harmonious interpretation).

It is easy to characterise this body of case law as a power-grab by the CJEU. Wallerman, however, offers a more nuanced analysis. Focusing on national jurisprudence and the courts, she finds that where national courts send preliminary references that are receptive to a finding that national practices are not consistent with EU law, the CJEU tends to take up that invitation to intervene. Conversely, it tends to be duly cautious and to respect the autonomy of national courts when the latter articulate reasons why national practices should be left untouched.[92] Bobek agrees that remedies are best understood as a highly contextual area that depends on national legislation and the particular approach favoured by domestic judges.[93] The one-million-euro question nevertheless remains. Has the CJEU gone too far in ensuring that breaches of individual EU rights are remedied, thus disrespecting the principle of national procedural autonomy? Or has it not gone far enough?

---

[87] Case 33-76 *Rewe-Zentralfinanz eG and Rewe-Zentral AG v Landwirtschaftskammer für das Saarland* [1976] ECR 1989.

[88] TEU, Article 19(1): 'Member States shall provide remedies sufficient to ensure effective legal protection in the fields covered by Union law'.

[89] As well as the absence of any harmonising measures at the Union level: Case 45/76 *Comet BV v Produktschap voor Siergewassen* [1976] ECR 2043.

[90] Joined Cases C-392/04 and C-422/04 *i-21 Germany GmbH and Arcor AG & Co. KG v Germany* [2006] ECR I-8559 [62].

[91] Case C-326/96 *B.S. Levez v T.H. Jennings (Harlow Pools) Ltd* [1998] ECR I-7835.

[92] A Wallerman, 'Can two walk together, except they be agreed? Preliminary references and (the erosion of) national procedural autonomy' (2019) 44(2) EL Rev 159.

[93] Bobek (n 30), 'The effects of EU law in the national legal systems'.

(A) Too Far?

Perhaps the starkest example for those arguing that the CJEU can go 'too far' in insisting on remedial action for EU law breaches is the case of *Factortame*. In an attempt to protect its fishing industry, the UK's Merchant Shipping Act 1988 limited access to British waters to domestically registered vessels. British registration, in turn, required a majority-British ownership. This blatant breach of the Treaty was challenged by Spanish fishermen in a series of cases dealing with supremacy, damages, and state liability.[94]

Before things got anywhere that far, however, the claimants faced a significant procedural dilemma: pending the Court of Justice's ruling on the compatibility of the Act with EU law, their fleet was barred from fishing and would likely go bankrupt. No interim measures were available under domestic law against the government (Crown). In those circumstances, any notion that EU law would not require the creation of new remedies was swiftly despatched by the Court of Justice: in order to ensure 'the full effectiveness of [Union] law', interim relief was to be available, centuries of domestic constitutional law notwithstanding.

Together with the Court's finding that EU law overrides conflicting national law, even if that law is an Act of Parliament, the ruling thus caused significant constitutional disruptions in the UK's legal order, long marked by parliamentary sovereignty. Some constitutional lawyers went as far as to suggest that the doctrine had thus been abandoned – strong evidence (if true) of just how little genuine autonomy remains for the Member States.[95]

(B) Not Far Enough?

There are also plenty of instances, however, where EU law does not push far enough in protecting individuals' rights. Take the example of air quality legislation. Remember how states have to improve ambient air quality, and to 'draw up action plans' where there is a risk that limit values or alert thresholds are exceeded? This obligation, the Court decided in *Janecek*, has direct effect,[96] prompting litigation across Europe by those seeking to enforce the right to clean air.

The UK government has a long track record of failing to meet air quality standards as prescribed by the Directive. In the first round of litigation, where such a failing was established, the UK Supreme Court decided to take the unusual step of issuing a mandatory order to oblige the government to deliver an action plan as prescribed by the Directive. This particular remedy was influenced by the upcoming general election, and so the Court decided to signal to

---

[94] See Case C-213/89 *The Queen v Secretary of State for Transport, ex p Factortame Ltd and ors* [1990] ECR I-2433 and *Factortame III* (n 60).

[95] N Barber, 'The afterlife of parliamentary sovereignty' (2011) 9(1) Intl J Const L 144.

[96] *Janecek* (n 48).

the 'new Government, whatever its political complexion [...] the need for immediate action to address this issue'.[97]

The breach persisted, however, and the Government was taken to court once more, this time by an environmental NGO, ClientEarth. The High Court granted the claimant an exceptional 'continuing liberty to apply', explaining that:

> The Court itself cannot realistically monitor the performance by the government [...] but it can adapt its procedure to provide a quick, efficient and low cost means of enabling the current claimant, which has acted as a valuable monitor of the government's efforts to improve air quality to date, to bring the matter back before the Court [...] I [Mr Justice Garnham] acknowledge that this is a wholly exceptional course for the Court to take.[98]

Despite these remedial exceptions and the domestic courts' innovation, at the time of writing, the UK government has yet to comply with its legal obligations, recently delaying any implementation until 'after the Covid-19 outbreak response'.[99]

Bavaria in Germany has been similarly reluctant to implement its action plans as required by the Directive, even following a court's order requiring it to do so. Senior politicians furthermore 'publicly stated their intention not to comply'.[100] German law, however, does not provide effective remedies to force compliance by public authorities, leaving a procedural gap. National courts can issue orders and impose low-value financial sanctions, but there is no effective sanction if the authority refuses to comply with the court order. Could German courts go beyond these remedies and consider coercive measures under EU law? No, found the Court in *Deutsche Umwelthilfe*. The right to effective judicial protection

> is not an absolute right and may be restricted, in particular in order to protect the rights and freedoms of others. A coercive measure such as coercive detention entails a limitation on the right to liberty, guaranteed by Article 6 of the Charter.[101]

Although Member States are subject to judicial review in meeting their obligations under said directive,[102] the Court of Justice thus refused to insist on any

---

[97] *R (ClientEarth) v Secretary of State for Environment, Food and Rural Affairs* [2015] UKSC 28 [31].

[98] *R (ClientEarth) v Secretary of State for Environment, Food and Rural Affairs (No 3)* [2018] EWHC 398 (Admin) [14] and [16].

[99] K Nield, 'Air pollution and Covid-19: Clean air zones postponed across the UK' (*ClientEarth*, 24 April 2020), https://perma.cc/YPG9-2FLB.

[100] Case C-752/18 *Deutsche Umwelthilfe eV v Freistaat Bayern* EU:C:2019:1114 [18].

[101] *Deutsche Umwelthilfe* [44].

[102] Case C-723/17 *Lies Craeynest and ors v Brussels Hoofdstedelijk Gewest and Brussels Instituut voor Milieubeheer* EU:C:2019:533 [45].

specific remedial action to realise the right to clean air. National procedural architecture is preserved – at the expense of Bavarian lungs.

(C) A Middle Way

None of this is to suggest that there is no way of striking the right balance between the protection of individual rights and the effectiveness of EU law, on the one hand, and respect for national legal orders, on the other. Consider *Unibet*, a preliminary reference from Sweden concerning the prohibition on promoting lotteries organised domestically or abroad.

Unibet, a gambling provider, had purchased advertising space in Swedish media outlets to promote its services. It was against these outlets, not Unibet, that the Swedish state took legal action. Unibet argued that Swedish procedural rules infringed on the EU free movement provisions and demanded, before the domestic court, a declaratory judgment stating that the companies had the right, in EU law, to promote their gambling and betting services in Sweden. Swedish law did not provide for such a free-standing action, however. Could EU law require the creation of new national remedies?

The Court of Justice reiterated that the Treaty 'was not intended to create new remedies [...] other than those already laid down by national law'. But that was not the end of the story. The situation

> would be otherwise only if it were apparent from the overall scheme of the national legal system in question that no legal remedy existed which made it possible to ensure, even indirectly, respect for an individual's rights under [Union] law.[103]

On the facts of the case, the Court of Justice found that domestic law provided plenty of other venues through which the compatibility of national provisions with EU law could be challenged, including judicial review and actions for damages, all of which complied with the principles of equivalence and effectiveness. There was therefore no need to establish a new remedy.

Also at stake was the question of interim relief: the domestic court was under an obligation to set the national measure aside until a decision on compatibility with EU law. For this reason, *Unibet* has been called the 'Swedish *Factortame*'.[104] Upon closer inspection, however, the *Unibet* ruling is much more nuanced than *Factortame*. The Court explained that national courts must be able to grant interim relief, provided such relief 'is necessary, which it is a matter for the national court to determine'.[105] This gives national courts

[103] Case C-432/05 *Unibet (London) Ltd and Unibet (International) Ltd v Justitiekanslern* [2007] ECR I-2271 [40]–[41].

[104] X Groussot and H Wenander, 'Self-standing actions for judicial review and the Swedish *Factortame*: *Unibet (London) Ltd and Unibet (International) Ltd v Justitiekanslern*' (2007) 26 CJQ 376.

[105] *Unibet* (n 103) [76].

significant leeway in assessing procedural rules in light of the principle of effectiveness. What is more, the qualification that relief be provided *if necessary* suggests an 'element of proportionality in carrying out this balancing act'.[106]

Overall, then, *Unibet* represents a middle-way between securing the effectiveness of EU law and respecting national procedural autonomy. At first glance, this judgment may seem similar to the series of cases on the Clean Air Directive. After all, none of the cases saw the CJEU insist on a particular remedy, as it had done in *Factortame*. The noteworthy element in *Unibet*, however, is that national courts were given the discretion to decide whether relief is necessary. In entrusting national courts with carrying out this assessment, the CJEU respects them as independent actors which nonetheless form part of the EU legal body – precisely as envisaged by the Treaties.

***

It is tricky to determine the extent to which EU law needs to ensure a uniform approach to remedial action for individual rights breaches under EU law. Let us return to the example of equal pay. As we saw, that right has been laid down in the Treaty for more than 60 years; however, the way that states enforce it differs greatly across the Union. In some Member States, including Sweden, wages are set through collective bargaining, while in the UK or France, individual negotiation is expected. Remedies vary accordingly.[107] Surely it would be too draconian, counterproductive even, to overhaul all national procedures and practices in light of a Treaty provision. Yet, as some of the case law examined in this chapter shows, oversight of national practices is necessary to ensure that individuals can enjoy their EU rights. Obviously, a balancing act is necessary. How to achieve this, however, is less clear.

The tightrope runs from effectiveness, at the one end, to national procedural autonomy, at the other. What type of act the CJEU performs as a response will depend on the type of question asked and the particular legal context in which the case unfolds. The supremacy element underpinning *Factortame* could explain why the CJEU took a different approach in *Unibet*, where no such tension existed. Moreover, following *Unibet*, domestic judges and their proportionality assessment will increasingly have a role to play in this exercise.

Conclusion: Peaceful Coexistence Between the Species

Without remedies, any talk of rights is cheap. The crucial question is therefore how to make rights real, and who should be entrusted with this task. One way, as described in Chapter 2, is to legislate. Yet legislation on remedies, with the exception of private enforcement, is scarce. This leaves us with judicial action

[106] Groussot and Wenander (n 104), 'Self-standing actions for judicial review and the Swedish *Factortame*'.

[107] S Burri, L Senden, and A Timmer, 'A comparative analysis of gender equality law in Europe: 2019' (European Commission, February 2020), https://perma.cc/SB76-EMSJ.

as a key driver of legal protection, sharpening teeth and claws of this particular paper tiger. As seen in this chapter, the CJEU has been particularly imaginative and insists on the harmonious interpretation of national law in light of EU law, direct effect, and state liability. Although each has sought to protect individual rights, this pursuit must be balanced against the need to respect the autonomy of national procedures and the specific ways in which legal orders have developed: new predators need time to bed in as the ecosystem evolves around them. This is not an easy balancing act, not least when seen through the lens of legal certainty and predictability.

Further Reading

Read M Bobek, 'Why There Is No Principle of "Procedural Autonomy" of the Member States' in H-W Micklitz and B De Witte (eds), *The European Court of Justice and the Autonomy of the Member States* (Intersentia 2012). Do you agree with Bobek's argument that, once a Member State joins the EU, its national procedural autonomy ceases to exist? Could you make an argument, relying on the debates in this chapter, that there is still respect for diversity in the EU legal order?

How do the debates discussed in this chapter fit with the ever-increasing secondary legislation on EU remedies? See FG Wilman, 'The End of the Absence? The Growing Body of EU Legislation on Private Enforcement and the Main Remedies It Provides For' (2016) 53(4) CML Rev 887.

Much of the case law discussed in this chapter deals with individual rights on non-discrimination, especially concerning gender. Why do you think that is, and how has the EU helped further gender equality and construct a social programme for Europe by creating the remedies discussed? Consider C Hoskyns, *Integrating Gender: Women, Law and Politics in the European Union* (Verso 1996).

CHAPTER 6

Feminists vs Founding Fathers

Individual Rights, Obligations, and the Horizontal Effect(s) of EU Law

The direct effect of EU law is a unique feature of the 'new legal order'. In Chapter 5, we traced the grant of 'silent rights' to individuals. Rights are mirrored in obligations, so who should bear them? The Member States as Treaty signatories, of course. But what about individuals and private parties? Can EU law also impose silent burdens?

At first glance, the answer to this question is straightforward: the effective vindication of rights should not depend on who has violated them. Indeed, in *Van Gend en Loos*,[1] the CJEU explicitly described the 'new legal order' as conferring both rights *and* obligations on individuals. At the same time, however, this conclusion might leave us with a lingering sense of unease. Is it really fair to hold a private party who simply complied with domestic law responsible, if the latter turns out to be in violation of EU rules? In Debate 1, we will explore this tension, examining the case for and against direct effect in 'horizontal situations' – that is, in litigation between private parties.

Relatively early on, the CJEU came down firmly in favour of horizontal direct effect. In *Defrenne II*, the equal pay provision in the Treaty was found to apply not only to the Member States, but also to agreements between individuals. Rather than settling the issue, however, the case led to a host of new questions. Could all provisions of EU law be directly effective, as long as they met the basic test of clarity and precision discussed in Chapter 5? In the ensuing examination of different sources of law, the Court soon declared that horizontal direct effect was not limited to Treaty articles and: it extended to regulations, general principles, and the Charter of Fundamental Rights. In consequence, lingering unease grew into acute concern and outright resistance from senior courts in several Member States. This, in turn, led the CJEU to impose certain restrictions, notably as far as directives are concerned.

In exploring the horizontal effect of EU law, it can thus be tempting to focus on that particular ban: '[i]f it were not for directives, direct effect could have

[1] Case 26-62 *NV Algemene Transport- en Expeditie Onderneming van Gend en Loos v Netherlands Inland Revenue Administration* [1963] ECR 1.

become a rather marginal topic of academic interest to EU constitutional lawyers.'[2] As we will see in Debate 2, however, the Court has been remarkably consistent (in the face of much criticism) in denying their horizontal direct effect. Much more significant today are debates surrounding the horizontal application of other sources of EU law, particularly the Charter: some Charter provisions are applicable even in national court cases involving private parties,[3] whereas others are not.[4]

However, the vexed question of horizontality is by no means limited to direct effect. The interaction of EU law and domestic legal systems – from harmonious interpretation to supremacy – can impact private legal relations in manifold ways. This includes situations that might otherwise be covered by directives, raising the question of whether, despite strong protestations that they must not enjoy horizontal direct effect, the Court's jurisprudence has in fact achieved that very outcome. We look at this allegation in Debate 3 to determine whether horizontal effect has been introduced by the backdoor, or whether something altogether different is going on.

Debate 1

Should EU law impose obligations on individuals?

Article 119 of the Treaty of Rome provided that 'each Member State shall ensure that the principle of equal pay for male and female workers for equal work or work of equal value is applied' – a principle introduced to ensure fair competition, rather than any high-minded commitment to gender equality. France, at the time the only Member State mandating equal pay in its domestic law, had feared that its industry would be disadvantaged unless the Common Market took a joint approach to the issue. Yet, a decade after the Treaty of Rome had entered into force, little had changed in practice, with pay discrimination rampant – and entirely legal – in the majority of Member States.

Enter Éliane Vogel-Polsky,[5] a lawyer and feminist, who came up with an ingenious solution. As early as 1967, she argued that the right to equal pay, found today in Article 157 TFEU, should be directly enforceable in the Member States.[6] It took a while to find the perfect test case. Equal pay litigation

---

[2] M Bobek, 'The effects of EU Law in the national legal systems' in C Barnard and S Peers (eds), *European Union Law*, 3rd edn (Oxford University Press 2020).

[3] Case C-176/12 *Association de médiation sociale v Union locale des syndicats CGT and ors* EU:C:2014:2 (*AMS*); Case C-684/16 *Max-Planck-Gesellschaft zur Förderung der Wissenschaften e.V. v Tetsuji Shimizu (Max-Planck-Gesellschaft v Shimizu)* EU:C:2018:874; Joined Cases C-569/16 *Stadt Wuppertal v Maria Elisabeth Bauer (Bauer)* and C-570/16 *Volker Willmeroth v Martina Brossonn* EU:C:2018:871 *(Brosson)*.

[4] See, e.g., Case C-64/16 *Associação Sindical dos Juízes Portugueses v Tribunal de Contas* EU:C:2018:117.

[5] J-P Stroobants, 'Eliane Vogel-Polsky, jurist et militante féministe, est morte à 90 ans' *Le Monde* (Paris, 6 December 2015), https://perma.cc/TN7X-GBS2.

[6] For a fascinating account of the historical background to the case, see E Gubin and C Jacques, *Éliane Vogel-Polsky, une femme de conviction* (Institut pour l'égalité des femmes et des hommes 2007).

is notoriously tricky given occupational segregation: proving that (traditionally female-dominated) clerical jobs are 'work of equal value' to (historically male-dominated) maintenance jobs continues to be a formidable challenge. These problems could be sidestepped, however, in a workplace where men and women did *exactly* the same job and yet were treated differently – which is precisely what Belgian airline Sabena did to its cabin crew.

Along with her legal team, Éliane Vogel-Polsky was thus able to put Article 157 TFEU to the test in an action by Gabrielle Defrenne, a flight attendant. At the time, female cabin crew working for Sabena had to be unmarried, widowed, or divorced, as well as childless. They were also forced to retire by the age of 40, while male stewards working alongside them could work until 55, and after 23 years of service were entitled to an extra pension.[7] This was entirely legal under Belgian law. It was only when the CJEU recognised that the Treaty provision could enjoy direct effect that equal pay for equal work was transformed into an individual right that domestic courts had to protect, irrespective of 'whether [the employer is] public or private'.[8] *Defrenne II* is a landmark ruling: not only did it lay the foundations for a social Europe, it also recognised horizontal direct effect.

(A) The Case for Horizontal Direct Effect

In *Defrenne II*,[9] recognising that the right to equal pay under Article 157 TFEU had horizontal effect meant that its prohibition on discrimination between men and women applied 'not only to the action of public authorities, but also … to contracts between individuals'. Consequently, Gabrielle Defrenne could insist on her EU rights irrespective of the fact that her employer was a private body.[10]

Despite its immense practical significance, 'horizontality' is not a concept used or expanded on by the Court. As Walkila notes,[11] the CJEU instead speaks of 'a provision which is capable of conferring rights on private actors and which may be relied on against other private actors'[12] with reference to 'a fundamental freedom applying to a private actor'[13] or a certain 'conduct' of a private

[7] Gubin and Jacques, *Éliane Vogel-Polsky*.

[8] Case 43-75 *Gabrielle Defrenne v SABENA* [1976] ECR I-455 (*Defrenne II*) [22].

[9] See also Case 36-74 *B.N.O. Walrave and L.J.N. Koch v Association Union cycliste internationale and ors* [1974] ECR 1405; Case C-281/98 *Roman Angonese v Cassa di Risparmio di Bolzano SpA* [2000] ECR I-4139 *(Angonese)*.

[10] *Defrenne II* (n 8) [39].

[11] S Walkila, *Horizontal Effect of Fundamental Rights in EU Law* (Europa Law Publishing 2016), p. 30.

[12] Case C-438/05 *International Transport Workers' Federation and Finnish Seamen's Union v Viking Line ABP and OÜ Viking Line Eesti* [2007] ECR I-10779 (*Viking Line*).

[13] Case C-94/07 *Andrea Raccanelli v Max-Planck-Gesellschaft zur Förderung der Wissenschaften eV.* [2008] ECR I-5939.

actor.[14] This suggests not only that situations where horizontality is found are rarely uniform,[15] but also that the CJEU's approach to determining what counts as horizontality, which EU provisions enjoy it, and the underlying legal method for each categorisation is rather ad hoc.

But why does the CJEU insist on horizontality? After all, other international organisations, such as the European Convention on Human Rights, cover only violations committed by states.[16] Remember the powerful finding in *Van Gend en Loos*: the 'new legal order' was taken to concern not only the Member States but also their nationals. Limiting the application of EU law to cases involving the state could be seen as denying individuals their promised 'legal heritage', even if it means creating obligations for them too. Ultimately, cases dealing with horizontality tend to involve 'rights of deep value to the individuals claiming them',[17] including those touching on work and family life. Granting horizontality to such rights signals 'the extent to which the EU affects these questions'.[18]

There are also 'clear constitutional overtones'.[19] In order to secure the supremacy of its laws, the Union had to demonstrate a level of individual rights protection worthy of, and common to, national constitutional traditions. Horizontality is thus a further crucial building block in the 'new legal order', allowing EU law to claim its unique position in domestic legal systems.

(B) The Case Against Horizontality

At the same time, however, the recognition of horizontal direct effect has not been without controversy. Remember the wording of Article 157 TFEU: '[e]ach Member State shall ensure that the principle of equal pay for male and

[14] Case C-415/93 *Union royale belge des sociétés de football association ASBL v Jean-Marc Bosman, Royal club liégeois SA v Jean-Marc Bosman and ors* and *UEFA v Jean-Marc Bosman* [1995] ECR I-4921.

[15] Indeed, in some cases, such as *Defrenne II* (n 8), it is a matter of determining the extent to which EU law enforcement can be pursued in domestic private legal settings, while in other instances, such as *Viking Line* (n 12) and Case C-341/05 *Laval un Partneri Ltd v Svenska Byggnadsarbetareförbundet, Svenska Byggnadsarbetareförbundets avdelning 1, Byggettan and Svenska Elektrikerförbundet* [2007] ECR I-11767 (cases involving the right of a trade union to take collective action against a private undertaking seeking to reallocate to a different Member State to benefit from lower wages) horizontality meant that the CJEU had to balance and ultimately decide between two EU norms – the right to collective action, and the freedom of establishment – both applicable in disputes between private parties.

[16] Note, however, that this includes a duty imposed on contracting parties to protect individuals against violations of ECHR rights committed by other individuals. See, e.g., *Young, James and Webster v United Kingdom* [1981] 4 EHRR 38.

[17] E Frantziou, 'The horizontal effect of the charter of fundamental rights of the EU: Rediscovering the reasons for horizontality' (2015) 21(5) Eur LJ 657, 658.

[18] Frantziou, 'The horizontal effect of the charter of fundamental rights of the EU'.

[19] G de Búrca and B Aschenbrenner, 'The development of European constitutionalism and the role of the EU Charter of Fundamental Rights' (2003) 9 Columbia J of Eur L 355, 372.

female workers for equal work or work of equal value is applied.' Reading a 'silent right' for individuals into this provision is a big step in and of itself, as discussed in the previous chapter. Might extending it to include a 'silent burden' on private parties – employers, in this case – be a step too far?

The horizontal effect of EU law has always raised domestic concerns, with several Member States and domestic courts continuing to push back against it. We will see in the next chapter how the French judiciary rebelled against the CJEU by resisting the case law on direct effect of directives.[20] Provisions contained in such legislative instruments were for the Member States to implement; the CJEU could not circumvent this division of responsibilities by interfering directly in horizontal relationships. The CJEU relented, in part, and refused litigants' invitations to grant directives horizontal direct effect. The French Courts in turn would eventually accept the supremacy of EU law in general, and the *vertical* direct effect of directives in particular.[21] Resistance continues, though, as the Danish Supreme Court's approach in *Ajos* shows.[22]

What makes the application of EU law to private conflicts so controversial? In addition to the textual difficulty of reading private rights and burdens into provisions addressed to the Member States, legal certainty looms large. As the Treaties do not specify which provisions can apply horizontally, the CJEU has had to decide this on a case-by-case basis. More significantly, horizontal direct effect has allowed the CJEU to sidestep concrete legislative outcomes, in particular national measures implementing EU directives, thus undermining Member States' regulatory competence. Horizontality furthermore blurs traditional demarcations between public and private legal spheres – and although it offers individuals a greater chance of enjoying of their EU rights, it also imposes a burden on them to observe EU law.

Imagine a private employer who dutifully complies with national legislation, which, nevertheless, is contrary to EU law. Should she be liable for damages, even in the obvious absence of fault? A final difficulty thus arises in the remedial dimension: should the claimant, relying on such a right, proceed directly against her employer, or is she limited to an action in damages against the state?[23] Economic theory suggests that employers *are* best placed to bear such burdens;[24] but then again, 'not all employers…in the European Union, are proverbial faceless multinational corporations. Many companies are run by

[20] Chapter 7, Debate 2.

[21] See M Rasmussen, 'How to enforce European law? A new history of the battle over the direct effect of directives, 1958 – 1987' (2017) 23(3-4) Eur LJ 290.

[22] UfR 2017.824H (Case no. 15/2014, *DI, acting on behalf of Ajos A/S v Estate of A*) (DK).

[23] Case C-193/17 *Cresco Investigation GmbH v Markus Achatzi* EU:C:2018:614, Opinion of AG Bobek [179] *(Cresco)*.

[24] J Adams-Prassl, 'A case for remedies against employers? Horizontality and the effective enforcement of EU employment law' in E Brameshuber, M Friedrich and B Karl, *Festschrift Franz Marhold* (Manz 2020).

single individuals or small numbers of people. Why should they bear the cost of applying faulty national legislation?'[25]

***

Horizontality clearly creates both winners and losers: it is a victory for individuals to whom it grants rights that are enforceable against employers irrespective of their status, but it is a liability risk to employers in the private sector. The debate continues to rage, even amongst Members of the Court, most recently in the context of the Charter. To AG Bobek, for example, its horizontal applicability would involve 'a deeply *ideological* choice on risks and costs allocation',[26] whereas AG Cruz Villalón sees it as simply 'reasonable' that the burden of an eventual action for damages against the Member State should fall on the person who has benefited from the unlawful conduct, and not on the holder of the right that has been violated.[27]

Debate 2

Should all EU law apply horizontally?

Despite these controversies, the Court has never wavered in its insistence on the horizontal direct effect of EU law *in principle*. The battleground thus shifted to another question: should *all* EU law apply horizontally? On some level, the answer is a clear 'of course not': the requirements of sufficient clarity and precision encountered in the previous chapter still apply. The precise tests vary, but as a rule of thumb, 'as long as there is a clear rule of behaviour which can be extracted' from a provision of EU law, it has the potentially to be directly effective.[28]

The key question in horizontal cases, then, is as to the source of the EU provision a private litigant is seeking to rely on. We have already seen that if the right is found in the Treaties themselves, horizontal effect will be granted. The same applies for rights set out in regulations, given that they 'shall have general application ... [and] be binding in ... entirety and directly applicable in all Member States.'[29] But what about more open-textured norms, including in particular directives, general principles, and, most recently, the Charter? It is here that domestic courts and scholars voice fears that the Court may begin to head 'down a slippery slope that ultimately disturb[s] both the institutional balance and the economy of the treaties [and departs from the] intentions of the founding fathers'.[30]

---

[25] *Cresco* (n 23), Opinion of AG Bobek [183].
[26] *Cresco*, Opinion of AG Bobek [183].
[27] *AMS* (n 3), Opinion of AG Cruz Villalón [79].
[28] Bobek (n 2), 'The effects of EU Law in the national legal systems', p. 160.
[29] TFEU, Article 288.
[30] Rasmussen (n 21), 'How to enforce European law?', 291.

(A) Directives

When it comes to directives, the line has been consistently firm: they do not have horizontal direct effect. In *Marshall*,[31] the applicant had been dismissed by her employer when she reached the age of 62, whereas male employees faced no such treatment. Domestically, there was no remedy for discrimination on the basis of sex in relation to retirement, and the directive that contained a relevant provision had not been implemented, despite the fact that the deadline had passed. The CJEU declared that 'where a person involved in legal proceedings is able to rely on a directive as against the State he may do so regardless of the capacity in which the latter is acting, whether employer or public authority'.[32] But, it continued, 'a directive may not of itself impose obligations on an individual and [...] a provision of a directive may not be relied upon as such against such a person'.[33]

This means that even a clear, precise, and unconditional provision of a directive seeking to confer rights or impose obligations on individuals 'cannot of itself apply in proceedings exclusively between private parties.'[34] But why should it matter whether your counter-party is a public or private entity when your rights have been violated by a non-implemented directive? At least four Advocates General have called for this public–private distinction to be abandoned on the grounds that it fragments the availability of remedies to individuals across the Union and so creates uncertainty and incoherence in the law.[35]

The CJEU, however, has not wavered in its position, which it argues is rooted in the Treaty stipulation that directives are addressed to states, not individuals.[36] In *Dori*, the Court added a constitutional dimension to this refusal, explaining that '[t]he effect of extending that case-law to the sphere of relations between individuals would be to recognize a power in the Community to enact obligations for individuals with immediate effect, whereas it has competence to do so only where it is empowered to adopt regulations'.[37] But quite how persuasive are these arguments? The fact that only Member States were addressees of the equal pay provision had not been a deterrent in *Defrenne*.[38]

[31] Case C-152/84 *M. Helen Marshall v Southampton and South-West Hampshire Area Health Authority* [1986] ECR 723.
[32] *Marshall* [49].
[33] *Marshall* [48].
[34] Joined Cases C-397/01 to C-403/01 *Bernhard Pfeiffer and ors v Deutsches Rotes Kreuz, Kreisverband Waldshut eV* [2004] ECR I-8835.
[35] *Marshall* (n 31), Opinion of AG Van Gerven; Case C-316/93 *Nicole Vaneetveld v Le Foyer SA v Fédération des Mutualités Socialistes et Syndicales de la Provence de Liège* [1994] ECR I-763, Opinion of AG Jacobs *(Vaneetveld)*; Case C-91/92 *Paola Faccini Dori v Recreb Srl* [1994] ECR 3325, Opinion of AG Jenz *(Dori)*; Case C-413/15 *Elaine Farrell v Alan Whitty and ors* EU:C:2017:745, Opinion of AG Sharpston (*Farrell*).
[36] Case 148/78 *Criminal proceedings against Tullio Ratti* [1979] ECR 1629 [23]; *Marshall* (n 31) [48].
[37] *Dori* (n 35) [24].
[38] See also *Farrell* (n 35) [31].

(B) General Principles

Nor has the Court expressed similar unease in finding horizontal effect of general principles. These principles are developed by the CJEU with the underlying promise of providing structure and coherence to a legal system of which the Union, the Member States and their citizen rights are all part. The 'general principles family' continues to expand, with prominent members including proportionality,[39] legitimate expectations,[40] and equal treatment and non-discrimination.[41] In their application, these principles 'fill gaps' where the existing legal texts provide no clear answer. Being intrinsic to the 'new legal order', general principles enable EU law to claim supremacy and are key in ensuring that individual rights are directly applicable in the domestic legal settings.[42]

Concern about the role of general principles stems from the fact that they are often developed by the CJEU without any explicit Treaty support – a point highlighted by the Danish Supreme Court in *Ajos*. It is often unclear how the CJEU 'spots' general principles, what criteria they must meet, and how the force of their application should be judged. When it comes to general principles, then, the CJEU ultimately engages in law-making. This is not necessarily illegitimate: many of these principles have subsequently been codified in the Treaty.[43] However, the extent to which individuals in private disputes can rely on general principles, including fundamental rights, remains unclear.

This legal obscurity was brought to the fore in *Mangold*.[44] The case concerned national legislation that authorised the renewal of fixed-term contracts, without any restriction, once an employee had turned 52. Mr Mangold, then 56 years old, challenged this law on the basis of various directives, including a directive on equal treatment in employment and occupation that lays down 'a general framework combating discrimination on the grounds of religion, or belief, disability, age or sexual orientation'.[45] Significantly, the implementation period for the directive had not yet expired, and the dispute was between two private parties. Considering the CJEU's established case law denying direct effect to directives, one would therefore expect the CJEU to rule that Mr Mangold's claim could not succeed.

---

[39] Case 114/76 *Bela-Mühle Josef Bergmann KG v Grows-Farm GmbH & Co. KG* [1977] ECR 1211.

[40] Case 120/86 *J. Mulder v Minister van Landbouw en Visserij* [1988] ECR 2321.

[41] Joined Cases 117/76 *Albert Ruckdeschel & Co. and Hansa-Lagerhaus Ströh & Co. v Hauptzollamt Hamburg-St. Annen* and 16/77 *Diamalt AG v Hauptzollamt Itzehoe* [1977] ECR 1753.

[42] S Weatherill, 'From myth to reality: The EU's "new legal order" and the place of general principles within it' in S Vogenauer and S Weatherill (eds), *General Principles of Law: European and Comparative Perspectives* (Hart 2017).

[43] See notably TEU, Article 6.

[44] Case C-144/04 *Werner Mangold v Rüdiger Helm* [2005] ECR I-9981.

[45] Council Directive 2000/78/EC of 27 November 2000 establishing a general framework for equal treatment in employment and occupation [2000] OJ L303/16, Article 1.

Instead, the CJEU found that the principle of non-discrimination on grounds of age was a general principle of EU law which, as such, could not be conditioned upon the expiry of a transposition period.[46] Consequently, the national court was asked 'to guarantee the full effectiveness' of the general principle, including by setting aside any provision of national law that may conflict with EU law, 'even where the period prescribed for transposition of that directive has not yet expired'.[47] This is some seriously impressive legal pirouetting. How did the CJEU swing it?

The key move was a linking of the principle of non-discrimination on grounds of age to the general principle of equal treatment whose source, it pointed out, was *not* the directive but 'various international instruments' and 'the constitutional traditions common to the Member States'.[48] This, then, is the (supposed) distinction between the case law on directives and their horizontal (non)application, on the one hand, and the idea of general principles enjoying horizontal force, on the other – even though the point was never addressed head-on. Instead of focusing on obligations for private parties, the Court's emphasis shifted to the 'responsibility of the national court ... to provide ... the legal protection which individuals derive from the rules of [EU] law and to ensure that those rules are fully effective'.[49]

The judgment in *Mangold* was welcomed for securing individual rights,[50] but it also attracted much scorn for creating uncertainty as to when general principles apply horizontally and for jumping ahead of national legislative processes.[51] Roman Herzog, a former German President, went as far as publicly calling for a 'stop to the European Court of Justice' on the basis that the Court had turned into a legislature that had empowered itself to overturn national legislation where and when it saw fit.[52]

In response, the CJEU seemed to become somewhat more reticent in recognising general principles, let alone endowing them with horizontal applicability. In *Audiolux*, for example, it refused to identify the protection of minority shareholders as a general principle on grounds that 'the general, comprehensive character which is otherwise naturally inherent in general principles of law'[53] was missing. It similarly declined to recognise non-discrimination on grounds of illness as a general principle.[54] Although it accepted that discrimina-

---

[46] *Mangold* (n 44) [74]–[76].

[47] *Mangold* [77].

[48] *Mangold* [65], [74].

[49] *Mangold* [77].

[50] See, e.g., T Tridimas, 'Fundamental rights, general principles of EU law, and the Charter' (2014) 16 CYELS 361, 367.

[51] See, e.g., Editorial Comments, 'Horizontal direct effect – A law of diminishing coherence?' (2007) 43(1) CML Rev 1.

[52] R Herzog and L Gerken, 'Stoppt den Europäischen Gerichtshof' *Frankfurter Allgemeine Zeitung* (Frankfurt, 8 September 2008).

[53] Case C-101/08 *Audiolux SA e.a. v Groupe Bruxelles Lambert SA (GBL) and ors and Bertelsmann AG and ors* [2009] ECR I-9823 [42].

[54] Case C-13/05 *Sonia Chacón Navas v Eurest Colectividades SA* [2006] ECR I-6467.

tion on the basis of disability may include obesity (and thus may be caught by the Framework Directive 2000/78), it refused to classify this as a general principle.[55] Would *Mangold* turn out to be a one-hit wonder?

No. The Court's findings in *Mangold* were confirmed and further developed in *Kücükdeveci*.[56] That case similarly concerned the Framework Directive 2000/78 (which Germany had by then implemented) and a private dispute with an age discrimination claim at its heart. Here, the CJEU reiterated the idea that the principle of nondiscrimination on grounds of age is a general principle of EU law, adding that it was also protected by the Charter, Article 21 of which prohibits discrimination based on age. The role of the Directive, the Court explained, was merely to give 'expression' to the aforementioned principle. The obligation on national courts to set aside any conflicting national law thus derived not from the Directive, but from the general principle as inspired by the Charter.[57]

***

General principles are a significant means of protecting individuals, 'breath[ing] extra life into the EU legal order'.[58] At the same time, however, their horizontal application potentially disrupts EU and national law. Even if a directive is incapable of horizontal application, a claimant may succeed if she is able to find, embedded in or beyond the directive, a general principle of EU law on which it is possible to rely horizontally. This is problematic for several of the reasons discussed in our first Debate. Most obviously, it blurs traditional borders between private and public parties and upsets legal certainty. It also empowers the CJEU to rely on unwritten legal principles as the basis for insisting that domestic legislative efforts be set aside.

Today, judicial debates on general principles are increasingly becoming superseded by the enforcement of the Charter.[59] The CJEU's nod to the Charter in *Kücükdeveci* is significant. It showed that horizontal application of general principles can extend to Charter provisions, making the latter a potential new resource in resolving private disputes and overriding national legislation. At the same time, however, the Court did not explain which Charter provisions could have this effect, and so the Charter's potential as a new source of individual rights and obligations was left to be determined in future litigation. The legacy of *Kücükdeveci* lives on – both in terms of the effective vindication of fundamental rights, but also in terms of the uncertainty as to which

[55] Case C-354/13 *FOA v KL* EU:C:2014:2463.
[56] Case C-555/07 *Seda Kücükdeveci v Swedex GmbH & Co. KG* [2010] ECR I-365.
[57] *Kücükdeveci* [21].
[58] Weatherill (n 42), 'From myth to reality', p. 36.
[59] HCH Hofmann and C Mihaescu, 'The relation between the Charter's fundamental rights and the unwritten general principles of EU law: Good administration as the test case' (2013) 9(1) Eur Const L Rev 73. Although note that in areas where Charter protection is not particularly strong (e.g. Article 37 CFR), general principles still act as important 'gap fillers' in the case law. See, e.g., S Bogojević, 'Human rights of minors and future generations: Global trends and EU environmental law particularities' (2020) 29(2) RECIEL 191.

general principles found in the Charter may enjoy horizontality (beyond Article 21 CFR) and indeed whether other Charter provisions, independent of general principles, could have the same effect.

(C) The Charter of Fundamental Rights

Beyond the approach in *Kücükdeveci* – whereby Charter provisions are given horizontal applicability by linking them to general principles with horizontal application – it was initially unclear whether the Charter could act as an independent source of individual rights and obligations. On the one hand, cases such as *Walrave and Koch*, *Defrenne II* and *Angonese* had long asserted that Treaty provisions can have horizontal direct effect.[60] Given that the Charter has 'the same legal value as the Treaties',[61] it would be only fair to assume that the same would hold for the Charter's provisions.

Difficulty lurks, on the other hand, in Article 51(1) CFR, which lists the Charter's addressees – the EU institutions, bodies, offices, and agencies, as well as the Member States (when implementing EU law) – but does not mention private parties at all.[62] In a move that would have made Éliane Vogel-Polsky proud, the CJEU ruled that this silence should not be taken to imply a ban on horizontality: 'the fact that certain provisions of primary law are addressed principally to the Member States does not preclude their application to relations between individuals'.[63] With one fell swoop, the key hurdle to giving horizontal effect to the Charter was gone.

Just as in *Defrenne II*, however, the Court's approach raised more questions than it answered. Which Charter provisions could possess horizontality powers? The CJEU was quick to note that not *all* Charter provisions can be relied on in private disputes. Take *AMS*, a case concerning Article 27 CFR, which secures the right to information and consultation for workers or their representatives, as an example. The Court found that this particular provision could not be applied horizontally:

> It is ... clear from the wording of Article 27 of the Charter that for this article to be fully effective, *it must be given more specific expression in European Union or national law* ... the facts of the case may be distinguished from those which gave rise to Kücüdeveci in so far as the principle of non-discrimination on grounds of age at issue in that case, laid down in Article 21(1) of the Charter, is sufficient in itself to confer on individuals an individual right which they may invoke as such.[64]

---

[60] *Walrave and Koch* (n 9); *Defrenne II* (n 8); *Angonese* (n 9).

[61] TEU, Article 6(1).

[62] See, e.g., Case C-282/10 *Maribel Dominguez v Centre informatique du Centre Ouest Atlantique and Préfet de la region Centre* EU:C:2011:559, Opinion of AG Trstenjak [80]. See also K Lenaerts, 'The role of the EU Charter in the Member States' in M Bobek and J Adams-Prassl (eds), *The EU Charter of Fundamental Rights in the Member States* (Bloomsbury 2020).

[63] *Bauer* (n 3)[88]; *Max-Planck-Gesellschaft v Shimizu* (n 3).

[64] *AMS* (n 3) [45]–[57] [emphasis added].

Unsurprisingly, then, the classic requirements of clarity and unconditionality must be met before a Charter provision can confer rights on individuals in horizontal litigation. Furthermore, it is noteworthy that in examining whether France had breached EU law in its efforts to implement Directive 2002/14 on informing and consulting employees, the CJEU focuses its discussion on the Charter. This is in line with the ruling in *Åkerberg Fransson*[65] (when national legislation falls 'within the scope of European Union law', the Charter applies), but it also serves as an important reminder that any recognition of horizontality has to be based on primary law rather than the provisions of a directive.

In subsequent cases, the CJEU has recognised the horizontality of a number of Charter Articles, including Articles 21, 31(2) and 47 CFR. They provide for the following rights:

> *Article 21(1) CFR:* Any discrimination based on any ground such as sex, race, colour, ethnic or social origin, genetic features, language, religion or belief, political or any other opinion, membership of a national minority, property, birth, disability, age or sexual orientation shall be prohibited.
>
> *Article 31(2) CFR:* Every worker has the right to limitation of maximum working hours, to daily and weekly rest periods and to an annual period of paid leave.
>
> *Article 47 CFR:* Everyone whose rights and freedoms guaranteed by the law of the Union are violated has the right to an effective remedy before a tribunal in compliance with the conditions laid down in this Article.
>
> Everyone is entitled to a fair and public hearing within a reasonable time by an independent and impartial tribunal previously established by law. Everyone shall have the possibility of being advised, defended and represented.
>
> Legal aid shall be made available to those who lack sufficient resources in so far as such aid is necessary to ensure effective access to justice.

Let us look closely at some of the key cases in which the horizontality of these provisions was at stake, all of which arose in the field of (private) employment relations.

Article 21(1) CFR is concerned with protecting employees (including job applicants) against discrimination on a number of grounds, including religion and belief. In *Egenberger*, an atheist applicant for a policy research job challenged the employer's refusal to invite her to interview. Membership in a particular Protestant church had been explicitly stipulated as a selection criterion.[66]

[65] Case C-617/10 *Åklagaren v Hans Åkerberg Fransson* [2013] ECR I-9011, [21].

[66] Case C-414/16 *Vera Egenberger v Evangelisches Werk für Diakonie und Entwicklung eV* EU:C:2018:257 *(Egenberger)*. See also Case C-68/17 *IR v JQ* EU:C:2018:696, where a Catholic doctor (whose employment had been terminated when he remarried) similarly challenged the employer, a non-profit Catholic organisation, albeit on the technically distinct grounds of anti-discrimination as enshrined in the 'mandatory general principle of EU law' as the claimant's employment had been terminated nine months before the entry into force of the Charter [35]. Both employers acted in full compliance with German law.

In *Cresco*, an employee sought holiday pay for Good Friday afternoon – a national holiday reserved under Austrian law to members of the Evangelical Churches of the Augsburg and Helvetic Confessions, the Old Catholic Church and the United Methodist Church.[67] The claimants had grounded their arguments both in Directive 2000/78, which establishes a general framework for equal treatment in employment, and the broad equal treatment provision in Article 21 CFR.

But these were horizontal claims against private sector employers. In consequence, the Court was adamant that 'a directive cannot be relied on in a dispute between individuals for the purpose of setting aside legislation of a Member State that is contrary to that directive'.[68] Directive 2000/78 does not establish the principle of equal treatment in the field of employment and occupation, 'but has the sole purpose of laying down, in that field, a general framework for combating discrimination on various grounds, including religion and belief'.[69]

This left the claimants with recourse to general principles and the principle of nondiscrimination on grounds of religion or belief, which is embedded in the Charter. Here, the Court was much more receptive:

> The prohibition of all discrimination on grounds of religion or belief is mandatory as a general principle of EU law. That prohibition, which is laid down in Article 21(1) of the Charter, is sufficient in itself to confer on individuals a right which they may rely on as such in disputes between them in a field covered by EU law.[70]

Given the mandatory and sufficiently clear nature of the general principle and Article 21(1) CFR, there was no need for more specific provisions of EU or national law in order to confer rights on individuals in a private dispute. Domestic courts were to guarantee the full effectiveness of that right, even by disapplying any contrary provision of national law if necessary.

This raised a conundrum for the national court in *Egenberger*, as German law severely restricted their ability to scrutinise religious exemption claims: 'judicial review should be limited to a review of plausibility on the basis of the church's self-perception'.[71] Closer scrutiny was required, but how could this be achieved, given the horizontal context of the claim? Through the direct effect of the Charter, which allowed the claimant to overcome the traditional limitations placed on rights set out in directives alone. Article 47 CFR was found (similarly to Article 21(1) CFR) to be 'sufficient in itself and does not need to

[67] *Cresco* (n 23).

[68] *Cresco* [73]. See also, with reference to Article 31(1) CFR, *Bauer* (n 3) [76ff] and *Max-Planck-Gesellschaft v Shimizu* (n 3) [66].

[69] *Egenberger* (n 66) [75].

[70] *Egenberger* [76]; *Cresco* (n 23) [73], [76].

[71] *Egenberger*.

be made more specific by provisions of EU or national law to confer on individuals a right which they may rely on as such'.[72]

Although the horizontal application of the Charter thus enabled the national court to set aside conflicting national legislation, the CJEU followed its by now well-established approach and was careful to point out that a national court should first, in hearing a dispute between two individuals, aim for conform interpretation. Only if the relevant national law cannot be interpreted consistently with EU law does the national court have an obligation:

> to provide, within the limits of its jurisdiction, the legal protection which individuals derive from the general principles of EU law, such as the principle prohibiting discrimination on grounds of religion or belief, now enshrined in Article 21 of the Charter, and to guarantee the full effectiveness of the rights that flow from those principles, by disapplying, if need be, any contrary provision of national law.[73]

This suggests that the CJEU is keen to respect national legislative autonomy to the extent permitted by EU law. What is more, the CJEU recognised that in protecting the rights of parties in horizontal disputes, a national judge may be called on to strike a balance between competing rights, and in this review 'make sure that the principle of proportionality is complied with'.[74] This would mean that Articles 21 and 47 CFR may need to be balanced against various other interests involved, such as respect for the status of churches as laid down in Article 17 TFEU.[75]

Commentators have lauded this approach for 'not interfer[ing] with the freedom of national courts to balance competing fundamental rights according to national constitutional values',[76] as well as for offering a methodology for assessing the application of fundamental rights in disputes between private parties 'that is capable of reconciling the effectiveness of EU law with national constitutional structures'.[77] Whether the national courts would be subject to review if they appeared to strike the 'wrong' balance, however, remains a question left unaddressed.

Turning to Article 31(2) CFR, this provision has been litigated in the context of employment relationships in a pattern familiar from our discussion thus far. The substantive questions are relatively straightforward. Are employers under an obligation to provide pay in lieu of untaken holidays where the

[72] *Egenberger* [78]–[79].

[73] *Egenberger* [71]–[75]. This approach is confirmed in *Cresco* (n 23) [75] and *IR v JQ* (n 66) [67].

[74] *Egenberger* [80].

[75] *Egenberger* [8].

[76] A Colombi Ciacchi, 'The direct horizontal effect of EU fundamental rights' (2019) 15(2) Eur Const L Rev 294, 305.

[77] E Frantziou, 'Mangold recast? The ECJ's flirtation with Drittwirkung in *Egenberger*' (*European Law Blog*, 24 April 2018), https://perma.cc/LH5E-GS64.

former employee's fixed term contract has expired,[78] or where they have died?[79] The relevant answers can be found in Directive 2003/88 on working time, as well as in the Charter. Which one, if any, of these norms could be relied on in the respective disputes?

It depends on who you have been working for. *Bauer and Brossonn* brought an interesting factual twist – one of the deceased ex-employees, Herr Bauer, had worked for Stadt Wuppertal, a German municipality. The relevant provisions of the Directive could therefore have direct vertical effect, and his widow had the right to obtain compensation in lieu of paid annual leave from the public authority. Herr Brossonn, the second deceased employee, however, worked for a private employer, thus leaving his widow without similar recourse: 'a directive cannot of itself impose obligations on an individual and cannot therefore be relied upon as such against an individual', of course.[80]

But we are not left with this unsatisfactory outcome: the horizontal application of Article 31(2) CFR was able to offer protection where a mere directive could not. The right to paid annual leave 'constitutes an essential principle of EU social law',[81] the CJEU explained, drawing on various international instruments and the Charter. The right was 'mandatory', because derogations can be made only in compliance with the strict conditions in Article 52(1) CFR, and 'unconditional', because it need not be given concrete expression by the provisions of EU or national law.[82] As a result, the national court was empowered to set aside conflicting national law: both widows were entitled to payment in lieu of their deceased husband's unused holiday entitlements, albeit for fundamentally different legal reasons.

What does this mean for private employers? The annual leave saga continues to rumble on. In *Max Planck Gesellschaft v Shimuzu*, the CJEU clarified that, in these horizontal situations, the employer must be able to show that she has exercised all due diligence in enabling the worker to take the paid annual leave to which she is entitled to under EU law.[83] If the worker has refrained from taking her paid annual leave deliberately and in full knowledge of the consequences, on the other hand, the Charter does not preclude the loss of that right.[84]

More fundamentally, what does this line of cases tell us about the horizontal effect of Charter provisions? There is an increasing tendency to presume that mandatory and unconditional provisions of the Charter (including general principles, as now enshrined in a Charter provision) are horizontally applicable,[85]

[78] *Max-Planck-Gesellschaft v Shimizu* (n 3).

[79] *Bauer* (n 3).

[80] *Bauer* [76].

[81] *Bauer* [80].

[82] *Bauer* [84]–[85].

[83] *Max-Planck-Gesellschaft v Shimizu* (n 3) [94].

[84] *Max-Planck-Gesellschaft v Shimizu* [56].

[85] E Frantziou, '(Most of) the Charter of Fundamental Rights is horizontally applicable' (2019) 15(2) Eur Const L Rev 306; LS Rossi, 'The relationship between the EU Charter of Fundamental Rights and Directives in horizontal situations' (*EU Law Analysis*, 25 February 2019), https://perma.cc/5ZJH-PFA5; Lenaerts (n 62), 'The role of the EU Charter in the Member States'.

although it may be too early to draw firm conclusions on this point. To date, the provisions which have been gilded with horizontality have undeniably 'revolutionised the enforcement of employment norms'[86] and enabled individuals to realise rights which they would not have been able to enforce simply by reference to directives. Whether future litigation will continue to impact employment relations in this way is uncertain, however. Remember, for example, the resistance of AG Bobek we encountered in the first Debate.

We also know that Article 27 CFR is inapplicable in private disputes because it is conditional on further specification, both at the EU level as well as in domestic implementation. But so are the provisions on 'solidarity' in Chapter IV of the Charter – another example of employment-specific provisions, including the provisions on the right of collective bargaining and action (Article 28 CFR), protection in the event of unjustified dismissal (Article 30 CFR), and the entitlement to social security and social assistance (Article 34 CFR).[87] The extent to which the Court will continue to insist that only mandatory and unconditional Charter provisions entail horizontality remains to be seen.

***

The fact that certain Charter provisions enjoy horizontality is a game-changer for individual rights protection in the EU. It enables citizens to enforce their rights before national courts without further legislative effort, and to do so even against private entities. What is more, the Charter succeeds at protecting individuals where directives fail to confer directly enforceable rights. Yet we also see a Court recognising the need to respect the interests of the Member States, in particular as regards their national legislative space. The contortions in *Bauer and Bresson* ensured a defensible outcome – even though the reasoning left plenty of room for counter-intuitive decisions in the future. Imagine, for example, a claim along the lines of *AMS* against a local French municipality. Does the real problem lie in the Court's steadfast adherence to the ban on horizontal effect for directives? And more importantly, would jettisoning that hallowed refusal cure EU law's 'infant disease', as encountered in Chapter 1, once and for all?

Debate 3

Has the CJEU achieved horizontal effect of directives by the back door?

In the previous chapter, we saw that direct effect was but one of the constitutional principles which characterise the relationship between EU law and the Member States' legal orders. The supremacy of EU law and the obligation on

[86] J Adams-Prassl, 'Article 47 CFR and the effective enforcement of EU labour law: Teeth for paper tigers?' (2020) Eur Labour LJ 391.

[87] Adams-Prassl, 'Article 47 CFR and the effective enforcement of EU labour law'.

national courts to interpret national law in harmony with EU norms can be just as important in securing the effective judicial protection of rights.

The interaction of these different approaches has caused particular interest in the context of our present discussion. The Court continues to emphasise that directives cannot confer rights on litigants in horizontal scenarios, in the face of extensive academic criticism and a long line of Advocates General suggesting that the Court reverse its stance.[88] At the same time, however, this has not stopped the CJEU from recognising alternative routes to achieving a substantively identical outcome, as the widows *Bauer and Brossonn* found. In that case, it was the horizontal direct effect of a sufficiently clear and precise Charter provision that helped outflank the ban on horizontality.

Nor has the reticence to grant directives horizontal direct effect extended to allowing other doctrines to operate in a similar fashion, suggesting that the Court has abandoned any concerns about imposing obligations on individuals in all but principle. Let us explore three such scenarios in turn.

(A) Recognising a Broad Notion of the State

One long-standing way in which rights found in directives can be enforced in a private setting is by adopting an expansive definition of 'the state' in such disputes. This is evident in *Foster*,[89] where the applicant sought to rely on the Equal Treatment Directive against her employer, British Gas. The CJEU ruled that

> a body, whatever its legal form, which has been made responsible, pursuant to a measure adopted by the State, for providing a *public service under the control of the State and has for that purpose special powers beyond* those which result from the normal rules applicable in relations between individuals is included in any event among the bodies against which the provisions of a directive capable of having direct effect may be relied upon.[90]

The Court does not elaborate on what counts as a 'public service under the control of the state', or what 'special powers' consist of. This makes sense: any catch-all definition of state bodies is unrealistic in an administratively complex and diverse Europe.[91]

The CJEU nonetheless offered some valuable clarification in *Farell*:[92] the two conditions set out in *Foster* are not to be read cumulatively; the notion of a 'state' should be construed broadly. This lets us appreciate the general thrust of the Court's conception of the 'state', but it offers limited guidance as to what exactly should be considered 'special powers', and how substantial they

---

[88] *Marshall* (n 31), Opinion of AG Van Gerven; *Vaneetveld* (n 35), Opinion of AG Jacobs; *Dori* (n 35), Opinion of AG Jenz; *Farrell* (n 35), Opinion of AG Sharpston.

[89] Case C-188/89 *A. Foster and ors v British Gas plc.* [1990] ECR I-3313.

[90] *Foster* [20] [emphasis added].

[91] P Koutrakos 'Is there more to say about the direct effect of directives?' (2018) 43(5) EL Rev 621, 622.

[92] *Farrell* (n 35).

must be in order for a body carrying out tasks in the public interest by delegation of the state to be considered part of the state. More litigation on these points is bound to unfold.

(B) Horizontal Harmonious Interpretation ('Indirect Effect')

Beyond an expansive reading of direct effect itself, the duty of harmonious interpretation can lead to similar substantive results in horizontal litigation. As we saw in Chapter 5, the doctrine had its origins in vertical litigation against the state, filling a remedial gap where obligations had not been set out with sufficient clarity and precision.[93] This was soon extended to horizontal scenarios.

In *Marleasing SA*, the eponymous claimant alleged that another company, *La Commercial SA*, had been set up for fraudulent purposes, and sought to have its incorporation annulled. Given the horizontal nature of the claim, Directive 68/151, which provided an exhaustive list of situations in which such nullity could be ordered (and would thus have provided a comprehensive answer to the claim), was inapplicable. But this did not mean that it was irrelevant to the case:

> The Member States' obligation arising from a directive to achieve the result envisaged by the directive and their duty ... to take all appropriate measures, whether general or particular, to ensure the fulfilment of that obligation, is binding on all the authorities of Member States including, for matters within their jurisdiction, the courts. It follows that, in applying national law ... the national court called upon to interpret it is required to do so, as far as possible, in the light of the wording and the purpose of the directive in order to achieve the result pursued by the latter.[94]

This approach was confirmed in *Webb*,[95] where the UK House of Lords found that an employer could not dismiss an employee on the grounds of pregnancy when she was a replacement for another employee on maternity leave. Significantly, this obligation did not exist prior to the domestic court's interpretation of national employment law in light of the Equal Treatment Directive. The same principle is applicable when the obligation on individuals arises not from EU but national law. That is, conflicting national law must be interpreted in conformity with EU law, even if that prevents national law from being enforced, and creates a new obligation for one of the parties.[96]

---

[93] Case 14/83 *Sabine Von Colson and Elisabeth Kamann v Land Nordrhein-Westfalen* [1984] ECR 1891.

[94] Case C-106/89 *Marleasing SA v La Comercial Internacional de Alimentacion SA* [1990] ECR I-4135 [8].

[95] Case C-32/93 *Carole Louise Webb v EMO Air Cargo (UK) Ltd* [1994] ECR I-3567.

[96] See, e.g., C-456/98 *Centrosteel Srl v Adipol GmbH* [2000] ECR I-6007. See also *Pfeiffer* (n 34), where the litigants had been pushed to work more than 48 hours per week on average, which was in accordance with national law but in conflict with EU rules on safety and health.

(C) The Knock-On Effects of Supremacy ('Incidental Effect')

The fact that directives have no horizontal direct effect, then, does not mean that directives will never prejudice one party in a private dispute. Another avenue for such effects to manifest themselves is as a result of knock-on consequences of the supremacy of EU law. If a party is attempting to rely on a domestic provision that has been adopted in breach of a superior EU norm, then their action will be unable to succeed: given the supremacy of the latter, the domestic court has to disapply any offending provisions.

One measure that is not infrequently at the basis of such disputes is the Commission's notification system. Based on the Notification Directive,[97] it is an important motor in market construction – it helps prevent trade barriers by requiring that Member States notify the Commission and other Member States before introducing new product standards and specifications, allowing for time to 'react and to propose amendments for lessening restrictions to the free movement of goods'.[98]

This means that, if a Member State ignores the notification procedure and introduces new product specification for, say, burglar alarms or short-term holiday rentals, then their national rules will be inapplicable. This, in turn, could have an effect on individuals who have relied on the national law, as was the case in *CIA*[99] and, more recently, in *Airbnb Ireland.*[100] This is so even though the directive in question creates 'neither rights not obligations for individuals',[101] which has led academic commentators to describe its impact on private litigation as *incidental.*

***

Looking at the interaction between EU law and domestic legal systems in horizontal scenarios, 'it is often difficult to distinguish these cases convincingly from direct horizontal effect'.[102] This has led many commentators to wonder whether we are looking at 'Derivative Horizontal Direct Effect for Directives'[103] or, more straightforwardly, whether the CJEU has given up on anything other than paying lip service to the ban on horizontal direct effect for directives.

---

[97] European Parliament and Council Directive 2015/1535/EU of 9 September 2015 laying down a procedure for the provision of information in the field of technical regulations and of rules on Information Society services [2015] OJ L241/1, which has been subject to numerous amendments since its first iteration as Directive 83/89/EEC.

[98] Case C-194/94 *CIA Security International SA v Signalson SA and Securitel SPRL* [1996] ECR I-2201 [50].

[99] *CIA Security International.*

[100] Case C-390/18 *Criminal Proceedings Against X* EU:C:2019:1112.

[101] Case C-443/98 *Unilever Italia SpA v Central Food SpA* [2000] ECR 7535.

[102] P Craig and G de Búrca, *EU Law: Text, Cases, and Materials*, 7th edn (Oxford University Press 2020), p. 259.

[103] LS Rossi, 'The relationship between the EU Charter of Fundamental Rights and Directives in horizontal situations' (*EU Law Analysis*, 25 February 2019), https://perma.cc/5ZJH-PFA5.

In substance, there is much to this argument: the widows Bauer and Brossonn were both entitled to financial compensation, and Mrs Webb could bring an action against her (private sector) employer just as Mrs Marshall had done against her public sector one. In terms of legal mechanisms, on the other hand, these cases could not be more different. It is important to keep these distinctions in mind, lest we confuse cause and effect. Direct effect is about conferring rights (and imposing obligations) directly on individuals. The doctrines we have encountered in the preceding Debates will have various impacts on litigation, whilst not necessarily conferring any rights directly.

Remember also that they operate just as much in vertical as in horizontal scenarios – so the cases where they interact with directives are but a subset of a much larger range of possibilities. Any suggestion that the recognition of 'indirect' and 'incidental' effect furthermore involves a degree of subterfuge – creating a deliberate way around ban on horizontal effect of directives – struggles with chronology: the duty of harmonious interpretation can already be found in the case law some years before the horizontality of directives was ever discussed.[104]

Conclusion: Legal Certainty vs Effectiveness

The potential horizontal application of EU law adds another layer of complication to the tensions we explored in Chapter 5. In addition to balancing the effective protection of individual rights and Member State regulatory competence, we also need to consider the obligations imposed on individuals. In one sense, the Court's answer has been straightforward: as long as a norm is sufficiently clear and precise, and not found in a directive alone, it will confer rights on individuals and impose concomitant obligations.

The reality, of course, is much messier and Pollockian. Ongoing litigation is required to tease out which provisions so qualify, and the overlapping effects of different constitutional doctrines can muddy the waters. This is not without irony: legal certainty was one of key planks in the Court's argument for refusing horizontal direct effect of directives. In reality, it may well have achieved the opposite. In *Farell*, AG Sharpston concluded her opinion with a postscript in which she criticised the Court for jeopardising individual rights by insisting on non-horizontality for directives, arguing that that the present situation 'creates complexity for plaintiffs and uncertainty for defendants'.[105] Joining a long line of Advocates General past and present,[106] she invited the Court to revisit its position. True to form, it refused.

This stance, however, is increasingly at odds with the CJEU's insistence that *national* courts do everything within their powers 'to provide … the legal protection which individuals derive from [EU law] and to ensure that those rules

[104] We are grateful to Stefan Enchelmaier for this point.

[105] *Farrell* (n 35), Opinion of AG Sharpston [150].

[106] Opinions of Van Gerven, AG Jacobs, and AG Jenz (see n 35 herein).

are fully effective, setting aside any provision of national law which may conflict'.[107] In the same spirit, perhaps the time has come for Luxembourg, too, to set aside any provisions which may conflict – that is, its commitment to ruling out the horizontal direct effect of directives. In practice, this would not lead to a much deeper encroachment on national regulators than we have already seen, and it would at long last remove the curious juxtaposition of legal certainty and the protection of individual rights.

Further reading

'2018 was a glorious year for scholars who ... have long been advocates of the direct horizontal effect of (EU) fundamental rights', suggests Aurelia Colombi Ciacchi – not least because the cases came from Germany, whose legal system has known long battles about the horizontal effect even of domestic rights. See 'The direct horizontal effect of EU fundamental rights: ECJ 17 April 2018, Case C-414/16, *Vera Egenberger v Evangelisches Werk Für Diakonie Und Entwicklung E.V. and ECJ* 11 September 2018, Case C-68/17, *IR v JQ*' (2019) 15 European Constitutional Law Review 294, especially pages 302–04.

Who should carry the responsibility of ensuring a safe workplace where Charter rights are observed – the state or the employer? In thinking about horizontality, consider findings in labour economics that employers are best placed to ensure efficient risk distribution. See L. Summers, 'What Can Economics Contribute to Social Policy? Some Simple Economics of Mandated Benefits' (1989) 79 Am Econ Rev 177.

The horizontality debate is by no means limited to the context of general principles and the Charter. Another important area in which the debates play out is the internal market. Stefan Enchelmaier explores the extent to which the fundamental economic freedoms can impose restrictions on private parties in 'Horizontality: the application of the four freedoms to restrictions imposed by private parties' in P. Koutrakos and J. Snell, *Research Handbook on the Law of the EU's Internal Market* (Edward Elgar 2017).

[107] *Mangold* (n 44) [77].

CHAPTER 7

Umpire or Emperor?
Preliminary References, Supremacy, and the Court of Justice

The CJEU is a key player in European integration. Its decisions have laid the foundations for market liberalisation and put individuals at the centre of EU law. In a series of early landmark cases, the Court quickly established itself as a powerful yet discreet actor in shaping the new legal order, 'tucked away in the fairyland Duchy of Luxembourg'.[1]

Today, the CJEU no longer enjoys this privilege of seclusion. Gone are the days when judges, Advocates General, and their teams all fit in the picturesque Villa Vauban – the Court's original seat.[2] Today, the Court is housed in a brutalist 'Palais' on the Kirchberg – 'a complex collection of buildings [with] two high-rise towers (making unfortunate allusions to Tolkien difficult to suppress)'.[3] This physical expansion is a reflection of jurisdictional growth, frequently in tandem with the expansion of EU competences. Throughout this book, we encounter a wide range of situations where the Court's case law digs deep into 'hitherto jealously guarded'[4] domains, from national procedural law to fundamental rights. The CJEU has placed itself at the heart of EU law as a dynamic legal enterprise, which quite naturally sparks debates and inquiries into its role and the proper distribution of responsibilities between the Union and its constituent Member States. Is the CJEU a supreme court? If so, where does this leave domestic (supreme) courts? And more importantly, '*[q]uis custodiet ipsos custodes*'[5] – who is tasked with ensuring that the Court does not venture outside its competence or jurisdiction?

Ultimately, the following debates centre on different visions of the CJEU's role. Does it favour a top-down approach, as an emperor would, issuing decrees

[1] E Stein, 'Lawyers, judges, and the making of a transnational constitution' (1981) 75(1) AJIL 1.

[2] A historical photo-presentation of the CJEU through the years is available at https://curia.europa.eu/jcms/jcms/P_93450/en.

[3] N Nic-Shuibhne, 'A court within a court: Is it time to rebuild the Court of Justice?' (2009) 34(2) EL Rev 173, 174.

[4] JH Mance, 'The interface between national and European law' (2013) 38(4) EL Rev 437, 437–38.

[5] L Watson and P Watson (eds), *Juvenal: Satire 6* (Cambridge University Press 2014), p. 65.

and actively shaping the Union? Or is it better understood as an umpire, mediating and resolving disputes and neutrally enforcing the rules of the game? These are very different types of authority, and they give rise to very different relationships with their subjects. We can explore the true nature of the Court of Justice through its relationship with other actors: citizens, courts and tribunals, and Member States in preliminary reference rulings across all domains of EU law (Debate 1); and national supreme courts when it comes to the vexed question of EU law's supremacy (Debate 2).

Debate 1

Is the CJEU a Supreme Court?

To Koen Lenaerts, President of the Court of Justice, the CJEU is a 'mere umpire' with restricted powers: it 'simply clears up any confusion left over in the bloc's treaties, steering clear of politics'.[6] This description certainly fits some of the CJEU's functions, but not all.

In line with Article 19 TEU, the CJEU has one overarching mission: to 'ensure that in the interpretation and application of the Treaties the law is observed'. It also has three more specific tasks, relating to annulment actions (Article 263 TFEU); infringement actions (Article 258 TFEU); and preliminary references (267 TFEU). As we saw in Chapters 3 and 4, the first two functions are indeed umpire-like. In infringement actions, the CJEU is asked to preside over disputes between the Commission and the Member States on whether the latter have breached EU law. These are classic interinstitutional battles, where the CJEU enforces the rules of the game. Annulment actions allow for a more heterogeneous group of litigants – the Member States and EU institutions may in principle be joined by individuals, including NGOs, if they meet the tough standing criteria – to review EU acts based on specific grounds.

In all of these scenarios, the CJEU acts as an umpire, making sure that the EU follows its own rulebook. The Court continues to be called upon to arbitrate institutional battles, deciding whether any of the institutions have overstepped their powers.[7] In recent years, for example, the Commission has challenged what was perceived as the Council's power-grab to negotiate an international agreement that would link the EU emissions trading scheme to an Australian equivalent.[8] The Council has also been accused of sidelining the European Parliament in adopting the first set of procedural rules governing Article 7(1) TEU hearings (to which we return in Chapter 11).[9] These con-

[6] 'The wizards of Luxembourg' (*The Economist*, London, 21 May 2020), https://perma.cc/M4CZ-NL98.

[7] Although they are much rarer today as a result of the wide adoption of the ordinary legislative procedure; see Chapter 3.

[8] Case C-425/13 *Commission v Council* EU:C:2015:483.

[9] However, the matter is not yet brought before the CJEU: L Pech, D Kochenov and S Platon, 'The European Parliament sidelined: On the Council's distorted reading of Article 7(1) TEU' (*Verfassungsblog*, 8 September 2019), https://perma.cc/N2RT-Q7TX.

frontations are significant for interinstitutional balance and cooperation, but they are not constitutionally disruptive for national legal orders.

(A) Article 267 TFEU: Procedural Innovation or Revolutionary Constitutionalism?

Matters are different when it comes to preliminary references, especially when the CJEU not only reviews EU law, but interprets its interactions with domestic norms. According to President Lenaerts, in doing so the Court merely fills constitutional lacunae left by the Treaty and legislative compromise. '[O]ne man's lacuna-filling, [however], is another man's power grab.'[10] After all, it was in the exercise of its interpretative powers that the CJEU laid down many of the major constitutional milestones we encounter throughout this book – from direct effect and supremacy to state liability. Article 267 TFEU does not just provide a vital route, via the national courts, for individuals to review national measures implementing EU acts: it is key to ensuring the effectiveness of EU law. Ultimately, its objectives are to secure uniformity of EU law throughout a jurisdictionally distinct Union,[11] avert 'the risk of an incorrect interpretation of EU law',[12] and ensure that the law established by the Treaties is observed within all corners of the EU.[13] The Court is not a mere umpire; rather, it is a forceful and imaginative actor, shaping the contours of the EU legal order.

The CJEU's powers are considerable, especially from an historical perspective. Prior to World War II, only a handful of courts world-wide had ever exercised 'the power of the constitutional judicial review'.[14] The Court was modelled after the *Conseil d'État*, a senior French judicial body designed to hold the government to account.[15] But why add a preliminary reference procedure to the Treaties?

The interpretive task assigned by Article 267 TFEU was proposed at the negotiations leading up to the Treaty of Rome by Nicola Catalano, the Italian representative and later a judge at the CJEU. It was inspired by judicial mechanisms known to the Italian and German legal system, where similar processes allowed references from junior courts to be sent to domestic constitutional

[10] 'The wizards of Luxembourg' (n 6).

[11] Case 166/73 *Rheinmühlen-Düsseldorf v Einfuhr- und Vorratsstelle für Getreide und Futtermittel* [1974] ECR 33. See also Case C-62/14 *Peter Gauweiler and ors v German Bundestag* EU:C:2015:7, Opinion of AG Cruz Villal [40].

[12] Case C-160/14 *João Filipe Ferreira da Silva e Brito and ors v Portugal* EU:C:2015:565 (*Ferreira da Silva*) [44].

[13] Opinion 2/13 of the Court on the compatibility of the draft agreement with the EU and FEU Treaties EU:C:2014:2454, [176].

[14] A Stone Sweet, 'The European Court of Justice' in P Craig and G de Búrca (eds), *The Evolution of EU Law*, 2nd edn (Oxford University Press 2011), p. 122.

[15] KJ Alter, *The European Court's Political Power: Selected Essays* (Oxford University Press 2010), p. 186.

courts.[16] Pierre Pescatore, the Luxembourgian representative and another subsequent Member of the Court, recalled that other representatives '*n'avaient pas conscience de l'importance de cette innovation*'[17] – although the mechanism's Treaty inclusion was closely scrutinised by all.[18] Today, Article 267 TFEU is the 'jewel in [EU law's] crown';[19] it is one of the main reasons why the CJEU is thought to be 'the most active and influential international legal body in existence'.[20] Vesterdorf, a former President of the General Court, goes even further: the fact that the CJEU not only observes Member State compliance with the Treaties, but actively advises national courts through preliminary rulings and thereby promotes the 'unity and the consistency' of EU law, elevates the CJEU to Europe's supreme court.[21]

Not quite so fast. What about the national courts, on whom the preliminary reference procedure depends, and who are therefore arguably just as powerful as the CJEU? Article 19 TEU makes explicit reference to national legal systems in setting out the EU's judicial system, and the CJEU has long set down 'a clear separation of functions':[22] national courts refer questions to the CJEU and apply the Court's ruling domestically, whereas the CJEU interprets EU law and enjoys exclusive competence to review the legality of EU acts. Is this balance of responsibilities maintained in practice? Or is the relationship inevitably stacked in the CJEU's favour, acting like an emperor with little regard for domestic judicial sensitivities?

(B) Asking the (Right) Question

Preliminary rulings can only be requested by national judges. If questions about the validity or interpretation of EU law are raised in the course of domestic proceedings, the issue is referred to Luxembourg for a preliminary ruling. The Court's attitude to referrals is generally welcoming: it operates as a helpline in the interpretation of all manners of EU acts.[23] But there are limits. In *Foglia I*, the Court refused to admit a preliminary reference request in the

[16] P Pescatore, 'Les travaux de "groupe juridique" dans la négotiation des traités de Rome' (1981) 34(1) Studia Diplomatica 159.

[17] ('didn't realise the importance of this innovation'): Pescatore, 'Les travaux de "groupe juridique" dans la négotiation des traités de Rome' 173.

[18] M Rasmussen, 'From *Costa v. ENEL* to the treaties of Rome: A brief history of a legal revolution' in MP Maduro and L Azoulai (eds), *The Past and Future of EU Law: The Classics of EU Law Revisited on the 50th Anniversary of the Rome Treaty* (Hart 2010), p. 81.

[19] P Craig, *EU Administrative Law*, 2nd edn (Oxford University Press 2012), p. 263.

[20] Alter, *The European Court's Political Power* (n 15), p. 186. See also Stone Sweet (n 14), 'The European Court of Justice', p. 121.

[21] B Vesterdorf, 'A constitutional court for the EU?' (2006) 4(4) Intl J Const L 607, 610–11.

[22] Case 6/64 *Costa v ENEL* [1964] ECR 585.

[23] Note that with regard to questions of validity, the CJEU rules only in relation to legally binding acts, whereas with regard to interpretation requests, its jurisdiction covers non-legally binding acts, too: Case C-322/88 *Salvatore Grimaldi v Fonds des maladies professionnelles* [1989] ECR 4407; Case 135/77 *Robert Bosch GmbH v Hauptzollamt Hildesheim* [1978] ECR 855.

absence of a genuine dispute: two enterprising Italians, 'in agreement as to the result to be attained', had engineered an indirect attack on French tax law.[24] The local *Pretore* was not impressed, and sent off another request. Surely it was a matter for the referring court alone to decide what questions should be referred? The Court stood firm in *Foglia II*: its duty under Article 267 TFEU was 'not that of delivering advisory opinions on general or hypothetical questions but of assisting in the administration of justice in the Member States'.[25]

The *Foglia*-series divides commentators: some see it as significantly circumscribing national courts' discretion to determine referrals;[26] others hail the Court's restraint in not extending its jurisdiction to advisory opinions.[27] *Foglia* lives on,[28] even though outright refusals are rare in practice – not least because of the Court's narrow definition of 'hypothetical' cases. In *Wightman,* for example, the UK Government argued that the unilateral revocability of Article 50 TEU was not an admissible question, since it 'addresse[d] events that have not occurred and may not occur'.[29] The Court of Justice, however, insisted that 'questions relating to EU law enjoy a presumption of relevance'[30] – it was 'not for the Court to call into question the referring court's assessment of the admissibility of the action in the main proceedings'.[31]

In addition to rejecting hypothetical cases,[32] the CJEU has also refused to rule on questions it considers irrelevant or unnecessary to the actual facts of the main action,[33] questions that lack the factual or legal material necessary to give a useful answer,[34] and questions that are not articulated with sufficient clarity.[35] In the latter scenario, the Court has not been afraid to reframe or combine the questions asked, thereby (re-)defining the relevant legal dilemma. This runs the risk of undermining national courts' authority to determine the relevant

---

[24] Case 104/79 *Pasquale Foglia v Mariella Novello* [1980] ECR 745 [10].

[25] Case 244/80 *Pasquale Foglia v Mariella Novello (No 2)* [1981] ECR 3045 [18].

[26] G Bebr, 'The existence of a genuine dispute: An indispensable precondition for the jurisdiction of the Court under Article 177 EEC treaty' (1980) 17(4) CML Rev 525.

[27] D Wyatt, '*Foglia (No 2)*: The Court denies it has jurisdiction to give advisory opinions' (1982) 7 EL Rev 186.

[28] See, e.g., Case C-318/00 *Bacardi-Martini SAS and Cellier des Dauphins v Newcastle United Football Company Ltd* [2003] ECR I-905 [44].

[29] Case 621/18 *Andy Wightman and ors v Secretary of State for Exiting the European Union* EU:C:2018:999 [21].

[30] *Wightman* [27].

[31] *Wightman* [30].

[32] Case C-72/15 *PJSC Rosneft Oil Company v Her Majesty's Treasury and ors* EU:C:2017:236 [50]. See also Rules of Procedure of the Court of Justice [2012] OJ L265/1, Article 94.

[33] Case 126/80 *Maria Salonia v Giorgio Poidomani and Franca Baglieri, née Giglio* [1981] ECR 1563; Joined Cases C-52/16 *'SEGRO' Kft. v Vas Megyei Kormányhivatal Sárvári Járási Földhivatala* and C-113/16 *Günther Horváth v Vas Megyei Kormányhivatal* EU:C:2018:157 [43].

[34] Case C-235/95 *AGS Assedic Pas-de-Calais v François Dumon and Froment, liquidator and representative of Établissements Pierre Gilson* [1998] ECR I-4531; Joined Cases C-320-322/90 *Telemarsicabruzzo SpA v Circostel and ors* [1993] ECR I-393.

[35] Case C-83/91 *Wienand Meilicke v ADV/ORGA F. A. Meyer AG* [1992] ECR I-4871.

queries, as well as rendering useless the dialogue that Article 267 TFEU seeks to establish. Take *ClientEarth* as an example:[36] the Court's reformulation of the question referred, the UK Supreme Court explained with some exasperation, had 'the unfortunate effect of enabling each party to claim success on the issue'.[37]

(C) Giving the Correct Answer: Interpretation vs Application of EU Law

In responding to preliminary reference requests, the Court's ruling must make 'every effort to give a reply which will be of assistance in resolving the dispute in the main proceedings',[38] but it is for the national courts to apply these recommendations to the facts of the case. Under no circumstances can Luxembourg directly interpret or (dis)apply national law.[39]

This is a line easily drawn in principle and quickly crossed in practice. Given the supremacy of EU law, the interpretation of relevant Treaty provisions will not infrequently leave little wriggle room for the referring court.[40] On occasion, the Court of Justice will even give an answer so specific as to resolve the dispute. In *Mickelsson & Roos* (the 'jet skis' case explored in detail in Chapter 10), for example, the Court was concerned with the proportionality of Swedish environmental law – a question which as with 'any assessment of the facts in the case is a matter for the national court'.[41] However, 'in a spirit of cooperation', the Court of Justice then provided a detailed assessment, analysing alternative outcomes with a view to providing the national court with 'all the guidance that it deems necessary'.[42] Critics are unimpressed: what role does this leave for national courts?[43]

It depends not least on what type of preliminary ruling the Court hands down. Tridimas identifies three categories: 'outcome cases', such as *Mickelsson*, where national courts are given specific instructions that essentially dispose of the case; 'guidance cases', where the Court of Justice furnishes guidelines; and

---

[36] Case C-404/13 *The Queen on the Application of ClientEarth v Secretary of State for the Environment, Food and Rural Affairs* EU:C:2014:2382.

[37] *R (ClientEarth) v Secretary of State for Environment, Food and Rural Affairs* [2015] UKSC 28 [6]. A similar point, relying on a different set of case law, was made by Lord Mance (n 4).

[38] Recommendations of the Court of Justice of the European Union to national courts and tribunals in relation to the initiation of preliminary ruling proceedings [2018] OJ C257/01, paragraph 11.

[39] See, e.g., C-237/02 *Freiburger Kommunalbauten GmbH Baugesellschaft & Co. KG v Ludger Hofstetter and Ulrike Hofstetter* [2004] ECR I-3403 [22].

[40] *Costa* (n 22), p. 593.

[41] C-142/05 *Åklagaren v Percy Mickelsson and Joakim Roos* [2009] ECR I-4273 [15]–[16], [39].

[42] *Åklagaren* [35].

[43] See, e.g., S Enchelmaier, 'Moped trailers, *Mickelsson & Roos, Gysbrechts*: The CJEU's case law on goods keeps on moving' (2010) 29 YEL 190, 212–13.

'deference cases', where the answer is cast in terms so general as to leave significant leeway to the referring court.[44]

But it takes two to tango: the precise way questions are posed is key to the kind of answer desired.[45] Remember also that, in practice at least, national courts *do* get the ultimate say. A close investigation of two decades' worth of preliminary references in Swedish environmental law revealed a wide range of domestic responses – from loyal absorption and application to simply ignoring the CJEU's ruling.[46]

(D) Tension in the Air

All parties involved will therefore on occasion stray beyond the strict separation of responsibilities. The ensuing tension is palpable: the CJEU needs to ensure appropriate respect for domestic judicial autonomy, but not at the cost of denying the effective vindication of citizens' rights. Two very different doctrines help tread this fine line: *acte clair* and *Köbler* liability.[47]

Acte clair: *Safe Harbour or Rogue Hideout?*

Acte clair provides an important exception to the operation of the preliminary reference procedure. Where a text is so clear that it requires no interpretation or further elucidation to resolve the dispute before a national court, the latter does not have to refer the question to the CJEU. The doctrine, long rooted in Italian and German law, was incorporated into EU law in *CILFIT*.[48] The Italian Court of Cassation, faced with a question of grave importance (is wool an animal product for purposes of import levies?), enquired about the scope of its duty to enlist the Court of Justice's interpretative help: surely the answer was obvious?[49]

The intervening Member States, supported by the Commission, agreed. A high degree of autonomy for domestic judges 'would bear witness to [the CJEU's] confidence in national courts'.[50] AG Capotorti, however, was not impressed. Pointing to a long list of French cases in which the *Conseil d'État* had sought to rely on *acte clair* to avoid preliminary referrals, even in cases where the Court of Justice's involvement was patently required, the AG highlighted the dangers of excessive interpretative leeway at the domestic level.[51]

---

[44] T Tridimas, 'Constitutional review of Member State action: The virtues and vices of an incomplete jurisdiction' (2011) 9(3–4) Intl J Const L 737.

[45] A Wallerman, 'Can two walk together, except they be agreed? Preliminary references and (the erosion of) national procedural autonomy' (2019) 44(2) EL Rev 159.

[46] S Bogojević, 'Judicial dialogue unpacked: Twenty years of preliminary references on environmental matters initiated by the Swedish judiciary' (2017) 29(2) JEL 263.

[47] At least, this is how Rasmussen explains the introduction of *acte clair* to EU law: H Rasmussen, 'The European Court's *acte clair* strategy in CILFIT' (1984) 9 EL Rev 242.

[48] Case 283/81 *Srl CILFIT and Lanificio di Gavardo SpA v Ministry of Health* [1982] ECR 3415.

[49] Wool is not an animal product, or at least it was not included as such in the relevant annex on 'animal products' as set out in the case, *CILFIT*.

[50] *CILFIT*, p. 3425.

[51] *CILFIT*, Opinion of AG Capotorti, p. 3435.

Given that national judges already enjoyed a 'wide margin of discretion' under Article 267 TFEU, Capotorti concluded that there was no need to adopt the *acte clair* doctrine at the EU level.

Perhaps surprisingly, the Court sided with the Member States. It softened national courts' referral obligations, even in the absence of further judicial remedies, as long as the correct application of EU law was 'so obvious as to leave no scope for any reasonable doubt as to the manner in which the question raised is to be resolved'.[52] This was not to be mistaken for a *carte blanche*: the national court 'must be convinced that the matter is equally obvious to the courts of the other Member States and to the Court of Justice', and bear in mind the 'characteristic features of [EU] law and the particular difficulties to which its interpretation gives rise'.[53] This includes the fact that EU acts and legislation are issued in several languages; EU law uses terminology particular to it and legal concepts may have a specific EU meaning; and that EU law must be construed in its textual, purposive, and temporal context.

When read in conjunction with the CJEU's earlier recognition of the doctrine of *acte éclairé* – exempting national courts from the duty to request a preliminary ruling where a case is 'materially identical with a question which has already been the subject of a preliminary ruling in a similar case', as in *Da Costa*[54] – should we interpret *CILFIT* as a broad grant of interpretative competence to the national courts?

The answer depends on your reading of the *CILFIT* criteria. To some, they are 'sisyphean',[55] 'not for the fainthearted',[56] and 'draconian',[57] robbing *acte clair* of all practical relevance. David Edwards, a former CJEU judge, disagrees: the conditions as 'caveats rather than strict criteria', suggesting that they are 'no more than common sense'.[58] This view is shared by senior domestic judges, not least given the danger that 'an over-literal application of the *CILFIT* test could inundate the Court … The chimera of unseen language versions or unforeseeable future decisions by other national courts should not oblige a court to make a reference.'[59]

---

[52] *CILFIT* [16].

[53] *CILFIT* [17].

[54] Joined Cases 28-30/62 *Da Costa en Schaake NV and ors v Netherlands Inland Revenue Administration* [1963] EU:C:1963:6, 38. National courts retain the right to refer, should they deem it necessary: Joined Cases C-569/16 *Stadt Wuppertal v Maria Elisabeth Bauer* and C-570/16 *Volker Willmeroth v Martina Brossonn* EU:C:2018:871 [28].

[55] Case C-461/03 *Gaston Schul Douane-expediteur BV v Minister van Landbouw, Natuur en Voedselkwaliteit* [2005] ECR I-10513, Opinion of AG Ruiz-Jarabo Colomer [2]–[4].

[56] Joined Cases C-72/14 and C-197/14 *X* EU:C:2015:319, Opinion of AG Nils Wahl [53].

[57] A Albors-Llorens, 'Judicial protection before the Court of Justice of the European Union' in C Barnard and S Peers (eds). *European Union Law*, 3rd edn (Oxford University Press 2017), p. 291.

[58] D Edwards, '*CILFIT* and *Foto-Frost* in their historical and procedural context' in MP Maduro and L Azoulai (eds), *The Past and Future of EU Law: The Classics of EU Law Revisited on the 50th Anniversary of the Rome Treaty* (Hart 2010), p. 179.

[59] Lord Mance (n 4), 'The interface between national and European law', 444.

It has also been endorsed by the CJEU itself: national courts have 'sole responsibility for determining whether the correct application of EU law is so obvious as to leave no scope for any reasonable doubt'.[60] Neither contradictory decisions in other countries nor referrals on point from lower courts constitute 'a conclusive factor capable of triggering the [Article 267] obligation'.[61]

A broad interpretation of the *CILFIT* criteria shows significant deference and respect to domestic judiciaries – but there are other consequences, not least a less centralised application of EU law.[62] Remember also AG Capotorti's warning about national courts' sheltering behind *acte clair* to avoid their duty to refer, even when faced with demands for clarity from both parties. In the *Laval* saga (to be encountered in Chapter 10), a Swedish court relied on *CILFIT* to decide, without Luxembourg involvement, the highly complex, novel, and contentious question of whether private parties would have to pay damages for infringing Article 49 TFEU.[63]

Köbler *Liability*

Does this mean that the national courts can duck their Article 267 TFEU obligations, simply by pronouncing the magical word *CILFIT*? Not quite. We have already encountered *Köbler*,[64] the Court's ruling that a manifest disregard of EU law by a national court adjudicating at final instance will attract (financial) state liability – which, in principle, is a strong deterrent against domestic courts' excessive reliance on *acte clair*. In practice, however, *Köbler*-type claims have been met with limited success,[65] largely due to the high threshold required for liability to kick in (itself a sign of respect for domestic judicial autonomy, albeit potentially at the expense of effective judicial protection for individuals).[66] That is not to say that lightning never strikes: in *Ferreira da Silva e Brito,* the Court found for the first time in its history that a domestic supreme court had breached its duty to make a preliminary reference under Article 267 TFEU.[67]

[60] *Ferreira da Silva* (n 12) [40]–[41].

[61] *Ferreira da Silva* [40]–[41]. The Court added that if there is evidence of conflicting lines of case law at the national level regarding the use of a particular EU term, or law, and that this interpretation has frequently given rise to difficulties of interpretation in other Member States, then that is an indication that a referral needs to be issued [44]. See also Case C-390/18 *Criminal proceedings against X* EU:C:2019:1112 [59], [63].

[62] A Kornezov, 'The new format of the acte clair doctrine and its consequences' (2016) 53(5) CML Rev 1317. National procedural autonomy must always be weighed against effective judicial protection, of course: Case C-322/16 *Global Starnet Ltd v Ministero dell'Economia e delle Finanze and Amministrazione Autonoma Monopoli di Stato* EU:C:2017:985.

[63] Dom nr 89/09, Mål nr A 268/04, 2009-12-02 57 (SE): '*EU-domstolens praxis ger tillräcklig ledning vid bedömning av de nu aktuella skadeståndsfrågorna*'.

[64] Case-224/01 *Gerhard Köbler v Austria* [2003] ECR I-10239.

[65] Z Varga, 'Why is the *Köbler* principle not applied in practice?' (2016) 23(6) Maastricht J Eur Comp L 984.

[66] Kornezov (n 62), 'The new format of the acte clair doctrine and its consequences'.

[67] *Ferreira da Silva* (n 12).

The incentive to refer is not exclusively underpinned by *Köbler* liability. The Commission may pursue infringement actions against Member States for not using the preliminary reference procedure with sufficient frequency – whether because of a culture of judicial reluctance to refer,[68] or concerns about additional delays to proceedings.[69] In 2004, for example, the 'discomfort' of Swedish courts in dealing with EU law and in acting as EU judiciaries[70] led to infringement proceedings being initiated against Sweden on the grounds that its national courts, and especially the Supreme Court, were too restrictive in their application of Article 267 TFEU.[71] In what has been described as a 'unique' episode in EU law,[72] Sweden was led to enact legislation requiring its national courts of last resort to give reasons in cases involving EU law in which they do not use Article 267 TFEU. The infringement action was duly withdrawn.[73]

More recently, the CJEU for the first time found that a Member State had infringed the Treaties by judicial malpractice in the context of Article 267 TFEU. French tax rules, as interpreted and applied by the *Conseil d'État*, violated EU free movement law: the *Conseil* ought to have made a preliminary reference.[74]

***

So is the CJEU a mere umpire, clarifying ambiguities, or is it a mighty institution, with a stature similar to an Emperor's? The preliminary reference procedure provides an excellent case study in the dynamic vacillation between these roles. The Court is umpire-like insofar as it is based on a 'carefully crafted division of competences that requires the close cooperation of the two interlocutors and promotes a model of dual judicial sovereignty'.[75] National courts are

[68] M Bobek, 'Learning to talk: Preliminary rulings, the courts of the new Member States and the Court of Justice' (2008) 45(6) CML Rev 1611.

[69] See, e.g., V Heyvaert, J Thornton, and R Drabble, 'With reference to the environment: The preliminary reference procedure, environmental decisions and the domestic judiciary' (2014) 130 LQR 413. Note that Article 267(4) TFEU allows for an urgent preliminary ruling procedure.

[70] See, e.g., U Bernitz, *Förhandsavgöranden av EU-domstolen: Svenska domstolars hållning och praxis* (Sieps 2010); M Wind, 'The Nordics, the EU and the reluctance towards supranational judicial review' (2010) 48(4) JCMS 1039.

[71] *Procedure against the Kingdom of Sweden* (COM 2003/2161) [2005] Eur L Reporter 445.

[72] U Bernitz, 'Preliminary references and Swedish Courts: What explains the continuing restrictive attitude?' in P Cardonnel, A Rosas, and N Wahl (eds), *Constitutionalising the EU Judicial System: Essays in Honour of Pernilla Lindh* (Hart 2012), p. 179.

[73] See *Lag (2006: 502) med vissa bestämmelser om förhandsavgörande från Europeiska unionens domstol (SE)*, §1. As explained by Lundius, who served as the Chairwoman of the Swedish Supreme Court from 2010 to 2016, the Swedish courts have almost doubled their preliminary referrals since the enactment of the set law. See M Lundius, 'The changing role of national courts' (2015) 148 Europarättslig Tidskrift 761, 763.

[74] Case C-416/17 *Commission v France* EU:C:2018:811.

[75] T Tridimas, 'The ECJ and the national courts: Dialogue, cooperation, and instability' in A Arnull and D Chalmers (eds), *The Oxford Handbook of European Union Law* (Oxford University Press 2015), p. 407.

entrusted with decisions about the necessity to refer and applying the ensuing ruling to the facts of the case, while the CJEU interprets EU law and enjoys exclusive competence to review the legality of EU acts – even if each court occasionally steps into the other's role. Yet there is also a clear sense of hierarchy in this relationship: in *Köbler*, the Court's role resembles that of an Emperor.

This may well be 'inherent in a governance model premised on supremacy', where the national courts acquire the role of 'EU law apostles'.[76] But to what extent are national courts dutiful followers of the word of the Treaties as interpreted by the Court – particularly when they have to consider the domestic sacredness of national constitutions faced with a corpus of supreme EU law? We have seen plenty of mechanisms allowing the CJEU to re-establish an equilibrium when domestic courts threaten to tip the balance too far towards national (judicial) sovereignty, but what about the opposite scenario?

Debate 2

Who should have the ultimate say?

In signing the Treaty of Rome, the six founding Member States proceeded 'on the assumption that they had [only] bound themselves by classical international agreements' – binding in international law, without direct implications for their domestic legal systems or individual citizens.[77] The CJEU's primary task was to help the Member States 'keep the other supranational bodies of the EU in check'.[78] The preliminary ruling mechanism would allow private litigants and national courts to refer cases to the CJEU 'so that they too could challenge the validity of EU law and thus hold EU legislative executive bodies in check'.[79]

(A) The Supremacy of EU Law

Things took a dramatic turn in *Costa v ENEL*, a seemingly[80] banal dispute over an electricity bill worth 1,925 lire (roughly €1 in today's money).[81] Could Italy's nationalisation of the sector be challenged as incompatible with the Treaty of Rome before a Milan judge? Absolutely not, suggested the Italian

[76] Tridimas, 'The ECJ and the national courts: Dialogue, cooperation, and instability', p. 407.
[77] N Fennelly, 'The European Court of Justice and the Doctrine of Supremacy: *Van Gen den Loos; Costa v ENEL; Simmenthal*' in MP Maduro and L Azoulai (eds), *The Past and Future of EU Law: The Classics of EU Law Revisited on the 50th Anniversary of the Rome Treaty* (Hart 2010), p. 39.
[78] Alter, *The European Court's Political Power* (n 15) p. 186.
[79] Alter, *The European Court's Political Power*, p. 186. See also Stone Sweet (n 14), p. 127.
[80] Mr Costa, it turns out, was not just 'an electricity customer', but also a shareholder in Edison Volta, an energy company whose assets had been nationalised.
[81] €1 equated circa 1936 Italian lira when Italy joined the Eurozone in 1999.

government: the claim that a domestic court was to apply anything other than national law was 'absolutely inadmissible.'

The Court of Justice, on the other hand, quickly put the idea that the Union was based on an ordinary international treaty to rest:

> By creating a [Union] of unlimited duration, having its own institutions, its own personality, its own legal capacity … and, more particularly, real powers stemming from a limitation of sovereignty or a transfer of powers from the States to the [Union], the Member States have limited their sovereign rights, albeit within limited fields, and have thus created a body of law which binds both their nationals and themselves.[82]

As a result, EU law was to enjoy primacy, or supremacy, over domestic rules:

> [T]he law stemming from the Treaty, an independent source of law, could not, because of its special and original nature, be overridden by domestic legal provisions, however framed, without being deprived of its character as Community law and without the legal basis of the Community itself being called into question.[83]

Thus was established one of the foundational pillars of European integration: without supremacy, the entire edifice would crumble. Subsequent cases fleshed out the contours of supremacy. There were to be no exceptions, not even for Member States' constitutional fundamental rights guarantees.[84] Even more importantly, the Court confirmed in *Simmenthal*, the duty to disapply[85] conflicting national law was not limited to supreme courts:

> Every national court must, in a case within its jurisdiction, apply [Union] law in its entirety and protect rights which the latter confers on individuals, setting aside any provision of national law which may conflict with it, whether prior or subsequent to the [Union] rule.[86]

It is important, in retrospect, not to underestimate just how revolutionary these early decisions must have seemed to domestic observers. A first instance judge in a small provincial court could suddenly find herself obliged to disapply national law, up to and including the Constitution – a power (if available at all) normally reserved for the uppermost echelons of the judiciary.[87]

---

[82] *Costa* (n 22) p. 593.

[83] *Costa*, p. 594.

[84] See Chapter 8.

[85] Rather than strike it down; national law remains valid outside the scope of EU law.

[86] Case 106/77 *Amministrazione delle Finanze dello Stato v Simmenthal SpA* [1978] ECR 629, as summarised in Case C-10/97 *Ministero delle Finanze v IN.CO.GE.'90 Srl and ors* [1998] ECR I-6307 [20].

[87] This point in particular continues to rumble on: Joined Cases C-188/10 *Aziz Melki* and C-189/10 *Sélim Abdeli* [2010] ECR I-5667.

Was this a rogue move by a 'runaway court', the first step towards a 'juristocracy' transferring power from representative bodies to judiciaries?[88] The Treaty, after all, is silent on the question of supremacy.[89] How could the CJEU give unequivocal preference to transnational law over democratically legitimised national rules? Why should EU law be able to interfere so deeply with established constitutional structures?

Or were the early decisions merely 'accidental', decided by judges drawn from across the Member States who shared a common understanding of the powers inherent in Article 267 TFEU and the ensuing vision of EU law?[90] The Court's dogged pursuit of effectiveness would prove vital for the Union's success, as Nial Fennelly, a former judge at the Supreme Court of Ireland, explains: '[t]he [Union] could not have functioned if its treaties and laws had not taken precedent over the laws and constitutions of the Member States'.[91]

***

The judgment in *Costa* was delivered in 1964. Supremacy might have been news for the six founding states, but the same cannot be said for subsequent members of the club. So why is supremacy still causing a stir? It turns out that the real issue is not so much one of the doctrine's operation in practice, but rather its theoretical underpinnings. Is supremacy a matter of EU constitutional law, and thus ultimately within the Court's jurisdiction? Or does it depend on the interpretation of the transfer of competence to the Union by national constitutions, a question that can only be settled by national (supreme) courts?

The official answer to this question will come as no surprise: '[t]he final word on EU law is always spoken in Luxembourg. Nowhere else'.[92] Senior domestic judges across the Union beg to differ: it is in their (constitutional) courts, from Karlsruhe to Copenhagen, that the matter is ultimately settled.

(B) Dogs That Bark

Most, if not all, national supreme or constitutional courts have struggled to accept unreservedly the principle of supremacy as espoused by the Court of Justice in *Costa*. This does not mean that the principle has been ignored in practice: it is the constitutional underpinning which has caused consternation. From the perspective of domestic courts, the supremacy of EU law will always

---

[88] I Solanke, '"Stop the CJEU"? An empirical analysis of activism at the Court' (2011) 17(6) Eur LJ 764, 765–66.

[89] A supremacy clause in the draft Constitutional Treaty was quietly dropped during its metamorphosis into the Treaty of Lisbon.

[90] Rasmussen (n 18), 'From *Costa v. ENEL* to the treaties of Rome', p. 83. See also A Grimmel, 'Judicial interpretation or judicial activism? The legacy of Rationalism in the studies of the European Court of Justice' (2012) 18(4) Eur LJ 518.

[91] Fennelly (n 77), 'The European Court of Justice and the Doctrine of Supremacy', p. 39.

[92] President von der Leyen, 'European Commission Statement 20/846' (Brussels, 10 May 2020), https://perma.cc/TA8T-A5YT.

be conditioned by national constitutions as the 'highest mandatory reference'.[93] These are no Basenjis[94] – they bark, but they do not bite.

Take France as an example. It took the *Conseil d'Etat* 25 years following *Costa* to embrace supremacy.[95] When it did, its findings were firmly based on the French Constitution – and not the Treaties, as the CJEU would have it.[96] This defiance found expression in disputes about directives to which it refused to grant direct effect. The first shot was fired in *Cohn-Bendit*. The litigant was a German citizen who had been deported by the French authorities as a ring-leader of the May 1968 student revolt. Years later, wanting to re-enter France to take up employment, he challenged that deportation. In line with Article 288 TFEU, however, the relevant directive was only 'binding...upon each Member State'. The *Conseil d'Etat* thus ruled that it was for the national authorities under the supervision of national courts to decide the appropriate means to give effect to the relevant provisions.

In subsequent years, the *Conseil d'État* was to become notorious in Luxembourg for finding ways to avoid making a referral in circumstances where it clearly should have done so.[97] Yet it is important to note that the former revolutionary was not stripped of his EU rights: the decision simply had to be based on the national implementing measure. The initial refusal by *Conseil d'Etat* to admit the direct effect of directives was thus 'always more limited in scope than at first seemed'.[98] Eventually, the *Conseil d'Etat* 'brought its position into line with that advocated by the European Court' in later cases, and in *Arcelor* – the first case challenging the validity of the emissions trading scheme – it turned to the CJEU to carry out a fundamental rights guarantee check on EU legislation, as opposed to relying on the French constitution.[99] All in all, then, lots of *grogner* – but no bite.

***

Why have domestic courts continued to cooperate with Luxembourg, despite deep constitutional misgivings? Weiler suggests that it was the siren song of judicial empowerment to review a much broader range of measures that incentivised national courts to cooperate.[100] This possibility, as Alter explains, appealed in particular to lower courts, who could free themselves from judicial

[93] I Pernice, '*Costa v ENEL* and *Simmenthal*: Primacy of European law' in MP Maduro and L Azoulai (eds), *The Past and Future of EU Law: The Classics of EU Law Revisited on the 50th Anniversary of the Rome Treaty* (Hart 2010), p. 55.

[94] If curious about barkless dogs, see B Bickering Jr and RJ Brach, *The Barkless Dog: A Handbook for the Basenji Owner* (Exposition Press 1962).

[95] *Arrêt Nicolo*, CE, ass., 20 Oct. 1989, n° 108243 (FR).

[96] For broader background, see A Tatham, 'Effect of European community directives in France: The development of the Cohn-Bendit jurisprudence' (1991) 40(4) ICLQ 907, 908.

[97] *CILFIT* (n 48), Opinion of AG Capotorti, p. 3437.

[98] Tatham (n 96), 'Effect of European community directives in France,' 919.

[99] Case T-16/04 *Arcelor SA v European Parliament and Council* [2010] ECR II-211.

[100] A-M Slaughter, A Stone Sweet, and JHH Weiler (eds), *The European Court and National Courts—Doctrine & Jurisprudence: Legal Change in Its Social Context* (Hart 1998).

hierarchy in this way.[101] But What about domestic constitutional and supreme courts? Here, Dyevre provides a plausible explanation: '[a]s with superpowers during the Cold War, the threat of mutually assured destruction gives human players a powerful incentive to cooperate'.[102]

But what happens when someone presses the nuclear button?

(C) Dogs That Bite

Whilst most domestic constitutional and supreme courts have found ways to reconcile and mediate collisions between EU law and their constitutional set up on the facts of individual cases, a few have gone further and declared CJEU judgments to be *ultra vires* – that is, beyond the powers conferred on the Union.

The first strike was delivered by the Czech Constitutional Court in its response to the Court of Justice's ruling in *Landtova*.[103] Scrutinising the co-ordination of social security and pension regimes, the Court insisted on a non-discriminatory scheme, irrespective of the arrangements between the Czech and the Slovak Republics following the dissolution of Czechoslovakia. This, the Czech Court suggested, was a major *faux pas*, 'a failure to respect European history ... comparing matters that are not comparable.' As a result,

> in this case a European Union body acted in excess of the law, resulting in a situation where an act enacted by a European body overstepped the powers which the Czech Republic had transferred to the European Union by virtue of Article 10a of the [Czech] Constitution; the act ignored the limits of the powers thereby delegated and was thus ultra vires.[104]

This is more than just a loud bark. But just like an optimistic dog owner who insists that their puppy is usually well trained, commentators quickly expressed their hope that *Landtova* would 'remain an isolated episode'.[105] One could argue, after all, that it concerned a specific historic issue, did not challenge the legislative powers of the EU, and may well have been motivated by domestic intra-judicial skirmishes.[106] A nibble, perhaps, but without drawing blood.

---

[101] K Alter, 'Explaining national courts acceptance of European Court jurisprudence: A critical evaluation of theories of legal integration' in A-M Slaughter, A Stone Sweet, and JHH Weiler (eds), *The European Court and National Courts—Doctrine & Jurisprudence: Legal Change in Its Social Context* (Hart 1998).

[102] A Dyevre, 'Domestic judicial defiance in the European Union: A systemic threat to the authority of EU law?' (2016) 35(1) YEL 106.

[103] Case C-399/09 *Marie Landtová v Česká správa socialního zabezpečení* [2011] ECR I-05573.

[104] This translation is taken from J Komarek, 'Czech Constitutional Court playing with matches: The Czech Constitutional Court declares a judgment of the Court of Justice of the EU Ultra Vires; Judgment of 31 January 2012, Pl. U' S 5/12, *Slovak Pensions XVII*' (2012) 8(2) Eur Const LR 323.

[105] Dyevre (n 102), 'Domestic judicial defiance in the European Union', 109.

[106] Tridimas, 'The ECJ and the national courts' (n 75), p. 421.

The same cannot be said of the Danish Supreme Court's challenge to Luxembourg's insistence on supremacy. The clash followed the Court of Justice's ruling in *Ajos*,[107] a case concerning the application of the general principle of non-discrimination on grounds of age, which the Court had found to be applicable to (horizontal) disputes between private parties.

The Danish Supreme Court, however, simply disregarded the preliminary ruling, applied domestic law, and refused to grant the contested general principle horizontal effect.[108] In so doing, it purported to create a broad *contra legem* exception to supremacy: the legal position under Danish law was clear and could not be interpreted in any other way. There was nothing in the Danish Accession Act to suggest that unwritten principles could take precedence over national law without specific action on part of the Danish legislator.

This was not the first time that the Danish Supreme Court had articulated limitations to the principle of supremacy – it had done so following both the Maastricht and the Lisbon Treaties. However, thus far it had always accepted that as long as the CJEU was not manifestly trespassing beyond its boundaries, it would accept the CJEU's evolving and dynamic case law and implement decisions accordingly.[109] The *Ajos*-saga offers no such margin of appreciation and, even more disturbingly, it leaves the status and impact of general principles – a key part of the EU's constitutional scaffolding – in the domestic legal order uncertain.

Why did the national court rule in this way? And why now? Denmark, after all, has been an EU member since 1972. Some commentators have pointed to the changing composition of the Danish Supreme Court, now populated with more critical voices, which 'over the last 20 years [have] shown signs of a greater willingness to engage with the more fundamental question about the limits of implementation and application of EU law in Denmark'.[110] Remember also the broader discontent when it comes to the applicability of general principles, especially following *Mangold*, as discussed in the previous chapter. As such, *Ajos* might illustrate a turn towards 'a greater national patrolling of the limited mandate given to the EU, including its judicial organ', resulting from 'a growing irritation with international courts over their perceived legal micro-management'.[111]

---

[107] Case C-441/14 *Dansk Industri acting on behalf of Ajos A/S v Estate of Karsten Eigil Rasmussen* EU:C:2016:278.

[108] See the Danish judgment following *Ajos*: UfR 2017.824H (Case no. 15/2014, *DI, acting on behalf of Ajos A/S v Estate of A*) (DK).

[109] R Holdgaard, D Elkan, and G Krohn Schaldemose, 'From cooperation to collision: The CJEU's *Ajos* ruling and the Danish Supreme Court's refusal to comply' (2018) 55(1) CML Rev 17, 49.

[110] Holdgaard and others, 'From cooperation to collision', 48.

[111] M Madsen, HP Olsen, and U Šadl, 'Competing supremacies and clashing institutional rationalities: The Danish Supreme Court's decision in the *Ajos* case and the national limits of judicial cooperation' (2017) 23(1-2) Eur LJ 140, 148–49.

At the same time, calls have been made not to exaggerate this conflict,[112] and not to extrapolate too much from a single breakdown in judicial dialogue.[113] Whilst *Ajos* has not (yet) been repeated in Denmark, however, a recent and even more forceful decision by the German Federal Constitutional Court (BVerfG) suggests that the issue is far from settled.

Since the early days of the principle of supremacy, German courts have been consistently vocal in challenging the CJEU's jurisdiction. In the course of scrutinising the constitutionality of Germany's ratification of the Maastricht Treaty, for example, the BVerfG made sure to remind the Union that its common powers derived from domestic constitutions – the Member States are the 'Masters of the Treaties', who give the Union power, subtly stressing that they could just as easily take them away.[114] Yet, despite much barking, there were no bites: Karlsruhe accepted EU law could provide fundamental rights protection comparable to the *Grundgesetz*. So long as the EU upholds such rights protection, it would allow EU law to take precedent.[115] There was no wavering in the BVerfG's insistence that supremacy could only stem from domestic constitutional law, however.[116] Even though the German court went on to qualify its *ultra vires* review and ratchet up the threshold,[117] it never found the Court to have acted beyond the scope of its powers on the facts of individual decisions. The justices of Karlsruhe even coined a catchy motto for what they were up to: '*Europafreundlichkeit*' (friendliness towards Europe).

Then came the Court of Justice's decision in *Weiss*.[118] Only the second-ever request for a preliminary ruling from the BVerfG,[119] it questioned the legality of the European Central Bank (ECB)'s 'secondary markets public sector asset purchase programme'. The technicalities are complex, centred essentially on the wisdom, or rather the legality, of quantitative easing to help stimulate the Eurozone and create price stability in specific sectors. In response to German concerns, the Court engaged in a detailed examination of Article 123 TFEU (which could be construed to prohibit the ECB's actions), but ultimately found the programme to be Treaty-compliant. When the case returned to Karlsruhe, the BVerfG disagreed in a decision with potentially enormous

112 Holdgaard and others (n 109) 53.

113 U Neergaard and K Engsig Sørensen, 'Activist infighting among courts and breakdown of mutual trust? The Danish Supreme Court, the CJEU, and the *Ajos* case' (2017) 36 YEL 275.

114 BVerfG, 12.10.1993 – 2 BvR 2134/92, 2 BvR 2159/92 (DE).

115 *Re Wunsche Handelsgesellschat* [1987] 3 CMLR 225, 265 (*Solange II*) (DE).

116 BVerfG, 6.07.2010 – 2 BvR 2661/06 (*Honeywell*).

117 In the Lisbon judgment, the domestic court singles out five areas – criminal law, war and peace, public expenditure and taxes, welfare, and culture and religion – as signifying 'national identity' for which the state must be able to develop its own legislative agenda: BVerfG, 30.06.2009 – 2 BvE 2/08 [252].

118 Case C-493/17 *Proceedings brought by H Weiss and ors* EU:C:2018:1000.

119 The first reference was Case C-62/14 *Peter Gauweiler and others v German Bundestag* EU:C:2015:400, on not dissimilar facts. In that case, however, the BVerfG had accepted the Court's position.

consequences: '[t]he CJEU [has] acted ultra vires, which is why, in that respect, its Judgment has no binding force in Germany'.[120]

This is far beyond previous barks, or even the nibbles in *Landtova* and *Ajos*. To start with, the decision explicitly contradicts the *Foto-Frost* doctrine, which entrusts the CJEU with exclusive competence to review the validity of EU acts. To share this competence with national courts is to jeopardise the effectiveness and uniformity of the EU legal order. The BVerfG rejected the Court of Justice's judgment on validity on the basis of a failed proportionality review, claiming that the latter's assessment 'does not satisfy the requirements of a comprehensible review as to whether the [European System of Central Banks] and the ECB observe the limits of their monetary policy mandate'.[121] The BVerfG seemed keen to see a more stringent proportionality test applied – not necessarily an unreasonable demand, as recognised by senior scholars in the field.[122]

The real problem lies in how the BVerfG conveyed its message. Its attack is stark, savage even, describing the Court of Justice's ruling as 'simply not comprehensible'[123] and 'objectively arbitrary'.[124] At first glance, this smacks of *Europafeindlichkeit* rather than *freundlichkeit* (enmity, rather than friendliness), striking right at the heart of judicial cooperation and collaborative dialogue as envisaged by the Treaties, and threatening the very foundations of the Union by disregarding the principle of supremacy. But is that really what is going on?

There is a flood of commentaries on the case.[125] Some media coverage sees it 'as an attack on ... the legal order of the EU',[126] while others choose to point to a silver lining, which is that it will hopefully lead to 'clearer and more detailed reasoning in the CJEU's case-law'.[127] Of particular interest are the musings of Andreas Vosskuhle, the BVerfG's Chief Justice who retired on the very day that *Weiss* was handed down. In an unprecedented interview following the ruling, he insisted that 'German judges don't question the CJEU's role or importance, they just want it to consult more with national constitutional courts', and expressed hopes 'for a quick "de-escalation"'.[128]

---

[120] BVerfG, 5.05.2020 – 2 BvR 859/15 [163].

[121] 2 BvR 859/15 [123].

[122] Editorial comments, 'Not mastering the Treaties: The German Federal Constitutional Court's PSPP judgment' (2020) 57(4) CMLR 965, 973.

[123] 2 BvR 859/15 (n 120) [116].

[124] 2 BvR 859/15 [118].

[125] See. e.g., the special issue 'The German Federal Constitutional Court's *PSPP* judgment' (2000) 21(5) German LJ 944.

[126] M Wolf, 'German court decides to take back control with ECB ruling' (*Financial Times*, London, 12 May 2020), https://perma.cc/JH22-5XAG.

[127] P Koutrakos, 'Longing for less interesting times? The German Federal Constitutional Court and the supremacy of EU law' (2020) 45(3) EL Rev 293, 294.

[128] M Karnitschnig, 'German judges take ECB fight to court of public opinion' (*Politico,* 13 May 2020), https://perma.cc/EVU8-BP9W.

Considerably more subtle ways would have been available to that end. The BVerfG could have asked the Court of Justice to explain its reasoning in a second preliminary reference, for example, following in the footsteps of the Italian Constitutional Court.[129] Then again, the Court of Justice was clearly on notice about German concerns surrounding the ECB's liquidity programme – not least following *Gauweiler* – and so a 'threshold has now been crossed',[130] with potentially dangerous consequences. As noted in a terse press release put out by the Court of Justice:

> In order to ensure that EU law is applied uniformly, the Court of Justice alone – which was created for that purpose by the Member States – has jurisdiction to rule that an act of an EU institution is contrary to EU law. Divergences between courts of the Member States as to the validity of such acts would indeed be liable to place in jeopardy the unity of the EU legal order and to detract from legal certainty.[131]

What happens next is unclear at the time of writing. One option is for the Commission to pursue infringement actions against Germany. Politically speaking, this would be a huge gamble. Another is for the ECB, in collaboration with Germany's *Bundesbank,* to rework key elements of the economic assessment. In any case, a new challenge awaits EU law – not only as to what will happen in this specific instance. Might increased national judicial defiance punch holes into legal integration? We return to this in the concluding chapter. There is a risk that a trend may be picked up and amplified beyond esoteric matters of fiscal and monetary policy by compromised courts in Member States where the rule of law is in peril. Hungary and Poland have been identified as the 'obvious candidates'.[132]

***

Ultimately, the debate surrounding supremacy and its impact on the relationship between the EU and national courts is one defined by pushes and pulls: the CJEU pushing its authority to define and (in)validate EU law, as stemming from the Treaties, and domestic courts pulling back by insisting on their own jurisdiction and domestic constitutional frameworks. It is an enormous debate, but also one that needs to be seen in proportion. Most of the time, judiciaries engage in a respectful dialogue and multilevel governance. *Weiss*, however, may have created more fundamental challenges, the magnitude of which we are not yet able to assess.

One possible conclusion is that we should rethink the Union's judicial architecture for contentious constitutional questions: resolving these through

---

[129] As the *Corte Costituzionale* did in Case C-42/17 *Criminal proceedings against M.A.S. and M.B.* EU:C:2017:936, following the CJEU's decision in Case C-105/14 *Criminal proceedings against Ivo Taricco and ors* EU:C:2015:555. See further 'Not mastering the Treaties' (n 122), 978.

[130] 'Not mastering the Treaties' (n 122), 965, 973.

[131] Court of Justice of the European Union, 'Press release No 58/20 following the judgment of the German Constitutional Court of 5 May 2020' (Luxembourg, 8 May 2020), https://perma.cc/7EUJ-L7B4.

[132] Wolf, 'German court decides to take back control with ECB ruling' (n 126).

formal dialogue and the preliminary reference procedure, which dichotomises interpretation and application, might not be the easiest way of settling thorny issues. Although the CJEU speaks with authority, its reasoning is condensed and often limited, as its 'committee style of judgment' restricts the Court's ability to introduce nuance or to express itself always with absolute clarity.[133] A 'Mixed Grand Chamber' could be set up, for example, to bring together Members of the Court and senior domestic judges in examining the validity of contested EU measures.[134]

Another way to view this debate is as an example of legal pluralism where 'adjudicating means establishing the culture of measure, of balance, of co-operation, not dominance, subordination and rejection'.[135] But is that not simply another way to claim that 'anything goes'? Indeed, the notion of pluralism is critiqued for justifying national courts' rebellion against EU law, but it has also been embraced for capturing legal reality – even if it requires considering its political and legal underpinnings.[136] After all, the Lisbon Treaty recognises the plurality of the EU legal order, for example through its reference to national identity.[137] If supremacy is simply taken to mean that rules and jurisprudence are imposed top-down, then it is hardly a principle fit to sit at the very core of EU law.

Conclusion: The Court of Justice as an S&M Dungeon?

The CJEU's central role in moulding the EU legal order and furthering European integration is undisputed. That does not mean that Luxembourg is an activist court, however. Its extensive powers derive from the generous wording of Article 267 TFEU, which provides it with exclusive competence to validate and to interpret EU law. Remember also the complex interinstitutional dynamics at play, and in particular the fact that national (supreme) courts' interests are by no means consistently aligned with their governments' politics.

The CJEU's case law on supremacy, direct effect, state liability, and individual rights has undoubtedly cut deep into the national legal systems, whilst being tolerated, acquiesced, and even encouraged by national governments. As *The Economist* pointedly put it,

> [i]f legislators did not like the court's actions, they could always change the law. That they hardly ever do suggests that they do not object strongly to the court's rulings. In this sense the ECJ resembles an S&M dungeon. National governments are happy to be tied up and slapped around in a dimly lit room by people

[133] Lord Mance (n 4), 'The interface between national and European law'.
[134] 'Not mastering the Treaties' (n 122), 976.
[135] P Kirchhof, 'The balance of powers between the national and European institutions' (1999) 5(3) Eur LJ 225, 241.
[136] N Walker, 'Constitutional pluralism revisited' (2016) 22(3) Eur LJ 333.
[137] TEU, Article 4(2): 'The Union shall respect the equality of Member States before the Treaties as well as their national identities, inherent in their fundamental structures, political and constitutional, inclusive of regional and local self-government'.

in odd outfits. However, they would prefer not to mention this fact to their jealous spouses back home: domestic courts and domestic voters.[138]

It is unsurprising, then, that judicial rebellion against the Court of Justice's rulings in *Landtova* and *Ajos* was quickly followed by national legislation reestablishing conformity. The Court does not operate through duress *vis-à-vis* the national legal systems: Member States have authorised its creation through their respective constitutions, and consent to its rulings, demand for which continues to grow unabated. In 2018, the most recent year for which data is available, new cases reaching the Court rose to 849 (from 739 in 2017), primarily due to an increase in the number of preliminary references.[139]

Further reading

Have a look at the most recent annual report of the CJEU[140] and especially the Court's activity log. How does the CJEU differ from your national (supreme) court, and what effect do you think its unique legal mission and physical setup have on its judgments? You may have noticed that one area that the CJEU does not cover is criminal prosecutions; in 2017, however, 20 Member States agreed to 'enhanced cooperation' – a special procedure under Article 86 TFEU – to establish the European Public Prosecutor's Office. See Council Regulation (EU) 2017/1939 of 12 October 2017 implementing enhanced cooperation on the establishment of the European Public Prosecutor's Office [2017] OJ L283/1, and A Novokmet, 'The European Public Prosecutor's Office and the Judicial Review of Criminal Prosecution' (2017) 8 New J Eur Crim L 374. What does this institutional addition tell us about the development of the EU judicial landscape?

Perhaps the most prominent theoretical framework to understand competing supremacy claims has been constitutional pluralism. Neil Walker argues that it offers 'better explanatory and justificatory accounts of the EU than any of the singularist (or monist), holist or federalist alternatives': 'Constitutional pluralism revisited' (2016) 22(3) Eur Law J 333. Do you agree?

For a flavour of different legal theories, as well as conceptual and doctrinal starting points bound to the nation-state perspective of law, try K Tuori, 'Transnational Law: On Legal Hybrids and Perspectivism' in M Maduro, K Tuori and S Sankari (eds), *Transnational Law: Rethinking European Law and Legal Thinking* (CUP 2014). Why does it matter that we can understand the EU legal order through different lenses?

---

[138] 'The wizards of Luxembourg' (n 6).

[139] Court of Justice of the European Union, 'Annual Report 2018: Judicial Activity' (European Union, February 2019), https://perma.cc/696S-ZGMG, p. 9.

[140] Available at http://curia.europa.eu

CHAPTER 8

Get Up, Stand Up – Stand Up for Your Rights!

EU Human Rights Protection

Article 6 TEU is one of the most important innovations in the Lisbon Treaty. It sets out a three-pronged framework for human rights protection in the European Union:

> 1. The Union recognises the rights, freedoms and principles set out in the Charter of Fundamental Rights … which shall have the same legal value as the Treaties. …
> 2. The Union shall accede to the European Convention for the Protection of Human Rights and Fundamental Freedoms. Such accession shall not affect the Union's competences as defined in the Treaties.
> 3. Fundamental rights, as guaranteed by the European Convention for the Protection of Human Rights and Fundamental Freedoms and as they result from the constitutional traditions common to the Member States, shall constitute general principles of the Union's law.

In this chapter, we take a closer look at the Union's broader commitment to fundamental or human rights, focusing on the Charter of Fundamental Rights in particular. The overall message is clear like a Mondrian: the EU citizen is not merely a consumer, but she also enjoys fundamental rights as an individual. Behind this high-level commitment in the Treaties, however, we quickly find a Pollockian world of heated debates and disagreements. Why should the EU protect human rights at all? How should it go about it? And, perhaps most worryingly, is the Union's relatively new-found commitment to human rights doing more bad than good, bringing about confusion by cramming ever more sources and methods into an already 'crowded house'?[1]

[1] P Cruz Villalón, 'Rights in Europe: The crowded house' (King's College London 2012, Working Paper in European Law 01/2012).

Debate 1

Why should the EU protect human rights?

Fundamental rights sit at the very core of the European project today. Article 2 TEU proudly proclaims that the 'Union is founded on the values of respect for human dignity, freedom, democracy, equality, the rule of law and respect for human rights'. This commitment to human rights protection comes even before the Internal Market[2] – a significant change when compared with the Treaty of Rome 60 years earlier, which was focused on establishing an *economic* community. What happened?

The careful crafting of the EU's commitment to human rights as a 'foundational myth', suggests Smismans, adopted in order to 'claim *retrospectively* that fundamental rights are and have always been inherent in the EEC/EU.'[3] Is that true? Yes, at least at first glance. The Treaty of Rome created an '*economic* community': other than a brief reference to equal pay, there is no mention of human rights.[4] This silence, however, should not be taken as evidence that human rights were not hotly discussed at the time. Indeed, their role may well be one of the longest-standing debates in EU law, preceding the Treaty of Rome.

In tracing historical sources, Gráinne de Búrca finds that plans for a sophisticated human rights regime at the supranational level were met with fierce resistance from several countries, and 'in particular [by] one of the influential German parliamentarians, Max Becker, [who] countered that the issue of fundamental rights protection was better left to the nation states.'[5] Their arguments *against* human rights protection in the Treaty of Rome? Each Member State already had its own domestic constitutional structures in place; and, in any event, another Treaty system had set up an international organisation specialised on fundamental rights protection several years earlier.[6] Herr Becker and co. won the argument. Fearing insurmountable political resistance, plans for Community-level human rights protection were dropped.

But the debate was far from put to rest. How did fundamental rights end up in a central place within the new legal order? Are we witnessing a cynical power grab by the EU, or the natural evolution of a constitutional system under the rule of law? The Union's role as a human rights institution is far from settled. Indeed, the lingering uncertainty left behind by these (potentially) competing explanations continues to shape the debate to this day.

---

[2] TEU, Article 3(3).

[3] S Smismans, 'The European Union's fundamental rights myth' (2010) 48(1) JCMS 45, 47.

[4] The equal pay saga is explored in depth in Chapter 6, Debate 1.

[5] G de Búrca, 'The evolution of EU human rights law' in P Craig and G de Búrca (eds), *The Evolution of EU Law*, 2nd edn (Oxford University Press 2011), p. 468.

[6] Statute of the Council of Europe (adopted 5 May 1949, entered into force 3 August 1949) 87 UNTS 103; Convention for the Protection of Human Rights and Fundamental Freedoms (adopted 4 November 1950, entered into force 3 September 1953) 213 UNTS 222 (ECHR). Remember also Schuman's approach as encountered in Chapter 1 – what does the evolution of EU human rights law tell us about his vision?

(A) Shoring up Supremacy and Legal Autonomy

A first explanation sees the origins of EU human rights law as nothing short of a judicial power grab, shoring up the resolute assertion of EU law's supremacy over domestic law and the CJEU's role as the guardian of the Union's legal autonomy.

After a brief hiatus following the establishment of the European Economic Community, the human rights debate came back with a vengeance in the early 1970s. Remember how, in 1964, the CJEU had declared EU law to be supreme over all Member State law?[7] And not just any EU law: the Court's supremacy claim was absolute. In order to protect the integrity of its new legal order, even Member State constitutions could not stand above Community law. This, at its heart, is why Max Becker's approach of delegating human rights protection to the State level was unworkable in practice. All norms of EU law are to take precedence over all norms of domestic law and other international agreements.

But what appears to be a coherent and logic corollary of *Costa v ENEL* can in practice quickly turn counterintuitive. What if a minor matter of obscure market regulation clashes with fundamental rights anchored in national constitutions? More specifically, could it really be true that Community measures dealing with, say, the distribution regime for butter,[8] licence deposits for grain exports,[9] or minimum purchase amounts of coal[10] could trump the rights to dignity and property enshrined in Germany's hallowed *Grundgesetz* (basic law)?

Yes, of course, according to CJEU's early decisions. But when faced with increasing unrest from senior courts, particularly in Germany, Luxembourg soon changed its tack. In a trio of cases in the early 1970s, the Court set out to address the tension that had become apparent. Instead of affording precedence to domestic constitutional rights, however, the Court insisted on developing its own fundamental rights apparatus, embedded in the Community legal system. Take a look at the two paragraphs at the heart of *Internationale Handelsgesellschaft*:

> Recourse to the legal rules or concepts of national law in order to judge the validity of [EU Law] would have an adverse effect on [its] uniformity and efficacy ... In fact, the law stemming from the Treaty, an independent source of law, cannot because of its very nature be overridden by rules of national law, however framed, without being deprived of its character as [EU] law and without the legal basis of the [EU] itself being called in question. Therefore the validity of [an EU]

[7] Case 6/64 *Costa v ENEL* [1964] ECR 585, see also Chapter 7, Debate 2.

[8] Case 29/69 *Erich Stauder v City of Ulm – Sozialamt* [1969] ECR 419.

[9] Case 11/70 *Internationale Handelsgesellschaft mbH v Einfuhr- und Vorratsstelle für Getreide und Futtermittel* [1970] ECR 1125 [3].

[10] Case 4/73 *J. Nold, Kohlen- und Baustoffgrosshandlung v European Commission* [1974] ECR 491.

> measure ... cannot be affected by allegations that it runs counter to either fundamental rights as formulated by the constitution of that State or the principles of a national constitutional structure.[11]

So far, so classic *Costa*: unconditional supremacy of EU law permits of no exceptions, not even for human rights protected in national constitutions, lest the entire edifice be undone. But that is not the end of the story. Here comes the twist:

> However, an examination should be made as to whether or not any analogous guarantee inherent in [EU] law has been disregarded. In fact, respect for fundamental rights forms an integral part of the general principles of law protected by the Court of Justice. The protection of such rights, whilst inspired by the constitutional traditions common to the Member States, must be ensured within the framework of the structure and objectives of the [EU]. It must therefore be ascertained ... whether [EU law] has infringed rights of a fundamental nature, respect for which must be ensured in the [EU] legal system.[12]

Domestic courts, in other words, need not worry about supremacy threatening constitutional guarantees. The CJEU itself would keep watch and ensure that Union measures do not infringe fundamental rights and liberties – scrutiny that was soon extended to include Member State actions, too.[13]

In recognising human rights as part of the European project, furthermore, the Court not only cemented the supremacy of EU law over Member State norms, including constitutions and fundamental rights – it also significantly increased its own standing *vis-à-vis* other Union and domestic institutions by putting 'itself in a position to assess any and every policy on any and every ground'.[14] The cynics' charge sheet does not end here. When faced with competition from international (rather than domestic) human rights law, the Court was similarly vigorous in upholding and defending EU fundamental rights – and thus its role as the ultimate arbiter of any ensuing disputes.

Following the attacks of 9/11, the UN Security Council put in place a system of economic sanctions targeted at Osama bin Laden and his supporters. The EU followed suit, eventually adding one Yassin Abdullah Kadi to its list of proscribed individuals and freezing his assets. When Mr Kadi sought to

---

[11] Case 11/70 *Internationale Handelsgesellschaft mbH v Einfuhr- und Vorratsstelle für Getreide und Futtermittel* [1970] ECR 1125 [3].

[12] *Internationale Handelsgesellschaft* [4].

[13] Case 5/88 *Hubert Wachauf v Bundesamt für Ernährung und Forstwirtschaft* [1989] ECR 2609 (*Wachauf*). At least within the scope of EU law (Case C-260/89 *Elliniki Radiophonia Tiléorassi AE and Panellinia Omospondia Syllogon Prossopikou v DImotiki Etairia Pliroforissis and ors* [1991] ECR I-2925 (*ERT*). The close link between the scope of the Court's scrutiny and fundamental rights has flared up again under the Charter – see Chapter 6 in particular.

[14] M Kumm, '*Internationale Handelsgesellschaft, Nold* and the new human rights paradigm' in MP Maduro and L Azoulai (eds), *The Past and Future of EU Law: The Classics of EU Law Revisited on the 50th Anniversary of the Rome Treaty* (Hart 2010), p. 117.

challenge this as a violation of his fundamental rights, the Court of First Instance rejected his claim: it did not have jurisdiction to review UN measures.[15] On appeal, the Court of Justice strongly disagreed, emphasising the autonomy of the Union's legal system, protected by the Court's exclusive jurisdiction, as well as the integral role played by fundamental rights across EU law.[16]

On the facts, the claimants succeeded in establishing that a number of their fundamental rights had been violated. Their victory, however, was short-lived, as the Court provided for a transitional period in which the EU institutions could rectify the sanctions regime.[17] The same cannot be said for *Kadi*'s broader significance: its 'constitutionalising thrust', Ziegler argues, is 'reminiscent of the [CJEU's] seminal cases of *Van Gend en Loos* and *Costa v ENEL*'.[18]

(B) With Great Power Comes Great Responsibility

That is certainly true, but still leaves us to work out where we are in the overarching debate. Is the Court's case law championing fundamental rights protection, even in the face of the mighty UN Security Council?[19] Or are we witnessing a 'rather cynical exercise in protecting EU law and the Court's own power'?[20]

Once *Kadi* is read in conjunction with *Internationale Handelsgesellschaft*, a clear and consistent logic emerges, at least within the confines of EU law: fundamental rights need to be included as norms at the highest constitutional level, as national and international norms are inevitably trumped by the supremacy and autonomy of EU law. The Court's recognition of fundamental rights cannot be explained solely as a utilitarian move, aimed at shoring up the supremacy of EU law.

---

[15] Case T-315/01 *Yassin Abdullah Kadi v Council and European Commission* [2005] ECR II-3649 [221]: 'The claim that the Court of First Instance has jurisdiction to review indirectly the lawfulness of [a UN security council decision] according to the standard of protection of fundamental rights as recognised by the Community legal order, cannot be justified either on the basis of international law or on the basis of Community law.' Read paragraphs [212]–[231] of the CFI's decision for a full exposition of its (ultimately rejected) arguments.

[16] Joined Cases C-402/05 P and C-415/05 P *Yassin Abdullah Kadi and Al Barakaat International Foundation v Council and European Commission* [2008] ECR I-6351 [281]–[283], [285]. We will encounter these points again in our discussion of Opinion 2/13 in Debate 3, below. There are ways in which international agreements that include adjudication mechanisms *can* be reconciled with the autonomy of EU law: see, e.g., Opinion 1/17 of the Court on the Comprehensive Economic and Trade Agreement between Canada and the EU (CETA) EU:C:2019:341.

[17] *Kadi* (n 16) [373]–[376].

[18] K Ziegler, 'Strengthening the rule of law, but fragmenting international law: The *Kadi* decision of the ECJ from the perspective of human rights' (2009) 9(2) HRLR 288, 295.

[19] C Gearty, 'In praise of awkwardness: *Kadi* in the CJEU' (2014) 10(1) Eur Const L Rev 15.

[20] S Weatherill, *Law and Values in the European Union* (Oxford University Press 2016), p. 148.

Instead, the development of fundamental rights can be understood as the logical corollary of an evolving 'new legal order', with the Treaties merely providing a framework to be fleshed out in an organic interplay between citizens, Member States, and Union institutions. The early members of the CJEU were deeply steeped in their own constitutional traditions, including the role(s) played by fundamental rights. The absence of any reference to such standards in the Treaty of Rome would have struck them as odd as they began the journey of 'constitutionalisation' – elevating the single market framework to an autonomous legal order. Given that human rights play an important role in any 'constitutionally complete system', Spaventa suggests, 'it is unlikely that experienced judges and jurists coming from countries with a strong constitutional ethos would be insensitive to such a major constitutional gap'.[21]

With the Union's evolution, this fundamental rights imperative only increased. The alleged fundamental rights violations in the early Internal Market cases were not infrequently specious. Today's competences, on the other hand, encompass just about every aspect of public powers, including areas which call for heightened sensitivity, such as social policy or criminal law, and thus an integrated approach right from the norm-setting stage. This was explicitly recognised by the Community institutions in 1977,[22] and the Member States in the Treaty of Amsterdam.

***

Ultimately, it is crucial to realise that the two explanations canvassed are not mutually exclusive. 'After the autonomous, supranational framework of Community law had been established, it had to be endowed with the principles inherent in the rule of law'[23] – of which courts are the ultimate guardians. The development of a fundamental rights regime was not merely a power grab, but also inevitable, necessary, and to be welcomed as a clear recognition that European integration was to serve not just the Internal Market, but also its individuals and citizens.

Debate 2

How should the Charter protect fundamental rights?

With the coming into force of the Lisbon Treaty, fundamental rights in the EU underwent a major shift in constitutional terms: Article 6 TEU clearly expressed Member States' commitment to elevate human rights protection to the very

[21] E Spaventa, 'Fundamental rights in the European Union' in C Barnard and S Peers (eds), *European Union Law*, 3rd edn (Oxford University Press 2020), p. 246.

[22] Joint Declaration by the European Parliament, the Council and the Commission concerning the protection of fundamental rights and the European Convention for the Protection of Human Rights and Fundamental Freedoms [1977] OJ C103/1.

[23] JN Cunha Rodrigues, 'The incorporation of fundamental rights in the community legal order' in MP Maduro and L Azoulai (eds), *The Past and Future of EU Law: The Classics of EU Law Revisited on the 50th Anniversary of the Rome Treaty* (Hart 2010), pp. 93, 96.

apex of EU norms. This does not mean, however, that old tensions and debates have gone away. If anything, they have become more prominent and played a crucial role in shaping the Charter. Every facet we encounter reflects elements of these competing considerations – whether it is the Charter's origins and path to Treaty status, the catalogue of rights it protects, or the detailed mechanisms deployed to that end.[24]

(A) The Journey from 'Solemn Proclamation' to Primary Treaty Status

Herr Becker's ghost overshadowed the Charter's life from the very beginning. In order to take account of competing anxieties – from ensuring adequate rights protection to respect for Member State autonomy – a 'revolutionary' new drafting body called the Convention was established.[25] Instead of the traditional approach to international negotiations (between senior diplomats, thrashing it out behind closed doors on behalf of their governments), the Member States involved both national and European parliamentarians, with NGOs and accession countries also given a voice to ensure broad representativeness.[26]

The ensuing document,[27] which closely resembles the Charter in force today, was 'solemnly proclaimed' in Nice in December 2000. What does that mean? Even a broadly established body such as the Convention had not been able to put old anxieties to rest. The result was a compromise – or a cop out, depending on your point of view. Perhaps the hardest question of all was shelved for future deliberation: whilst 'drafted so as to be capable of being legally binding, [t]he precise legal status of the Charter was left [...] undecided'.[28]

As a result, in its first decade the Charter's impact on Union law remained limited – at least beyond occasional citations in legislative preambles. It took the CJEU nearly six years to acknowledge the Charter's existence,[29] and even then the emphasis in subsequent cases was on continuity rather than radical change. The Charter had merely 'reaffirmed' fundamental rights, as recognised in long-established general principles.[30]

---

[24] G de Búrca, 'The drafting of the European Union Charter of Fundamental Rights' (2001) 26(2) EL Rev 126.

[25] Spaventa, 'Fundamental rights in the European Union' (n 21), pp. 239–40.

[26] We first encountered the Convection's work in the context of Union competences in Chapter 2, Debate 1.

[27] Charter of Fundamental Rights of the European Union [2000] OJ C364/01.

[28] P Craig, 'The Charter, the ECJ and national courts' in D Ashiagbor, N Countouris, and I Lianos (eds), *The European Union After The Treaty of Lisbon* (Cambridge University Press 2012), pp. 82–83.

[29] Case C-540/03 *European Parliament v Council* [2006] ECR I-5769.

[30] Case C-432/05 *Unibet (London) Ltd and Unibet (International) Ltd v Justitiekanslern* [2007] ECR I-2271 [37].

The Treaty of Lisbon brought about a sea-change, incorporating the Charter into primary Treaty law,[31] as first mooted in the failed Constitutional Treaty.[32] Litigants began to take notice, and familiar difficulties resurged once more, albeit in a new guise. When did the Charter apply? How should specific rights be interpreted? What, if anything, was off limits? The politicians had missed their chance to resolve potential contradictions, leaving the Charter's evolution to the Court.

(B) What Rights Should Be Protected?

The Charter's breadth is one of its most striking features. A total of 50 articles range from the fundamental (such as the right to human dignity and life, enshrined in Articles 1 and 2 CFR[33]) to the quixotic (including your right to placement services and to stand as a candidate at municipal elections, set out in Articles 29 and 40 CFR, respectively).

The Rights

The Charter is organised into six chapters: *Dignity* (including the prohibition of torture and slavery); *Freedoms* (such as respect for private and family life, data protection, and conducting a business); *Equality* (across a wide range of protected characteristics); *Solidarity* (key protections for workers, consumers, and the environment); *Citizens' Rights* (to ensure full participation in the democratic process); and *Justice* (covering the fundamentals of access to justice and procedural fairness).

It is a unique catalogue of fundamental rights. The Charter deftly overcomes the traditional divide between civil and political rights, on the one hand, and socio-economic rights, on the other. It also explicitly includes rights which have historically been limited to indirect protection (such as property and economic rights) or ignored altogether (data protection).

This is to be welcomed. The divide between different categories of rights by the Council of Europe between the European Convention of Human Rights (ECHR, with an emphasis on civil and political rights) and the European Social Charter (dedicated to the protection of economic and social rights) has long been criticised by scholars calling for an integrated approach.[34]

But it is also cause for potential concern. The longer the list of rights included, the higher the chance that EU or indeed Member State action is caught up in them (hello again, Herr Becker!), with the CJEU having to pronounce on some of the most controversial political issues of our time – from

[31] Treaty of Lisbon amending the Treaty on European Union and the Treaty Establishing the European Community [2007] OJ C306/1.

[32] Treaty establishing a Constitution for Europe [2004] OJ C310/1.

[33] Charter of Fundamental Rights of the European Union [2012] OJ C326/391.

[34] V Mantouvalou, 'Labour rights in the European Convention on Human Rights: An intellectual justification for an integrated approach to interpretation' (2013) 13(3) HRLR 529.

immigration control[35] and abortion,[36] to public protests[37] and the right to wear religious face coverings.[38] Even more importantly, the more rights we include in the normative and instrumental framework of Treaty-level human rights protection, the higher the chance that different rights will come into conflict with each other, leading to potentially counter-intuitive results. It is not difficult to see, for example, how creative corporate litigants could characterise environmental protection or labour rights as infringing on their freedom to conduct a business – and thus, *prima facie*, a human rights violation.[39]

The Principles

One way in which the Charter seeks to address these tensions is through a distinction between rights and principles. Article 52(5) CFR explains the difference:

> The provisions of this Charter which contain principles may be implemented by legislative and executive acts taken by [...] the Union, and by acts of Member States when they are implementing Union law, in the exercise of their respective powers. They shall be judicially cognisable only in the interpretation of such acts and in the ruling on their legality.

The political origins of this provisions are easily traced: the distinction between judicially enforceable rights and broader principles binding only the Union was key to ensuring the support of Convention members anxious about the inclusion of a wide range of social and economic rights.[40]

In reality, however, supposedly clean lines once more give way to fiendishly complex difficulties, which are far from resolved. Which Charter articles contain rights, and which ones contain principles? The answer can be relatively straightforward in some cases: Article 37 CFR,[41] for example, is a principle, whereas Article 2 CFR lays down a right.[42] There is no definitive catalogue,

---

[35] Case C-60/100 *Mary Carpenter v Secretary of State for the Home Department* [2002] ECR I-6279.

[36] Case C-159/90 *SPUC Ireland Ltd v Stephen Grogan and ors* [1991] ECR I-4685.

[37] Case C-112/00 *Eugen Schmidberger, Internationale Transporte und Planzüge v Austria* [2003] ECR I-5659 (*Schmidberger*).

[38] Case C-157/15 *Samira Achbita, Centrum voor gelijkheid van kansen en voor racismebestrijding v G4S Secure Solutions NV* EU:C:2017:203; Case C-188/15 *Asma Bougnaoui, ADDH v Micropole SA* EU:C:2017:204.

[39] See, e.g., J Prassl, 'Business freedoms and employment rights in the European Union' (2015) 17 CYELS 189 (labour rights); S Bogojević, 'Environmental (property) rights in market-based management' in S Bogojević and R Rayfuse, *Environmental Rights in Europe and Beyond* (Hart 2018) (environmental protection).

[40] Craig, 'The Charter, the ECJ and national courts' (n 28) p. 96.

[41] Article 37 CFR: 'A high level of environmental protection and the improvement of the quality of the environment must be integrated into the policies of the Union and ensured in accordance with the principle of sustainable development.'

[42] Article 2(1) CFR: 'Everyone has the right to life.'

though, and some rights (such as Article 35 CFR) might even contain both.[43] Does the distinction map on to the divide between civil and political versus social and economic rights? Not necessarily: the 'general justiciability of [the latter] means that one should not conclude that all Charter provisions containing [such] norms are automatically principles, or that all provisions in Title IV of the Charter should be presumed to contain principles and not rights.'[44]

And what is meant by 'judicially cognisable'? Is it a path to horizontal applicability in disputes between private parties, as discussed in Chapter 6? Or does it create a novel avenue for the judicial construction of a coherent European interpretation of fundamental rights – a path open, but ultimately not chosen, in *Carvalho*?[45] These questions are but the tip of an iceberg, and will ensure that fundamental rights protection stays at the forefront of EU law's great debates for years to come.

(C) How Far Should the Charter Go?

Who should be bound by EU fundamental rights? And when? The contours of this argument are well rehearsed: human rights should act as a clear break on Union action, as growing competences threaten interference in an ever-increasing range of human activity. Championing fundamental rights, however, can also come at a cost, insofar as respect for Member State autonomy is concerned.

Mary Carpenter's story provides a salutary tale. Having come to the United Kingdom as a tourist, she overstayed her visa, fell in love, and married Peter Carpenter. The Home Secretary sought to deport her, but an admittedly adventurous (and fundamentally sexist[46]) reading of free movement rules allowed the CJEU to bring the situation within the scope of Union law – and thus its fundamental rights jurisprudence.[47] On the facts, the proposed deportation was found to be an illegal infringement of the right to

---

[43] Article 35 CFR: 'Everyone has the right of access to preventive health care and the right to benefit from medical treatment under the conditions established by national laws and practices. A high level of human health protection shall be ensured in the definition and implementation of all Union policies and activities.'

[44] T Lock, 'Rights and principles in the EU Charter of Fundamental Rights' (2019) 56(5) CML Rev 1201, 1211. He cites the Opinion of AG Cruz-Villalón in Case C-176/12 *Association de médiation sociale v Union locale des syndicats CGT and ors* EU:C:2014:2 (*AMS*) [55] for the contrary view.

[45] Case T-330/18 *Armando Carvalho and ors v European Parliament and Council* EU:T:2019:324 (on appeal) (*Carvalho*). We return to this point in Chapter 11, and later in the current Debate.

[46] Finding, in essence, that she was required to stay at home to look after her husband's children in order to enable his occasional international business activities: *Carpenter* (n 35) [39].

[47] We will return to exploring this move in both Chapters 9 and 10; more recently, the Court has also recognised fundamental rights as a valid *limit* to market freedoms (*Schmidberger* (n 37)) – albeit inconsistently so: Case C-438/05 *International Transport Workers' Federation and Finnish Seamen's Union v Viking Line ABP and OÜ Viking Line Eesti* [2007] ECR I-10779).

respect for family life:[48] great news from the perspective of fundamental rights protection but rather disconcerting for Herr Becker's successors in national governments and parliaments, keen to preserve regulatory autonomy over difficult political choices. As a member of the German Constitutional Court argued in 2016, fundamental rights should not be protected 'in layers but by way of a division: citizens are protected vis-à-vis the Member States by national fundamental rights, while it is the Charter that protects them vis-à-vis the Union.'[49]

It comes as no surprise, then, that anxieties about the reach of fundamental rights had to be addressed (in principle, at least) in the Charter, with a dedicated Title VII providing a detailed user manual, and, for a small group of particularly anxious Member States, in a special Protocol annexed to the Treaty of Lisbon. But are these binding legal restrictions? Or is something else going on altogether?

Title VII: User Manual or Comfort Blanket?

Title VII is sometimes (and confusingly) referred to as the Charter's 'Horizontal Chapter'[50] – or, to give it its proper name, the 'General Provisions Governing the Interpretation and Application of the Charter'. Think of it as a user manual that provides a clarification of who the Charter is addressed to (its 'field of application': Article 51 CFR); the scope and interpretation of its rights (Article 52 CFR); and its relationship with the ECHR and national human rights instruments ('Level of Protection': Article 53 CFR).[51]

Upon closer inspection, however, it fails pretty miserably at clarifying anything.[52] Every time we look at Title VII in detail, the same conundrum becomes apparent. Seemingly clear and succinct words hide a much messier and complex reality: whether it is in distinguishing between rights and principles, above; the relationship with other sources of fundamental rights, discussed in Debate 3; or questions of horizontality and the scope of EU law as encountered in Chapter 6.

What is going on? It may well be that Title VII is aimed not so much at providing clear answers but first and foremost at providing (political)

---

[48] Based, at the time, on General Principles as inspired, *inter alia*, by the European Convention.

[49] J Masing, 'Unity and diversity of European fundamental rights protection' (2016) 41(4) EL Rev 490, 496.

[50] In this context, 'horizontal' means 'applicable across the Charter'. This is an important point of departure from the ECHR, especially when it comes to derogations. It should not be confused with 'horizontal' issues arising in litigation between private parties, explored in Chapter 6.

[51] There is also an official document designed to explain the Charter: Explanations relating to the Charter of Fundamental Rights [2007] OJ C303/17.

[52] For criticism, see, e.g., K von Papp, 'A federal question doctrine for EU fundamental rights law: Making sense of Articles 51 and 53 of the Charter of Fundamental Rights' (2018) 43 EL Rev 511.

reassurance for Member State anxieties. Take Articles 51(1) and (2) CFR as an example:

> The provisions of this Charter are addressed to the [...] Union with due regard for the principle of subsidiarity and to the Member States only when they are implementing Union law. They shall therefore respect the rights, observe the principles and promote the application thereof in accordance with their respective powers and respecting the limits of the powers of the Union as conferred on it in the Treaties.
>
> The Charter does not extend the field of application of Union law beyond the powers of the Union or establish any new power or task for the Union, or modify powers and tasks as defined in the Treaties.

The underlying concerns are palpable.[53] Restrict the scope of the Charter. Target its use against Union measures. Nip any thoughts of competence extension *via* human rights protection in the bud. Yet, as has quickly become apparent, these anxieties were never really translated into meaningful restraints. When Member States are 'implementing' EU law is an age-old debate.[54] The principle of conferral is open-ended, and subsidiarity has never succeeded as a (legal) constraint.[55] As Weatherill so aptly summarises, 'The *political* concern to signal to the Court (but not only the Court) that the Charter should not be used as a springboard to an extensive reading of the reach of the Charter is not matched by *legal* precision.'[56]

Given the Charter's intricate drafting process, that mismatch is unlikely to be an accident or oversight. What we are looking at instead is a careful compromise, struck between the competing aims and concerns that have shaped the Union's fundamental rights apparatus since its inception.

Protocol 30: A 'Fantasy Solution to a Fantasy Problem'

We can see this even more clearly when looking at Protocol 30 of the Lisbon Treaty: the much-vaunted 'opt-out' from the Charter, secured by the Polish and British governments. Its preamble notes 'the wish of Poland and the United Kingdom to clarify certain aspects of the application of the Charter' and emphasises that the Charter makes human rights 'more visible, but does not create new rights or principles' – but its two short articles then go on to provide no legal limitations whatsoever.[57]

---

[53] Weatherill (n 20), *Law and Values in the European Union*, p. 142.

[54] *Wachauf* (n 13); *ERT* (n 13).

[55] See Chapters 2 and 3.

[56] Weatherill (n 20), *Law and Values in the European Union*, p. 143.

[57] Protocol No 30 on the application of the Charter of Fundamental Rights of the European Union to Poland and to the United Kingdom [2016] OJ C202/312. Not everyone agrees entirely with this point: C Barnard, 'The opt-out for the UK and Poland from the Charter of Fundamental Rights: Triumph of rhetoric over reality?' in S Griller and J Ziller (eds), *The Lisbon Treaty: EU Constitutionalism without a Constitutional Treaty?* (Springer 2008).

Any remaining doubts on point were clarified by the Court in *NS*.[58] In the course of complex litigation surrounding the (now defunct) Dublin II regime for refugee resettlement, the UK Home Secretary sought to rely on Protocol XXX to avoid fundamental rights scrutiny under the Charter. The Court was not impressed, explaining that the Protocol could not 'call into question the applicability of the Charter in the United Kingdom or Poland, a position which is confirmed by the recitals in the preamble'; nor did it 'intend to exempt the Republic of Poland or the United Kingdom from the obligation to comply with the provisions of the Charter or to prevent a court of one of those Member States from ensuring compliance with those provisions.'[59]

This conclusion should not have come as a surprise to the British government. Critics had long been scathing about political attempts to sell the Protocol as a bulwark against EU fundamental rights, criticising 'a fantasy solution to a fantasy problem'.[60] As a contemporaneous Parliamentary report put it rather acerbically, Protocol XXX was there to provide (political) 'comfort rather than [act as a legal] safeguard'.[61]

(D) The Charter in Action

The Charter's first decade in legal force suggests that this may well be a price worth paying. The Court has become increasingly comfortable in its role as a human rights scrutineer, even though successful challenges remain the exception. Even more importantly, empirical evidence suggests that there has been little, if any, systemic upset to domestic human rights systems.

Vindicating Fundamental Rights

Article 52(1) CFR broadly divides fundamental rights violations into two categories: limitations that strike at the very essence of a protected right and are therefore impermissible *tout court*; and limitations that are provided for by law in pursuit of a legitimate objective, and may therefore be justified, subject to a detailed proportionality enquiry. The first category of cases is relatively rare, though not unheard of. In *Test-Achats*, a Belgian consumer association challenged a derogation in the EU directive designed to ensure equal access to goods and services, which (under certain circumstances) permitted insurers to

---

[58] Joined Cases C-411/10 *N. S. v Secretary of State for the Home Department* and C-493/10 *M. E. and ors v Refugee Applications Commissioner and Minister for Justice, Equality and Law Reform* EU:C:2011:865.

[59] *N. S. v Secretary of State for the Home Department* and *M. E. and ors v Refugee Applications Commissioner and Minister for Justice, Equality and Law Reform* [119], [120].

[60] M Dougan, 'Treaty of Lisbon 2007: Winning minds, not hearts' (2008) 45(3) CML Rev 617, 670.

[61] European Scrutiny Committee, 'The application of the EU Charter of Fundamental Rights in the UK: a state of confusion' (House of Commons, 26 March 2014), https://perma.cc/7583-FPJA.

charge women and men different premiums.[62] In a short ruling, the Court held that this derogation 'works against the achievement of the [Directive's] objective', and invalidated the offending provision as incompatible with Articles 21 and 23 CFR.[63]

In the vast majority of cases, on the other hand, a potentially legitimate aim can be adduced, thus requiring a detailed proportionality analysis. Take *Digital Rights Ireland* as an example, a case in which a number of claimants challenged sweeping data harvesting and storage powers in the Data Retention Directive.[64] The Court found that interference with Articles 7 and 8 CFR was 'wide-ranging' and 'particularly serious' – but that, by stopping short of accessing the actual content of communications, the Directive had not affected the very essence of those rights.[65] The enquiry thus turned to the measure's aim (fighting crime, a genuine objective of general interest) and a detailed proportionality enquiry. Whilst the retention of data was in principle an appropriate way of attaining the Directive's objectives, its sweeping provisions went beyond strict necessity, thus 'exceed[ing] the limits imposed by compliance with the principle of proportionality in the light of Articles 7, 8 and 52(1) of the Charter.'[66]

The examples thus far have focused on challenges to *Union* action. But Charter rights have also been applied in successful claims against Member State rules, in contexts ranging from paid annual leave to religious holidays.[67] Its use is not limited to cases involving the CJEU: within the scope of Union law, every national court is under a duty to provide effective judicial protection of Charter rights. This is powerfully demonstrated in *Benkharbouche*, a claim brought by workers abused in London embassies. Under UK law, their claims were barred by the State Immunity Act 1978. Insofar as their rights derived

---

[62] Case C-236/09 *Association Belge des Consommateurs Test-Achats ASBL and ors v Conseil des ministres* [2011] ECR I-773; Council Directive 2004/113/EC of 13 December 2004 implementing the principle of equal treatment between men and women in the access to and supply of goods and services [2004] OJ L373/37, Article 5(2).

[63] *Test-Achats* (n 62) [32]. The Court, however, delayed the effect of its ruling by nearly two years.

[64] Joined Cases C-293/12 and C-594/12 *Digital Rights Ireland Ltd v Minister for Communications and ors* [2014] ECR I-238 (*DRI*); European Parliament and Council Directive 2006/24/EC of 15 March 2006 on the retention of data generated or processed in connection with the provision of publicly available electronic communications services or of public communications networks and amending Directive 2002/58/EC [2006] OJ L105/54.

[65] *DRI* (n 64) [37], [39]–[40].

[66] *DRI* [44], [49]–[69].

[67] Case C-684/16 *Max-Planck-Gesellschaft zur Förderung der Wissenschaften e.V. v Tetsuji Shimizu* EU:C:2018:874 (German implementation of Directive 2003/88/EC in conflict with Article 31(2) CFR); Case C-193/17 *Cresco Investigation GmbH v Markus Achatzi* EU:C:2019:43 (Austrian Good Friday legislation in violation of Article 21 CFR). The employment context of these cases gives rise to a further difficulty – the horizontal application of charter norms, as discussed in Chapter 6.

from EU law were concerned, however, the Supreme Court disapplied the Act in order to give effect to Article 47 CFR.[68]

Respecting Regulatory Autonomy

It might be tempting to look at the materials surveyed and draw the conclusion that human rights have become powerful trumps in EU law, but that would be a misleading picture. Indeed, the reality is the opposite: the majority of fundamental rights challenges fail, with the Court deferring to domestic and Union-level regulatory autonomy.

A series of cases based on Article 16 CFR illustrate this development. The freedom to conduct a business has been deployed in an entertaining number of uphill struggles. Be it Ryanair's challenge to air passenger rights,[69] a German vineyard's insistence that their wines be marketed as healthy and wholesome,[70] or illegal casino operators trying to resist seizure of their gambling machines[71] – the Court has become increasingly weary of opportunistic litigants' attempts to frame attacks on market regulation as human rights challenges.[72]

Some genuine claimants may also be caught out by the Union's restrictive approach to standing. In *Carvalho*, a group of minors, backed by youth organisations and families across the Union and beyond, relied on a long list of different Charter rights – including the right to life, the rights of the child, and the right to property – in challenging the insufficient ambition of EU climate change policies, outlined in the 2030 Climate and Energy Policy Framework.[73] The General Court, however, found that the claimants lacked standing, even if it recognised that 'every individual is likely to be affected one way or another by climate change'.[74]

***

Where does this leave us? Think back to the competing anxieties underpinning EU fundamental rights protection: has the pendulum swung too far, in either direction? At least insofar as Member State autonomy is concerned, the answer seems to be in the negative. A few high-profile instances of conflict apart, the Charter has had surprisingly limited impact on domestic practice. An in-depth empirical study to mark its tenth anniversary found that the Charters' provisions were invoked in only the tiniest proportion (consistently less than 1 per cent) of cases before national courts.[75] This is not necessarily surprising: the

---

[68] *Benkharbouche v Secretary of State for Foreign and Commonwealth Affairs* [2017] UKSC 62.
[69] Case C-12/11 *Denise McDonagh v Ryanair Ltd* EU:C:2013:43.
[70] Case C-544/10 *Deutsches Weintor eG v Land Rheinland-Pfalz* EU:C:2012:526.
[71] Case C-390/12 *Robert Pfleger and ors* EU:C:2014:281.
[72] Parallels can be observed with the developments surrounding *Keck*: see Chapter 10, Debate 2.
[73] See, e.g., S Bogojević, 'Human rights of minors and future generations: Global trends and EU environmental law particularities' (2020) 29(2) RECIEL 191.
[74] *Carvalho* (n 45) [50]. For more on the standing puzzle, return to Chapter 4, Debate 2.
[75] M Bobek and J Adams-Prassl (eds), *The EU Charter of Fundamental Rights in the Member States* (Hart 2020).

Union's Charter was introduced in addition to, and much later than, Member States' own human rights instruments, domestically and internationally.

Debate 3

Too much of a good thing?

Whilst our focus thus far has been on the Charter, remember that Article 6 TEU set out multiple mechanisms of fundamental rights protection in the Union, including accession to the ECHR, and the 'general principles … as they result from the constitutional traditions common to the Member States'. Schütze refers to this setup as 'three bills of rights': an *unwritten* bill (the general principles); an *external* bill (the ECHR); and finally, a *written* bill (the Charter).[76] It is a unique approach. 'While the co-existence of an external and internal human rights bill is hardly unusual, the presence of two internal human rights regimes is a special feature of the Union legal order.'[77]

But is it a good idea? On the one hand, there are some clear advantages to a multi-layered approach. Different mechanism are designed for their respective constitutional settings, encourage development through dialogue between institutions, and can ensure there are no gaps. On the other hand, there can be too much of a good thing, especially when overlaps, differing interpretations, and competing claims to hermeneutic monopolies create confusion and complexity.[78] There are two central questions through which we can explore this debate. First, should the EU accede to the ECHR? And second, when (if ever) are Member States free to diverge from Union law in order to ensure a *higher* standard of fundamental rights protection?

(A) Should the EU Accede to the ECHR?

Article 6(2) TEU seems remarkably clear and straightforward: the Union 'shall accede' to the ECHR. Yet, over a decade later, nothing has changed or (at the time of writing) looks likely to change anytime soon. Let us take a quick look at the relationship pre-Lisbon in order to understand the complexities at hand.

Life Pre-Lisbon

We have already seen that the EU is not the only international institution when it comes to the protection of human rights. The most important instrument in this space, the ECHR, was created long before the Charter[79] and is administered through the Council of Europe and the European Court of Human

---

[76] R Schütze, 'Three bills of rights for the European Union' (2011) 30(1) YEL 131.

[77] Schütze, 'Three bills of rights for the European Union', 132.

[78] S Douglas-Scott, 'The EU and Human Rights after the Treaty of Lisbon' (2011) 11 HRLR 645, 682.

[79] See (n 6).

Rights (also referred to as the 'Strasbourg court', after its location). Today, the Council of Europe encompasses 47 countries, including all 27 EU Member States (and the United Kingdom).[80]

With the CJEU's recognition of fundamental rights as general principles, it quickly became important to manage the relationship. This was explicitly acknowledged as early as *Nold*, when the Court of Justice reassured the Member States that, in defining general principles, 'international treaties for the protection of human rights' would 'supply guidelines' to be followed.[81]

The indirect role of the ECHR in the Union's growing fundamental rights *acquis* was furthermore recognised in the Maastricht Treaty of 1992.[82] Given the rapid constitutionalisation of the EU and the CJEU's increasing confidence as a human rights adjudicator, however, the relationship between EU law and the ECHR became an increasingly complex dance – with a 'tendency to refer to each other's case law … but also the reluctance to give each other too much accreditation for fear of appearing too deferential and subservient to a rival transnational "constitutional" court'.[83]

Dancing together, in other words, requires moving in concert – but also keeping a respectful distance to avoid stepping on your partner's toes. Two difficulties in particular might emerge: the distinct evolution of norms, without any one court able to have the final say; and potential Member State liability for human rights violations 'forced' on them through the supremacy of EU law. In practice, however, both Courts have been careful to strike elegant compromises and avoid outright conflict.[84] In *Roquette Freres*, for example, the Luxembourg Court explicitly noted the ECHR's 'special significance' as a source of inspiration, and changed course on its interpretation of the scope of the right to privacy in order to align its jurisprudence with Strasbourg.[85]

The Strasbourg Court, too, has been accommodating: whilst it had long acknowledged that EU law 'as such cannot be challenged before the Court because the [EU] is not a Contracting Party', it also insisted that the Member States could only transfer competences 'provided that Convention rights continue to be secured. Member States' responsibility therefore continues even

[80] Council of Europe Treaty Office, 'Chart of signatures and ratifications of Treaty 005: Convention for the Protection of Human Rights and Fundamental Freedoms', https://perma.cc/M63U-SPGA.

[81] *Nold* (n 10) [13].

[82] TEU, Article F2 (as it then was): 'The Union shall respect fundamental rights, as guaranteed by the [ECHR]'.

[83] S Douglas-Scott, 'A tale of two courts: Luxembourg, Strasbourg, and the Growing European Human Rights *Acquis*' (2006) 43(3) CML Rev 629, 663.

[84] Our sister volume disagrees on this point: F de Londras and K Dzehtsiarou, *Great Debates on the European Convention on Human Rights* (Palgrave 2018), p. 37.

[85] Case C-94/00 *Roquette Frères SA v Directeur général de la concurrence, de la consummation et de la repression des frauds and Commission* [2002] ECR I-9011 [23]. The saga is documented in detail in Douglas-Scott (n 83), 'A tale of two courts', 648–49.

after such a transfer.'[86] In practice, however, such responsibility is unlikely to materialise. As long as the EU's fundamental rights apparatus 'can be considered at least equivalent' (but not necessarily identical) to the ECHR regime, Member States could benefit from a presumption of compliance – rebuttable only 'if, in the circumstances of a particular case, [...] the protection of Convention rights was manifestly deficient'.[87]

The Accession Saga

Close cooperation, then, but never through formalised channels. Indeed, for a while, the EU's accession to the ECHR seemed institutionally impossible: on the Council of Europe's side, Article 59 ECHR limited membership to nation states; and (as we have already seen in our discussion of competences in Chapter 2), when the Member States first tried to effect Union accession in the 1990s, the Court vetoed it on grounds of competence – accession 'could be brought about only by way of Treaty amendment.'[88]

Neither of these obstacles proved insurmountable in principle. In May 2004, the Council of Europe amended Article 59 ECHR to provide for EU Membership,[89] and the Lisbon Treaty explicitly conferred the necessary competence on the Union. Detailed and drawn-out negotiations ensued, and a final accession agreement was presented in the spring of 2013.[90] Hailed as 'the last step of a growing interlocked system of fundamental rights', the agreement set out a series of intricate innovations designed to address key procedural and institutional aspects.[91] One senior commentator even voiced his fear that the agreement would 'unfortunately deprive academics and lawyers involved in the European legal discourse of one of their favourite topics of discussion'.[92] As it quickly turned out, however, they need not have worried (whether fortunately or not, we leave for you to judge).

---

[86] *Matthews v United Kingdom* [1999] 28 EHRR 361 [32].

[87] *Bosphorus Hava Yollari Turizm Ve Ticaret Anonim SIrketi v Ireland* [2005] 42 EHRR 1 [155]–[156].

[88] Opinion 2/94 of the Court on the Accession by the Community to the European Convention for the Protection of Human Rights and Fundamental Freedoms [1996] ECR I-1759 [34–35].

[89] Protocol No. 14 to the Convention for the Protection of Human Rights and Fundamental Freedoms, Amending the Control System of the Convention (adopted 13 May 2004, entered into force 1 June 2010) CETS 194, Article 17.

[90] CDDH Ad Hoc Negotiation Group, 'Fifth negotiation meeting between the CDDH Ad Hoc Negotiation Group and the European Commission on The Accession of the European Union to the European Convention on Human Rights: Final report to the CDDH' (Council of Europe, 10 June 2013).

[91] P Gragl, 'A giant leap for European human rights? The final agreement on the European Union's accession to the European Convention on Human Rights' (2014) 51(1) CML Rev 13, 14. Gragl provides an excellent and extensive overview over key provisions.

[92] JP Jacqué, 'The accession of the European Union to the European Convention on Human Rights and Fundamental Freedoms' (2011) 48(4) CML Rev 995, 995.

In its mammoth *Opinion 2/13*, the CJEU held that the Accession Agreement as negotiated was incompatible with Article 6(2) TEU. That article required any accession to 'preserve the specific features of EU law' (such as its supremacy and direct effect), as well as respect for 'a set of common values on which the EU is founded', including in particular 'mutual trust between the Member States'.[93] Even more importantly, the Court suggested, the 'autonomy enjoyed by EU law requires that the interpretation of [EU] fundamental rights be ensured with the framework of the structure and objectives of the EU'.[94] Upon close inspection, however, the Accession Agreement fell afoul of both requirements: 'accession of the EU to the ECHR as envisaged [... was] liable adversely to affect the specific characteristics of EU law and its autonomy.'[95]

What should we make of this? For practical purposes, the Opinion proved to be a major setback to accession – and one that may yet turn out to be terminal, even though negotiations are understood to be ongoing once more.[96] The Court did not go as far as to say that accession would be impossible. The specific flaws identified by the Court, however, will make it very hard to ensure successful future negotiations.[97] From a broader normative perspective, we are in many ways back where we started in Debate 1. Is the autonomy of the Union's legal order fundamental to ensuring that the Union is founded on respect for the rule of law? Are fundamental rights once more wheeled out in a cynical attempt to prop up Luxembourg's 'splendid isolation'?[98]

Once more, there are elements of truth in both approaches. As de Londras and Dzehtsiarou argue in approaching this very set of questions from the perspective of the ECHR, in our sister volume on *Great Debates on the European Convention on Human Rights*, the extent to which accession is necessary to ensure fundamental rights protection has never been entirely clear. Benefits such as the 'streamlining' of key provisions have to be weighed against increased complexity and potential opacity. Ultimately, however, they conclude that accession *should* be pursued in order to ensure finality, equal treatment of EU and domestic law, and full EU accountability.[99]

We are perhaps less convinced that this ought to be the case. The pre-Lisbon system embodied a subtle balance which ensured fundamental rights protection

---

[93] Opinion 2/13 of the Court on the compatibility of the draft agreement with the EU and FEU Treaties EU:C:2014:2454, [162], [166] and [168].

[94] Opinion 2/13 [170] – including, of course, the role of the CJEU and the Preliminary Ruling procedure.

[95] Opinion 2/13 [200].

[96] Cf. the latest accession draft: Council of the European Union, 'Annex I: Synthetic Overview of the Required Amendments to the Negotiated Instruments' (European Union, 20 September 2019), https://perma.cc/M7VK-VBMR.

[97] See especially Opinion 2/13 (n 93) [184–99].

[98] B De Witte, 'Human rights' in M Evans and P Koutrakos (eds), *Beyond the Established Orders: Policy Interconnections Between the EU and the Rest of the World* (Hart 2011).

[99] Londras and Dzehtsiarou (n 84), *Great Debates on the European Convention on Human Rights*, pp. 40–42.

in distinct constitutional settings. From a *political* perspective, accession may well be desirable: it was easily written into the Lisbon Treaty, and some Member States might even have hoped that it would result in a reigning in of the Luxembourg Court. Weighed up against these benefits, however, the *legal* complexity we have uncovered might simply not be a price worth paying.

(B) Can Member States Diverge from Protective Standards?

It is not difficult to see how the interaction between three bills of rights provides for plenty of difficulty in practice. What happens when we add 27 Member State constitutions to the equation? On one level, the answer to this question is straightforward. We have seen the Court's consistent emphasis on the supremacy of Union law over all domestic law, including fundamental rights norms, right since *Internationale Handelsgesellschaft* in Debate 1. This has come at the cost of Member States' (and the EU's) regulatory competence, whilst also vindicating litigants' rights. Think of Mary and Peter Carpenter's right to respect for their family life, or Hans Åkerberg Fransson's (perhaps somewhat less meritorious) right not to be tried twice for his dodgy tax dealings.[100]

So far, the logic of supremacy, even if controversial from other perspectives, has at the very least operated in tandem with human rights protection thus far. But what about the opposite scenario? More specifically, what would happen in a situation where national law provided for a higher standard of fundamental rights protection than EU law, as read in light of the Charter? The framers of the Charter were clearly aware of this difficulty, and set out to address it in Article 53 CFR, stipulating:

> Nothing in this Charter shall be interpreted as restricting or adversely affecting human rights and fundamental freedoms as recognised [...] by the Member States' constitutions.

This is a twist on the *Internationale Handelsgesellschaft* anxiety, but not fundamentally different. Could Article 53 CFR really act as a break on supremacy, and thus the very core of the 'new legal order'? Of course not.

The *Melloni* saga revolves around another tax fraudster, tried *in absentia* after fleeing to Spain. When the Italian government tried to extradite him using a European Arrest Warrant (EAW), Mr Melloni sought to rely on the Spanish Constitution: given the impossibility of further appeals under Italian law, he suggested, the execution of an EAW would have run counter to his (domestic) constitutional right to a fair trial. The Court of Justice was not impressed. As long as the EAW regime was compatible with the Charter (as indeed the Court had previously found it to be),[101] the Spanish Government could not rely on

---

[100] Case C-617/10 *Åklagaren v Hans Åkerberg Fransson* [2013] ECR I-9011.

[101] Case C-399/11 *Stefano Melloni v Ministerio Fiscal* EU:C:2013:107 [54]. This would not have come as a surprise: see, e.g., Case C-303/05 *Advocaten voor de wereld VZW v Leden van de Ministerraad* [2007] ECR I-3633.

Article 53 CFR to resist the EAW. Any contrary reading of the Charter threatened to 'undermine the principle of the primacy of EU law'.[102]

Moreover, even where Member State authorities enjoyed a degree of discretion in implementing EU law, they could only rely on Article 53 CFR 'provided that the level of protection provided for by the Charter, as interpreted by the Court, and the primacy, unity, and effectiveness of EU law are not thereby compromised.'[103]

Having worked our way through a series of EU fundamental rights debates, this paragraph should not necessarily come as a shock. The tight link between supremacy and the Court's role as ultimate rights adjudicator has been a consistent theme in the jurisprudence.[104] Yet there is something about *Melloni* that might leave us with a sense of unease. This could simply be because of the counterintuitive outcome on the facts of the case. At least in principle, the worst-case scenario first envisaged in *Internationale Handelsgesellschaft* has come true.[105] More fundamentally, we are reminded once more of just how far EU law has come – from 'the esoteric joys of agricultural levies' to 'the heartland of criminal justice and individual protection'.[106] Weatherill hits the nail on its head: 'supremacy does not change – *Melloni* shows the Court's refusal to make any structural alterations in its approach – but the scope of its implications does.'[107]

Conclusion: The EU's Human Rights Paradox

Writing at the turn of the millennium, Alston and Weiler identified what they saw as the EU's human rights paradox: 'On the one hand, the Union is a staunch defender of human rights ... On the other hand, it lacks a comprehensive or coherent policy ... and fundamental doubts persist whether the institutions of the Union possess adequate legal competence in relation to a wide range of human rights issues.'[108]

Two decades on, can we safely conclude that this paradox has been resolved? From one perspective, absolutely. The Lisbon Treaty clearly put to rest any remaining questions of adequate legal competence. In addition to the provisions of Article 6 TEU surveyed in this chapter, a suite of measures are available

[102] *Melloni* [58].

[103] *Melloni* [60].

[104] D Sarmiento, 'Who's afraid of the Charter? The Court of Justice, national courts and the new framework for fundamental rights protection in Europe' (2013) 50(5) CML Rev 1267.

[105] The domestic Spanish situation turned out to be less dramatic than Mr Melloni's lawyers might have led us to believe: M Garcia, 'STC 26/2014: The Spanish Constitutional Court Modifies its case law in response to the CJEU's Melloni judgment' (*European Law Blog*, 17 March 2014), https://perma.cc/T5PT-N3RU.

[106] Weatherill, *Law and Values in the European Union* (n 20), p. 164.

[107] Weatherill, *Law and Values in the European Union*, pp. 164–65.

[108] P Alston and JHH Weiler, 'An "ever closer union" in need of a human rights policy' in P Alston (ed.), *The EU and Human Rights* (Oxford University Press 1999).

to deal with Member States in violation of the Article 2 TEU commitment (a process which we explore further in Chapter 11).

At the same time, however, as 'nation-building through economic integration has given way to nation-building through fundamental rights',[109] most of the underlying anxieties have not gone away – from Member State autonomy to the role of the CJEU. Fundamental rights protection has certainly become comprehensive, but there is still plenty of work to be done in order to ensure internal coherence and legal certainty.

Further reading

For the full history of human rights law in the EU and an account how things might have been very different, try G de Búrca, 'The Evolution of EU Human Rights Law' in P Craig and G de Búrca (eds), *The Evolution of EU Law*, 2nd edn (Oxford University Press 2011). As she points out, the first edition of that book did not have a chapter dedicated to human rights. Why the change?

Should EU fundamental rights provide a base line 'safety net' or full harmonization? E Spaventa advocates for the former in exploring human rights protection 'in the composite constitutional spaces of the European Union and its Member States': 'Should We "Harmonize" Fundamental Rights in the EU? Some Reflections about Minimum Standards and Fundamental Rights Protection in the EU Composite Constitutional System' (2018) 55(4) CML Rev 997.

The relationship between general principles, the Charter, and Member State legal systems links directly to the vexed question of the scope of EU law, as discussed in the preceding chapters. For a review of the evolving case law at the point of transition between the regimes, try M Dougan, 'Judicial Review of Member State Action under the General Principles and the Charter: Defining the "Scope of Union Law"' (2015) 52(5) CML Rev 1201.

[109] T Tridimas, 'Primacy, fundamental rights and the search for legitimacy' in MP Maduro and L Azoulai (eds), *The Past and Future of EU Law: The Classics of EU Law Revisited on the 50th Anniversary of the Rome Treaty* (Hart 2010).

CHAPTER 9

Ever Closer Union(s)

Free Movement of Persons and Citizenship

The free movement of persons is one of the four fundamental freedoms establishing the Internal Market,[1] and by far the 'most controversial'. For some, 'it is an article of faith, the defining feature of the EU. For others, it is a destructive force, with migrants competing with nationals for jobs and other limited resources … ultimately leading to a hollowing out of national identity'.[2]

In this chapter, we explore these tensions by looking at free movement rights, operating hand in hand with the principle of EU citizenship. It is an exciting topic: the law in this area keeps developing at a rapid pace. Many of the fundamental tensions that mark the evolution of EU law – be it the relationship between the economic and the social, the role of the Court as a driver of integration, or the trade-off between conferring rights on individuals and respecting Member State regulatory competence – come to the fore in a politically charged field.

In order to understand the twists and turns in the case law, we must first get a sense of what is at stake. Why is the free movement of persons essential to the Internal Market? Who are the winners and potential losers? And what does the empirical evidence tell us about the reality of movement amongst the 27 Member States (spoiler alert – it is not what xenophobe tabloids would have us think).

[1] Whilst the TFEU speaks of the free movement of persons in defining the Internal Market (Article 26), there are specific regimes in place to regulate the free movement of workers (Article 45 TFEU), the self-employed and legal persons (e.g. companies) (Article 49 TFEU), and the provision of services (Article 56 TFEU). The latter regulates scenarios where the cross-border activity is on a more short-term or intermittent basis: Case C-55/94 *Reinhard Gebhard v Consiglio dell'ordine degli Avvocati e Procuratori di Milano* [1995] ECR I-4165. Space limitations prohibit a detailed exploration of this point; for a full overview, see C Barnard, *The Substantive Law of the EU: The Four Freedoms*, 6th edn (Oxford University Press 2019), pt III.

[2] C Barnard, 'Free movement of natural persons and citizenship' in C Barnard and S Peers (eds), *European Union Law*, 3rd edn (Oxford University Press 2020), p. 398.

Against this backdrop, we can then turn to a detailed examination of the legal regime. What rights should we grant to the economically active, such as workers and students? What rights (if any) should we confer on everyone – not as an economic entitlement, but as a recognition of EU citizenship? And how, if at all, should we draw the distinction?

Debate 1

What is at stake?

Economists contrast the deep integration of the EU's goods markets with Member States' labour markets, which have remained surprisingly distinct. Potential explanations for this persistent heterogeneity range from differences in heritage, customs, and legal regulation, to (rather surprisingly) the fact that 'migration within the EU is very limited'.[3] As a result, key labour market indicators – from wage levels through to unemployment – vary dramatically across the Union, fuelling (potentially unfounded) perceptions of unfair competition and abusive migration.

(A) 'We Wanted Workers, and Humans Came'

'[M]an hat Arbeitskräfte gerufen, und es kommen Menschen', the poet Max Frisch famously quipped about the Swiss *Gastarbeiter* (guest worker) programme: 'We called for a labour force, and humans came'.[4] This tension is just as relevant today as it was in the last century. In economic terms, workers ('labour') are central to the operation of the economy (as a key 'factor of production').

In Chapter 10, we will encounter Ricardo's model of comparative advantage, which explains why countries are better off when trading with each other. Key to his model are relative labour costs, which will differ across nations. As a result, the free movement of goods is not independent from labour markets. Quite the opposite: free trade has potentially significant impacts on labour markets, which now have to 'indirectly compete against one another'.[5] Worker mobility helps smooth out this competition, allowing labour allocation to reach efficient levels across the Union.[6] At the same time, it is crucial to remem-

[3] R Baldwin and C Wyplosz, *The Economics of European Integration*, 6th edn (McGraw Hill 2020), p. 178.

[4] 'Überfremdung I' in M Frisch, *Öffentlichkeit als Partner (Edition Suhrkamp, 209)*, 3rd edn (Suhrkamp Verlag 1970), p. 100.

[5] Baldwin and Wyplosz (n 3), *The Economics of European Integration*, p. 187. At the simplest level, this will lead to a shift in industry concentration: jobs will be gained in exporting industries, and lost in sectors that have to compete with cheaper imports.

[6] Intergovernmental Committee on European Integration, 'The Brussels Report on the general common market' (Eng transl, commonly called the Spaak Report, June 1956), https://perma.cc/V5H2-HNFT.

ber that labour is not merely another commodity like coal or steel. Nowhere is the difficulty of creating an economic Union without a clear commitment to social aspects more evident.

Workers, then, are not simply a factor of production: they are humans, citizens, fathers, mothers, grandparents, children, and partners. As the International Labour Organisation's founding charter reminds us, 'labour should not be regarded merely as a commodity or article of commerce'.[7] This is the additional challenge – and joy – of free movement law where persons are concerned. Workers cannot be stored in a warehouse or shipped around at a moment's notice. They will have close family and social ties, seek education, and need medical care as well as provisions for retirement and old age.

In the absence of a comprehensive Union-wide social security, health, and/or pension regime, this has potentially significant resource implications for national governments. In addition to debates about 'product standards', such as academic, linguistic, or professional qualifications, the legal framework has to be able to accommodate these competing considerations – requiring complex and controversial balancing acts. The framers of the Treaty of Rome were acutely aware of this, envisaging an 'ever closer Union' of the peoples of Europe, as were their successors in creating EU citizenship in the Treaty of Maastricht. The Court's consistent expansive interpretation of the free movement provisions beyond their economic core similarly reflects a clear recognition that within the framework of the Treaties, the free movement of persons was never designed to serve economic ends alone.[8]

(B) Winners and (Potential) Losers

Another factor which complicates matters is the fact that the impacts of migration can be quite unequal. Free movement in the EU is not just a treat for economic elites, who tend to enjoy such freedoms in any event. In the short term and/or at the regional level at least, there will be clear winners – and potential losers.

On the positive side of the equation, free movement rights create opportunities for Europeans at all stages of their lives. Students across the EU owe a debt of gratitude to a young French woman who wanted to study cartoon design in Belgium without paying higher fees than her local counterparts. The Court of Justice agreed: Belgium could not discriminate against students from

[7] Treaty of Versailles (adopted 28 June 1919, entered into force 10 January 1920) UKTS 4, art 427 (establishing the predecessor institution to today's ILO). This commitment was emphatically restated in the ILO Declaration of Philadelphia: Declaration concerning the aims and purposes of the ILO (adopted at the 26th session of the ILO, Philadelphia, 10 May 1944).

[8] S O'Leary, 'Free movement of persons and services' in P Craig and G de Búrca (eds), *The Evolution of EU Law*, 2nd edn (Oxford University Press 2011), p. 500.

other EU countries.[9] Once you have finished your law studies, you might want to practise in different jurisdictions and encounter plenty of obstacles along the way. Who would want to instruct a German *Rechtsanwalt* to represent them before a Milan *Pretura*, instead of hiring an *avvocato* registered by the local bar?[10] Whether you are a Greek lawyer trying to practice in Germany,[11] or a British architect seeking to work in France,[12] EU free movement law will come to your rescue.[13]

The benefits of free movement and EU citizenship are by no means limited to these categories: tourists, for example, are entitled to protection as service recipients across the EU,[14] in addition to consular assistance overseas even if their own Member State does not maintain a diplomatic representation.[15]

Most importantly, just as with the theory of comparative advantage and international trade, there is the potential for us *all* to be better off in aggregate as a result of free movement. The (theoretical) economics of labour mobility are relatively straightforward, driven primarily by the levelling out of wage differentials once countries rid themselves both of explicit barriers (from immigration quotas to minimum income thresholds) and implicit barriers (from differences in health insurance and pension regimes to unemployment benefits and the recognition of professional and educational qualifications).[16] High-wage countries will then be able to attract workers from lower-wage countries, which in turn decreases workers' bargaining power and thus their wages. The opposite effect is observed in low-wage countries. As more and more workers emigrate, labour supply tightens, thus driving up the remaining workers'

[9] Case 293/83 *Françoise Gravier v City of Liège* [1985] ECR 593. Maintenance grants, student loans, and similar support measures, however, continue to be more contentious. The Court's initial emphasis on equal treatment in Case C-184/99 *Rudy Grzelczyk v Centre public d'aide sociale d'Ottignies-Louvain-la-Neuve* [2001] ECR I-6193 (*Grzelczyk*) has given way to a more cautious approach, allowing Member States to lay down integration requirements such as qualifying residence periods: Case C-209/03 *The Queen on the application of Dany Bidar v London Borough of Ealing and Secretary of State for Education and Skills* [2005] ECR I-2119; Case C-158/07 *Jacqueline Förster v Hoofddirectie van de Informatie Beheer Groep* [2008] ECR I-8507. For more on the treatment of students, see M Dougan, 'Cross-border educational mobility and the exportation of student financial assistance' (2008) 33(5) EL Rev 723.

[10] Case C-55/94 *Reinhard Gebhard v Consiglio dell'ordine degli Avvocati e Procuratori di Milano* [1995] ECR I-4165.

[11] Case C-340/89 *Irène Vlassopoulou v Ministerium für Justiz, Bundes- und Europaangelegenheiten Baden-Württemberg* [1991] ECR I-2357.

[12] Case 11-77 *Richard Hugh Patrick v Ministre des affaires culturelles* [1977] ECR 1199.

[13] As the directive consolidating the rules on the recognition of professional qualifications runs to nearly the same length as this entire book, we will spare you from detailed exploration: see European Parliament and Council Directive 2005/36/EC of 7 September 2005 on the recognition of professional qualifications [2005] OJ L255/22.

[14] Case 186/87 *Ian William Cowan v Trésor public* [1989] ECR 195.

[15] TFEU, Article 23.

[16] Baldwin and Wyplosz (n 3), *The Economics of European Integration*, p. 199.

wages. Eventually, this will lead to a new equilibrium, in which wages stabilise at a uniform level,[17] leaving both countries collectively better off.[18]

At the same time, however, remember that this is but an economic model – and that the distribution of these gains is not equal. Employers ('capital', in technical economics terms) in high-wage countries will gain from lower wages, as will high-skilled workers whose productivity is increased. Low-skilled workers, on the other hand, are more likely to suffer from wage competition. Empirical evidence for these claims is difficult to obtain with any degree of certainty. Overall, however, studies show that any wage impact of intra-EU migration thus far has been relatively minor.[19]

Regulation is nonetheless required to protect those who might otherwise lose out – whether it is by setting cross-European standards to remove unfair competition and other ways of 'social dumping',[20] or by creating carve-outs and limitations to certain entitlements with a view to protecting national regulatory choices.

(C) Schrödinger's Immigrant

These tensions, of course, are as old as migration itself, and were recognised in Union law right from the beginning. We will soon explore the various carve-outs laid down in the Treaties themselves. They have been brought back to the fore over the last two decades as a result of the Union's enlargement, intensifying concerns about 'Schrödinger's immigrant' – the mythical migrant worker who is out to steal your job whilst simultaneously being a lazy benefit scrounger.

The 'New Member States'

Since the early 2000s, the EU has nearly doubled in size – growing from 15 to 28 Member States (before shrinking back to 27 in 2020). The first and biggest wave of accessions saw ten countries (Poland, Hungary, Czech Republic, Slovakia, Estonia, Latvia, Lithuania, Slovenia, Malta, and Cyprus) join in 2004, followed by Romania and Bulgaria in 2007, and Croatia in 2013.[21]

A drawn-out accession process was designed to bring countries' legal arrangements in line with EU law (the *acquis*), but wage levels and the overall

---

[17] For a graphic illustration of this basic model, see Baldwin and Wyplosz, *The Economics of European Integration*, figure 8.11.

[18] Directorate-General of Employment, Social Affairs and Inclusion, 'Employment and social developments in Europe: Annual review 2019' (European Commission, June 2019), https://perma.cc/LY5L-VQB5.

[19] Baldwin and Wyplosz (n 3), *The Economics of European Integration*, pp. 196–97.

[20] This was the key reason for including equal pay as a provision in the Treaty of Rome, reflected today in Article 157 TFEU. See Case 43-75 *Gabrielle Defrenne v SABENA* [1976] ECR I-455, as discussed in Chapter 6, Debate 1.

[21] https://ec.europa.eu/neighbourhood-enlargement/node_en. At the time of writing, accession negotiations are pending with a number of countries in the Balkans, including in particular Montenegro and Serbia.

economic situation turned out to be somewhat stickier. At the extremes of the spectrum, at the moment of the Union's major enlargement in 2004, total labour cost per hour ranged from €28 in in France to €4 in Slovakia.[22] The ensuing migration flows have unsurprisingly taken place from east to west, with Germany and the UK in particular as popular destinations for workers from Poland, for example, and Italy and France for those from Romania.[23]

Accession thus had the potential for significant labour market impacts and political tension, not least in terms of narrowing wage ratios between 'old' and 'new' Member States,[24] and for reviving fears of 'social dumping', where businesses from low-wage countries undercut established operators by competing primarily on labour cost. In order to smooth the transition from one equilibrium to the next, the accession agreements provided for a tiered transitional regime, allowing Member States to abrogate free movement rights for citizens of the new Member States for up to seven years.[25]

Myth vs Reality

This did not stop populist fear mongering ('Benefits Britain Here We Come!', 'Wie viel kosten uns die neuen Zuwanderer?'),[26] even though these concerns are neither borne out in empirical data nor in the Court's jurisprudence.

When it comes to the economics of free movement, the evidence is clear. Intra-EU migrants are not lazy. Non-active EU migrants, for example, account for only 0.7 to 1 per cent of the EU population – and more than 70 per cent of those are pensioners, students, or job-seekers. They do not steal jobs: 'the empirical evidence we have to date does not support the notion that immigration has large, negative effects on European labour markets'.[27] And they are not interested in benefit scrounging: there is

> little evidence ... to suggest that the main motivation of EU citizens to migrate and reside in a different Member State is benefit-related as opposed to work or family-related. This is underpinned by data which show that in most countries, immigrants are not more intensive users of welfare than nationals.[28]

---

[22] Baldwin and Wyplosz (n 3), *The Economics of European Integration*, pp. 189–90.

[23] For a full overview, see the fascinating tables set out in Baldwin and Wyplosz, *The Economics of European Integration*, p. 192.

[24] Baldwin and Wyplosz, *The Economics of European Integration*, pp. 189–90.

[25] An overview of the (now expired) provisions can be found online at https://ec.europa.eu/eures/main.jsp?lang=en&acro=free&step=0.

[26] G Sheldrick, 'Benefits Britain here we come' (*Daily Express*, London, 1 January 2014), h https://perma.cc/3HHY-7LRE; 'Wie viel kosten uns die neuen Zuwanderer?' (*Bild Zeitung*, 30 January 2013), https://perma.cc/SV2P-52D7.

[27] Baldwin and Wyplosz (n 3), *The Economics of European Integration*, p. 198 highlight the non-infrequent instances of 'extreme ... complementarity', where immigrants fill jobs shunned by native workers, as a key explanation for this (counterintuitive) finding.

[28] ICF GHK and Milieu Ltd, 'A fact finding analysis on the impact on the Member States' social security systems of the entitlements of non-active intra-EU migrants to special non-contributory cash benefits and healthcare granted on the basis of residence' (*Directorate-General of Employment, Social Affairs and Inclusion*, 14 October 2013), https://perma.cc/VZM2-QHFE, p. 5.

If anything, migrants contribute significantly to their host states, 'pay[ing] more in taxes than they receive in benefits'.[29]

None of this comes as a surprise when we look at the detailed design of the free movement provisions. Far from opening the floodgates, EU law is specifically designed to 'prevent economically inactive EU citizens from using the host Member State's welfare system to fund their means of subsistence', as the Court of Justice asserted in *Dano*.[30]

The case concerned a Romanian national, Elisabeta Dano and her son Florin, whose benefits application had been rejected by the German government. The Court's response was surprisingly robust: any 'Member State must ... have the possibility ... of refusing to grant social benefits to economically inactive EU citizens who exercise their right to freedom of movement solely in order to obtain another Member State's social assistance although they do not have sufficient resources to claim a right of residence.'[31]

Right-wing tabloids duly celebrated the ruling as a 'crackdown on benefits tourism',[32] whilst legal commentators highlighted the disturbing consequence of giving in to the temptation of interpreting the limits on equal treatment in *Dano* broadly – not least, the 'end of free movement for the poor'.[33] Indeed, a closer look at the reality of many migrants' experiences quickly suggests a life quite distinct from the land of milk and honey depicted by xenophobic commentators – from struggling to enforce rights against exploitative employers[34] to state-sanctioned targeting of minority groups, such as Roma migrants in France.[35]

***

True or false, these controversies will continue to play an important role in debating the free movement of workers. As a result, it is perhaps more important than in any other area of EU law to consider competing perspectives. When discussing the negative impacts of labour migration, for example, we should not limit our focus to the 'old' Member States. What happens to eastern European health care systems that have invested significant resources into training doctors, only to see them leave to pursue opportunities in high-wage Member States?[36] Do immigrant workers undercutting established trade unions

---

[29] Migration Advisory Committee, 'EEA migration in the UK: Final report' (*MAC*, September 2018), https://perma.cc/B52L-JGWC, p. 71ff.

[30] Case C-333/13 *Elisabeta Dano and Florin Dano v Jobcenter Leipzig* EU:C:2014:2358 [76].

[31] *Dano* [78].

[32] P Bentley, 'The Roma gipsy who sparked a crackdown on benefit tourism: Elisabeta Dano, 25, tracked down to German city after finding herself at centre of landmark welfare case' (*Daily Mail*, 15 November 2014), https://www.dailymail.co.uk/news/article-2835442/The-Roma-gipsy-sparked-crackdown-benefit-tourism-Elisabeta-Dano-25-tracked-German-city-finding-centre-landmark-welfare-case.html.

[33] H Verschueren, 'Preventing "benefit tourism" in the EU: A narrow or broad Interpretation of the possibilities offered by the ECJ in *Dano*?' (2015) 52(2) CLM Rev 363, 377.

[34] For an important case study, see C Barnard and A Ludlow, 'Enforcement of employment rights by EU-8 migrant workers in employment tribunals' (2016) 45(1) ILJ 1.

[35] M Dawson and E Muir, 'Individual, institutional and collective vigilance in protecting fundamental rights in the EU: Lessons from the Roma' (2011) 48(3) CML Rev 751.

[36] P Collier, *Exodus: How Migration Is Changing Our World* (Oxford University Press 2013).

really represent a conflict between nationalities, or is it just a classic conflict between labour and capital, cynically recast as a cross-border issue by savvy employers?[37]

We also need to keep difficult questions in overall proportion. Baldwin and Wyplosz find in their assessment of the numbers that 'Europeans don't do much migrating'. Migration is limited to 0.2 per cent of the Union's population. Even amongst central and eastern European Member States, the numbers do not exceed 50 per 1000. More importantly, EU internal migration only makes up a small proportion of larger global patterns: 'seven out of ten foreign workers in EU Member States are from non-EU countries', they conclude, highlighting a stark 'mismatch between anti-EU rhetoric … and the reality of immigration'.[38]

Debate 2

Rights for the few (who are economically active)?

Article 45 TFEU is at the heart of free movement rights for individuals. 'Freedom of movement for workers', it declares, 'shall be secured within the Union.' The message is clear: work (i.e. economic activity) is a precondition to enjoying mobility and equal treatment rights. Over the course of the years, the case law of the CJEU and secondary legislation have expanded both the personal scope and the equal treatment implications of free movement – notably through the Citizen's Rights Directive (CRD)[39] – without, however, abandoning economic activity as the anchor point.

(A) Foundations: The Treaty

Article 45 TFEU is not limited to the high-level principle of free movement. It also begins to flesh out its contours, both through the abolition of existing barriers and the grant of specific rights:

> '2. Such freedom of movement shall entail the abolition of any discrimination based on nationality between workers of the Member States as regards employment, remuneration and other conditions of work and employment.

---

[37] Case C-438/05 *International Transport Workers' Federation and Finnish Seamen's Union v Viking Line ABP and OÜ Viking Line Eesti* [2007] ECR I-10779.

[38] Baldwin and Wyplosz (n 3), *The Economics of European Integration*, pp. 192–93.

[39] European Parliament and Council Directive 2004/38/EC of 29 April 2004 on the right of citizens of the Union and their family members to move and reside freely within the territory of the Member States amending Regulation (EEC) No 1612/68 and repealing Directives 64/221/EEC, 68/360/EEC, 72/194/EEC, 73/148/EEC, 75/34/EEC, 75/35/EEC, 90/364/EEC, 90/365/EEC and 93/96/EEC [2004] OJ L158/77 (Citizens' Rights Directive, CRD). The economically active are also covered by European Parliament and Council Regulation (EU) No 492/2011 of 5 April 2011 on freedom of movement for workers within the Union [2011] OJ L141/1. The provisions largely mirror each other, though on occasion workers will enjoy additional advantages. See further J Prassl, 'Migrants, citizens, aliens? Free movement rights for the economically inactive after *Brey* and *Dano*' (2016) 16 Rivista del Diritto della Sicurezza Sociale 311.

3. It shall entail the right, subject to limitations justified on grounds of public policy, public security or public health:
   (a) to accept offers of employment actually made;
   (b) to move freely within the territory of Member States for this purpose;
   (c) to stay in a Member State for the purpose of employment in accordance with the provisions governing the employment of nationals of that State laid down by law, regulation or administrative action;
   (d) to remain in the territory of a Member State after having been employed in that State, subject to conditions which shall be embodied in regulations to be drawn up by the Commission.'

The contours are relatively tightly defined. Equal treatment is limited to employment, remuneration, and employment conditions; residence granted 'for the purpose' of work; and derogations reserved for the Member States. The detailed implementation of these provisions was left to the EU legislature, as well as the CJEU.

The key to triggering the applicability of these rights is employment status. Remember that Article 45 TFEU is only directed at workers. The relevant definition is set out in what has become known as the '*Lawrie-Blum*' formula: 'The essential feature of an employment relationship … is that for a certain period of time a person performs services for and under the direction of another person in return for which he receives remuneration.'[40]

This formula clearly encompasses full-time employment in a factory or office. But what about individuals engaged in so-called atypical work – from part-time jobs to the gig economy? Domestic employment laws will often exclude such individuals from the scope of employment rights. Can they still be workers for purposes of free movement entitlements?[41] Yes, absolutely, explained the Court of Justice in *Levin*: the worker concept 'may not be defined by reference to the national laws of the Member States but ha[s] a Community meaning.' And that meaning was to be construed generously: 'concepts [which] define the field of application of one of the fundamental freedoms guaranteed by the Treaty … may not be interpreted restrictively', lest the 'achievement of the objectives of the Treaty … be jeopardized'.[42]

The CJEU has been broadly consistent in this generous approach to interpreting the scope of Article 45 TFEU,[43] raising the question of its outer boundaries. We will return to this difficulty imminently as well as in Debate 3. First, though, we need to explore the provisions of the CRD in some detail.

---

[40] Case 66/85 *Deborah Lawrie-Blum v Land Baden-Württemberg* [1986] ECR 2121 [17].

[41] Note that this is not necessarily the same definition of the worker as encountered in employment law. See N Kountouris, 'The concept of "worker" in European labour law: Fragmentation, autonomy and scope' (2018) 47(2) ILJ 19.

[42] Case 53/81 *D.M. Levin v Staatssecretaris van Justitie* [1982] ECR 1035 [11], [13], [15].

[43] Such as its move beyond discrimination in Case C-415/93 *Union royale belge des sociétés de football association ASBL v Jean-Marc Bosman, Royal club liégeois SA v Jean-Marc Bosman and ors* and *UEFA v Jean-Marc Bosman* [1995] ECR I-4921. For a discussion of market access in the free movement of persons context, try E Spaventa, 'From *Gebhard* to *Carpenter*: Towards a (non-)economic European constitution' (2004) 41(3) CML Rev 743.

(B) The Citizens' Rights Directive

Enacted in 2004, the CRD repeals a host of legislative measures with a view to providing a single, consolidated set of provisions.[44] But does it mark a clear point of departure from Article 45 TFEU's narrow focus on economic activity, inspired by the recognition of EU citizenship? A first glance suggest that this might be the case. Instead of free movement for workers, the CRD proclaims to set out 'the right of citizens of the Union and their family members to move and reside freely within the territory of the Member States'. But does it really strengthen rights, or merely provide clarification and restatement?[45] Upon closer inspection, we quickly see the nervousness which drove the initial focus on rights for the economically active re-emerge. Read the long list of preambles to get a sense of Member States' concerns.[46]

Mobility, Residence, and Equal Treatment

The CRD grants a suite of rights to EU citizens – nationals of the 27 Member States – as well as their family members (whose rights we explore separately, below). Articles 4 and 5 CRD provide for the preconditions of movement. Subject only to the basic requirement of valid travel documents, citizens are free to leave any Member State to travel to another, which in turn has to grant leave to enter its territory.[47]

Once arrived, Chapter III provides for a three-tiered system of residence rights, depending on length of stay. For an initial stay of up to three months, EU citizens enjoy residence rights 'without any conditions or any formalities other than the requirement to hold a valid identity card or passport.'[48] The right of residence beyond this period (and up to five years) is regulated by Article 7 CRD: workers and the self-employed enjoy it without further qualification; other categories of migrants need to jump through additional hoops.

---

[44] E Guild, S Peers, and J Tomkin, *The EU Citizenship Directive: A Commentary*, 2nd edn (Oxford University Press 2019).

[45] O'Leary (n 8), 'Free movement of persons and services', p. 515.

[46] These are also reflected in the fairly open-ended drafting, which has the short-term advantage of creating space for political compromise – whilst creating longer-term uncertainty and the need for judicial resolution of highly controversial points. One such example is the relationship between the CRD and the European Parliament and Council Regulation (EC) No 883/2004 of 29 April 2004 on the coordination of social security systems [2004] OJ L166/1. The measures were enacted on the same day and cover closely related questions, whilst not clarifying their interaction: Case C-140/12 *Pensionsversicherungsanstalt v Peter Brey* EU:C:2013:565.

[47] This should not be confused with the arrangements of the 'Schengen area', named after an independent Treaty providing for the abolition of frontier controls amongst its signatories: The Schengen acquis – Agreement between the Governments of the States of the Benelux Economic Union, the Federal Republic of Germany and the French Republic on the gradual abolition of checks at their common borders [2000] OJ L239/13. Whilst there is significant overlap in terms of membership, the provisions are not linked to the free movement of workers explored in this chapter.

[48] CRD, Article 6(1). The formulation is rather misleading: CRD, Article 14(1), clarifies that this right is only enjoyed 'as long as they do not become an unreasonable burden on the social assistance system of the host Member State.'

Students, for example, need to have comprehensive health insurance as well as sufficient means not to become a burden on the host state's social assistance system.[49] The CRD also makes provisions for various vicissitudes, from temporary illness and unemployment to death and divorce.[50]

After continuous,[51] lawful residence for a period of five years, finally, EU citizens are granted 'the right of permanent residence' in their host country. They no longer have to meet the conditions provided for in Chapter III, and the right can only be lost through absence 'exceeding two consecutive years'.[52]

Once lawfully resident, whether temporarily or permanently, 'all Union citizens residing on the basis of [the CRD] in the territory of the host Member State shall enjoy equal treatment with the nationals of that Member State within the scope of the Treaty.'[53] This is a potential game changer: no longer is the anti-discrimination norm limited to the employment context. The scope of the Treaties, as we discovered in Chapter 2, is very wide indeed.[54]

Family Life

The position of the worker herself is relatively straightforward, as are the various status extensions, such as for temporary illness or unemployment. Matters quickly become more complex – and potentially controversial – when family members are concerned. Remember the important realisation that labour is not a commodity. In order to incentivise movement, the CRD thus has to ensure that workers do not have to move alone. At the same time, however, Member States may well begin to worry about the cost of providing education, health care, and social assistance for workers' dependants.

This tension is reflected throughout the CRD. EU citizens' family members are explicitly listed as its beneficiaries, and defined widely to include spouses, direct descendants, and dependent relatives in the ascending line. Registered partnerships treated as equivalent to marriage by the host Member State are similarly included.[55] At the same time, however, we also find specific provisions for family members and limited carve-outs. When it comes to family members beyond the inner circle, such as long-term boyfriends and girlfriends, for exam-

[49] CRD, Article 7(1)(c).

[50] CRD, Articles 7(3), 12, and 13.

[51] CRD, Article 16(3) provides for certain exemptions, including pregnancy, vocational training, and compulsory military service.

[52] CRD, Articles 16(1) and 16(4). Article 17 provides another route to permanent residence, but is limited to certain edge cases (retirement, incapacity, and frontier workers).

[53] CRD, Article 24(1).

[54] CRD, Article 24(2) thus provides a series of explicit derogations, notably for social assistance and student grants and loans.

[55] C Bell and N Bačić Selanec argue that 'that the Court of Justice is fully competent to require that all Member States recognize same-sex marriages for the purposes of EU equality and free movement law where that marriage involves an EU citizen and was legally conducted in one of the EU Member States': 'Who is a "spouse" under the Citizens' Rights Directive? The prospect of mutual recognition of same-sex marriages in the EU' (2016) 41(5) EL Rev 655.

ple, Member States' obligations are limited to 'facilitating' entry and residence in line with national legislation.[56]

What happens in scenarios that are not explicitly covered by the CRD, such as asylum claims brought by citizens of non-EU states (usually referred to as 'third-country nationals' or 'TCNs')? Generally speaking, the admission of TCNs coming from outside the EU is a question of Member State competence,[57] unless an EU citizens' exercise of free movement rights brings a particular case within the scope of the Treaties.

One area in which this question has been repeatedly litigated is the so-called previous lawful residency requirement: a TCN spouse of an EU citizen could only claim subsequent protection under EU law if they were already 'lawfully resident in a Member State when [moving] to another Member State to which the citizen of the Union is migrating'.[58] This gives significant regulatory power to domestic immigration law: free movement rights only enter into the equation once lawful residence has been established according to national rules. At the same time, however, it also creates different conditions across the Member States, leading to potential free movement obstacles.

This was recognised in *Metock*. Mr Metock, a Cameroonian national, was married to Ms Ngo Ikeng, a British citizen working in Ireland. When his application for asylum was refused by the Irish authorities, Mr Metock applied for a residence permit as the spouse of an EU citizen. The application was again refused, this time on the basis that the applicant had come to Ireland directly and could not therefore demonstrate any previous lawful residence in another Member State. This scenario, the Irish Minister of Justice submitted, was a question of domestic competence, beyond the scope of the CRD.[59]

The Court of Justice disagreed. In reversing its previous case law on point,[60] it found that the grant of such exclusive competence

> would have the effect that the freedom of movement of EU citizens in a Member State whose nationality they do not possess would vary from one Member State to another, according to the provisions of national law concerning immigration, with some Member States permitting entry and residence of family members of an EU citizen and other Member States refusing them.[61]

---

[56] CRD, Article 3(2).

[57] Note that asylum claims are subject to the Dublin Regulations: European Parliament and Council Regulation (EU) No 604/2013 of 26 June 2013 establishing the criteria and mechanisms for determining the Member State responsible for examining an application for international protection lodged in one of the Member States by a third-country national or a stateless person [2013] OJ L180/31.

[58] Case C-109/01 *Secretary of State for the Home Department v Hacene Akrich* [2003] ECR I-9607 [50].

[59] Case C-127/08 *Blaise Baheten Metock and ors v Minister for Justice, Equality and Law Reform* [2008] ECR I-6241 (*Metock*) [44].

[60] *Metock* [58].

[61] *Metock* [67].

The prior lawful residence requirement was accordingly incompatible with the objective of establishing an Internal Market. The CRD conferred rights on TCN family members 'regardless of whether [they had] already been lawfully resident in another Member State' and 'irrespective of when and where their marriage took place.'[62]

Member State governments were outraged by this perceived intrusion into national immigration rules. Yet, from the perspective of the fundamental rights of the EU citizens involved, it is hard not to appreciate the importance of this reasoning. As we saw at the outset, the CJEU has consistently emphasised the need to interpret the fundamental freedoms broadly in order to ensure effective judicial protection for rights conferred by the Treaties.

Where Are the Limits?

That said, it is just as important to recognise that free movement rights *do* have their limits, provided in the Treaty and secondary legislation, and recognised in the case law of the CJEU. We have already encountered the Article 45(3) TFEU derogation: Member States can limit free movement rights if 'justified on grounds of public policy, public security or public health'. Article 45(4) TFEU further provides an exemption for employment in the public service.

As with all derogations from the fundamental freedoms, these provisions are to be interpreted strictly. The public sector employment derogation, for example, is limited to 'posts which involve ... [where the purpose of such exercise] the exercise of powers conferred by public law ... is to safeguard the general interests of the State ... and which therefore require a special relationship of allegiance to the State ... and reciprocity of rights and duties which form the foundation of the bond of nationality.' Limiting recruitment of spy chiefs to nationals is fine, in other words, but it does not cover the majority of public sector jobs, such as teachers.[63]

The CRD similarly provides for a number of limitations and restrictions, whilst also trying to ensure that any such derogation cannot be used to undermine core rights. Member States *are* allowed in principle to verify that a student meets her Article 7 CRD residence conditions, for example, but there must be 'reasonable doubt' in a specific case, as 'verification shall not be carried out systematically'.[64] Access to social assistance can similarly be curtailed in various scenarios, but must not be the trigger for automatic expulsion.[65] And whilst any right conferred by the CRD may be withdrawn

[62] *Metock* [68], [71], [99]. For a detailed annotation, see C Costello, '*Metock:* Free movement and "normal family life" in the Union' (2009) 46(2) CML Rev 587.

[63] *Lawrie-Blum* (n 40) [27]–[28], citing Case 149/79 *European Commission v Belgium* [1982] ECR 1845.

[64] CRD, Article 14(2).

[65] CRD, Articles 14(1), 14(3), and 24(2) CRD. See further Case C-67/14 *Jobcenter Berlin Neukölln v Nazifa Alimanovic and ors* EU:C:2015:597.

'in the case of abuse of rights or fraud, such as marriages of convenience', any punitive measure must be proportionate and subject to procedural safeguards.[66]

Chapter VI provides a detailed regime for the derogations derived from Article 45 TFEU, with a tiered approach which mirrors the acquisition of residence rights. Public health arguments, for example, can only justify expulsion during the first three months in a host state.[67] A series of general principles furthermore act as a break on state action: derogations on grounds of public policy or public security must comply with the principle of proportionality, and the alleged 'personal conduct of the individual concerned must represent a genuine, present and sufficiently serious threat affecting one of the fundamental interests of society.'[68]

Restrictions, finally, must 'not be invoked to serve economic ends'.[69] This reflects a broader concern in EU law that economic justifications cannot serve to abridge free movement rights, as illustrated in the student quota saga. Austria and Belgium are both in the peculiar situation of sharing a joint language with a much larger neighbour state that operates a *numerus clausus* system to restrict access to popular university courses such as medicine. The temptation for German and French students who have missed out on a place at home is therefore to hop across the border, leading to concerns 'that, having regard to the budgetary, human and material resources available to the teaching institutions concerned, this is jeopardising the quality of teaching'.[70] When faced with Belgium's quota system,[71] the Court was not impressed: 'the fear of an excessive burden on the financing of higher education cannot justify the unequal treatment of resident students and non-resident students.'[72] The 'objective of maintaining a balanced high-quality medical service open to all', on the other hand, was recognised as a valid justification in principle, subject of course to a detailed proportionality analysis.[73]

***

Despite its title, then, the CRD does not provide an unqualified entitlement to free movement and equal treatment. Its design evidences a continued commitment to prioritising rights for the economically active, the need for cross-border activity, and multiple possibilities for derogations and restrictions. This is a far cry from the universal promise inherent in notions of citizenship, which grants rights irrespective of whether you are a busy frequent flyer or have never left your hometown. Has the time come to embrace a very different approach?

---

[66] CRD, Articles 30, 31, and 35.

[67] CRD, Article 29.

[68] CRD, Article 27(2).

[69] CRD, Article 27(1).

[70] Case C-73/08 *Nicolas Bressol and ors and Céline Chaverot and ors v Gouvernement de la Communauté française* [2010] ECR I-2735 (*Bressol*), Opinion of AG Sharpston [19].

[71] Case C-147/03 *Commission v Austria* [2005] ECR I-5969 is the parallel case concerning Austrian limitations on student numbers.

[72] *Bressol* (n 70) [51].

[73] *Bressol* [62] ff.

Debate 3

Rights for all (citizens)?

EU law has come a long way since the original 'playboy directives', which extended free movement rights to those wealthy enough to sustain a life of leisure.[74] Perhaps the single most transformative moment was the recognition in the Maastricht Treaty, in what was then Article 8 EC, of Union citizenship. It is a powerful idea, pushing beyond the economic constitutionalism of the Internal Market: 'the Treaty on European Union', the Court explained in *Baumbast*, 'does not require that citizens of the Union pursue a professional or trade activity, whether as an employed or self-employed person, in order to enjoy the rights provided [by] citizenship of the Union.'[75] Citizenship has certainly expanded the reach of existing rights. But to what extent can it bring about a fundamental change in deeply entrenched legal structures, forging a unified model of equal treatment for all out of the fragmented categories characterising free movement law to date?

(A) Cives Europaeus Sum?

Article 20 TFEU establishes citizenship of the EU for every national of the Member States,[76] listing it as the EU's first substantive commitment, ahead even of the Internal Market in Article 26 TFEU. Citizens are entitled to 'enjoy the rights and be subject to the duties provided for in the Treaties', from 'the right to move and reside freely within the territory of the Member States' to 'the right to vote and to stand as candidates in elections to the European Parliament'.[77]

Even more importantly, they benefit from a prohibition, '[w]ithin the scope of application of the Treaties, and without prejudice to any special provisions contained therein, [of] any discrimination on grounds of nationality.'[78] When read together, these provisions promise formidable protection for EU citizens, with AG Jacobs evoking historical parallels with the protections granted to Roman citizens in ancient times. Could '*cives Europaeus sum*', ('I am a European citizen!') become as powerful a claim in 'oppos[ing] any violation of … fundamental rights' as the invocation '*cives Romanus sum*' had done 2000 years earlier?[79]

---

[74] C Barnard, *The Substantive Law of the EU: The Four Freedoms*, 6th edn (Oxford University Press 2019), p. 337.

[75] Case C-413/99 *Baumbast and R v Secretary of State for the Home Department* [2002] ECR I-7091 [83]

[76] The right is 'additional to', rather than replacing, existing nationalities.

[77] See TFEU, Articles 21–25, for details.

[78] TFEU, Article 18.

[79] Case C-168/91 *Christos Konstantinidis v Stadt Altensteig – Standesamt and Landratsamt Calw – Ordnungsamt* [1993] ECR I-1191, Opinion of AG Jacobs [46]; AN Sherwin-White, *The Roman Citizenship* (Clarendon Press 1939).

At the turn of the millennium, the potential seemed unlimited. In *Grzelczyk*, the Court held that 'Union Citizenship is destined to be the fundamental status of nationals of the Member States.'[80] In *Martinez Sala*, it enthusiastically embraced the combined reading of EU citizenship and the general anti-discrimination norm to grant a Spanish national resident in Germany access to child support. The Federal Republic's insistence on production of a formal residence permit constituted 'discrimination directly based on the appellant's nationality and, in any event, nothing to justify such unequal treatment [had] been put before the Court.'[81] This case, O'Leary explains, was a milestone in the sense that it 'exploded the notion that the introduction of EU citizenship was little more than a cosmetic exercise ... decoupled the application ... of free movement and non-discrimination from the need to exercise an economic activity'; and significantly broadened our understanding of the types of 'situation ... to be governed by EU law'.[82]

One straightforward illustration of this expansion can be found in the context of job-seekers' allowance – a benefit paid to unemployed workers looking for employment. Under a traditional economic analysis of free movement, the jobseeker traditionally found herself in a curious liminal position: economically active to enjoy free movement rights, but not entitled to any financial support from a putative host Member State. As the Court had confirmed in *Lebon*, 'the right to equal treatment with regard to social and tax advantages applies only to workers. Those who move in search of employment qualify for equal treatment only as regards access to employment'.[83]

Two decades later, the tune changed. In *Collins*, an Irish citizen had been unable to meet the UK government's residence requirements, and was therefore denied access to jobseekers' allowance payments. A straightforward case of applying *Lebon*? Not quite: the constitutional setup had evolved. 'In view of the establishment of citizenship of the Union and the interpretation in the case-law of the right to equal treatment enjoyed by citizens of the Union,' the Court explained, 'it [was] no longer possible to exclude from the ... fundamental principle of equal treatment ... a benefit of a financial nature intended to facilitate access to employment in the labour market of a Member State.'[84]

These illustrations should not be taken as a suggestion that citizenship will run a coach and horses through the careful limitations set out in the CRD and other EU measures. As the scope of citizens' rights expanded, so did the need for a 'safety valve ... to control who has access to benefits'.[85] In *Collins* itself,

---

[80] *Grzelczyk* (n 9) [31].

[81] Case C-85/96 *María Martínez Sala v Freistaat Bayern* [1998] ECR I-2691 [62]–[64].

[82] O'Leary (n 8), 'Free movement of persons and services', p. 500.

[83] Case C-316/85 *Centre public d'aide sociale de Courcelles v Marie-Christine Lebon* [1987] ECR 2811 [26]. Cf. Case C-292/89 *The Queen v Immigration Appeal Tribunal, ex p Gustaff Desiderius Antonissen* [1991] ECR I-745.

[84] Case C-138/02 *Brian Francis Collins v Secretary of State for Work and Pensions* [2004] ECR I-2703 (*Collins*) [63]

[85] Barnard (n 74), *The Substantive Law of the EU*, p. 259.

for example, the Court recognised that it was 'legitimate for the national legislature to wish to ensure that there is a genuine link between an applicant for an allowance in the nature of a social advantage ... and the geographic employment market in question', at least as long as any such requirement was proportionate and 'necessary in order for the national authorities to be able to satisfy themselves that the person concerned is genuinely seeking work in the employment market of the [UK].'[86]

(B) Purely Internal Situations

Perhaps the most adventurous – inspired or intrusive, depending on your perspective – deployment of citizenship to date has been in the context of so-called purely internal situations where there has been no cross-border activity whatsoever. It is one thing for the scope of EU law to be pushed to its edge on the facts of a particular case. Remember *Mary Carpenter* in Chapter 8: her husband Peter's (very) occasional commercial forays to France sufficed to bring their family life within the scope of the Treaty.[87] Dubious and sexist on the facts, but not particularly offensive to the orthodoxy of free movement law.

Purely internal situations are different.[88] EU free movement law simply does not apply in the absence of a cross-border element. Even the CRD makes it clear that its target beneficiaries are 'EU citizens who move to or reside in a Member State other than that of which they are a national'.[89] The classic illustration of this difference is university tuition fees in Scotland. Whereas English institutions charge significant amounts even to domestic students, the Scottish government continues to provide free higher education to its citizens. Until Brexit, at least, students from other EU countries enjoyed the same financial support: anything else would have constituted illegal discrimination on grounds of nationality. The same was not true for students from England and Wales, as moving from Oxford to Edinburgh does not cross any (EU Member) state boundaries. Scottish tuition fees for English students constitutes a purely internal situation, leaving Holyrood free to indulge in explicitly nationality-based discrimination.[90]

Could citizenship blow a hole into this bulwark? Potentially, yes. In *Ruiz Zambrano*, a Colombian family who had fled to Belgium sought to challenge the national government's refusal to grant them residence and work permits. Since their arrival, the family had been joined by two more children: Diego and

[86] *Collins* (n 84) [67], [72].

[87] Case C-60/100 *Mary Carpenter v Secretary of State for the Home Department* [2002] ECR I-6279.

[88] Not that they necessarily *should* be: see A Tryfonidou, 'Reverse discrimination in purely internal situations: An incongruity in a citizens' Europe' (2008) 35(1) Legal Issues of Econ Integration 43.

[89] CRD, Article 3(1).

[90] https://www.scotland.org/study/how-to-apply/funding-and-fees.

Jessica, Belgian citizens by virtue of the locality of their birth. As a result, the Ruiz Zambranos argued, the family could not be deported: they were entitled to protection as the dependents of EU citizens.

The Member States were up in arms. 'A situation such as that of Mr Ruiz Zambrano's ... children, where those children reside in the Member State of which they are nationals and have never left the territory of that Member State, does not come within the situations envisaged by the freedoms of movement and residence guaranteed under European Union law.'[91] The Court agreed that, given the lack of cross-border activity, the CRD was inapplicable.[92] It then, however, recalled the fundamental nature of EU citizenship, and went on to find that 'Article 20 TFEU precludes national measures which have the effect of depriving citizens of the Union of the genuine enjoyment of the substance of the rights conferred by virtue of their status as citizens of the Union.' Belgium's refusal of work and residence permits for Diego and Jessica's parents would lead to precisely such a 'situation where those children, citizens of the Union, would have to leave the territory of the Union in order to accompany their parents', and was therefore incompatible with EU law.[93]

Huge debates ensued. Had the Court pushed citizenship too far? What was the definition of the 'genuine enjoyment of the substance of the rights conferred by virtue of their status as citizens of the Union'? In subsequent litigation, the Court's jurisprudence seems designed to appease Member States by retrenching the scope of *Ruiz Zambrano* on the facts of different scenarios presented to it, whilst steadfastly re-affirming the underlying doctrine.

In *Shirley McCarthy*, a UK national who had never exercised any free movement rights, sought to protect her Jamaican husband by relying on *Ruiz Zambrano*. AG Kokott suggested that EU law was simply not engaged in the absence of cross-border activity. The Court of Justice disagreed. In principle, Mrs McCarthy could rely on her citizenship rights, even against her 'Member State of origin'.[94] On the facts, however, it turned out that the genuine enjoyment of the substance of EU citizenship does not extend to protection against broken hearts: the UK's refusal to grant her husband leave to remain would 'not have the effect of obliging Mrs McCarthy to leave the territory of the European Union'.[95]

A similar approach was adopted in subsequent cases,[96] eventually emboldening a number of Member States to argue that 'the principles stated by the Court in Ruiz Zambrano relate to altogether exceptional situations in which

[91] Case C-34/09 *Gerardo Ruiz Zambrano v ONEM* [2011] ECR I-1177 [37].
[92] *Ruiz Zambrano* [39].
[93] *Ruiz Zambrano* [42], [44].
[94] Case C-434/09 *Shirley McCarthy v Secretary of State for the Home Department* [2011] ECR I-3375 [48].
[95] *Shirley McCarthy* [50].
[96] See, e.g., Case C-256/11 *Murat Dereci and ors v Bundesminister für Inneres* EU:C:2011:734.

the application of a national measure would lead to the denial of the genuine enjoyment of the substance of the rights conferred by the status of citizen of the Union.' The Court refused to accept this high threshold, opting instead to emphasise the role of domestic courts in assessing the facts of individual cases in order to 'establish whether the refusal of the applications for residence permits submitted on the basis of family reunification … entails, for the EU citizens concerned, a denial of the genuine enjoyment of the substance of the rights conferred by their status.'[97]

Conclusion: Citizenship as a Metaphor or a Source of Rights?[98]

Where does this leave us? Looking at *Ruiz Zambrano*, on the one hand, and *Dano*, on the other, citizenship has not quite turned out to be the game changer it might have been. If at all possible, grounding challenges to unequal treatment on economic activity or a related status continues to promise higher chances of success.[99]

The debate is far from settled. Citizenship-driven constitutionalism, Shaw argues, does not only have an expansive dimension – there are also limits.[100] Kochenov strongly disagrees, suggesting that citizenship should be understood as nothing less than a 'systemic element of EU law endowed with foundational importance' in the project of European integration, all the way towards Federalism.[101]

Ultimately, the question boils down to a sharp choice, as AG Sharpston observed in *Ruiz Zambrano*:

> At a more conceptual level, is the exercise of rights as a Union citizen dependent – like the exercise of the classic economic 'freedoms' – on some trans-frontier free movement (however accidental, peripheral or remote) having taken place before the claim is advanced? Or does Union citizenship look forward to the future, rather than back to the past, to define the rights and obligations that it confers? To put the same question from a slightly different angle: is citizenship merely the non-economic version of the same generic kind of free movement rights as have long existed for the economically active and for persons of independent means? Or does it mean something more radical: true citizenship, carrying with it a uniform set of rights and obligations, in a Union under the rule of law in which respect for fundamental rights must necessarily play an integral part?[102]

---

[97] Joined Cases C-356/11 *O and S v Maahanmuuttovirasto* and C-357/11 *Maahanmuuttovirasto v L* EU:C:2012:776 [38] ff., [49].

[98] N Reich, 'Union citizenship: Metaphor or source of rights' (2001) 7(1) Eur LJ 4.

[99] C O'Brien, 'Social blind spots and monocular policy making: The ECJ's migrant worker model' (2009) 46(4) CML Rev 1107.

[100] J Shaw, 'Citizenship: Contrasting dynamics at the interface of integration and constitutionalism' in P Craig and G de Búrca (eds), *The Evolution of EU Law*, 2nd edn (Oxford University Press 2011).

[101] D Kochenov (ed.), *EU Citizenship and Federalism: The Role of Rights* (Cambridge University Press 2017).

[102] *Ruiz Zambrano* (n 91), Opinion of AG Sharpston [3].

Her answer, a mere 160 paragraphs later, will not come as a surprise when you think back to our opening debate in this chapter. Ultimately, she suggests, there would be many advantages to a broad reading of EU competence: 'the clearest rule would be one that made the availability of EU fundamental rights protection dependent neither on whether a Treaty provision was directly applicable nor on whether secondary legislation had been enacted, but rather on the existence and scope of a material EU competence', including the protection of citizens' fundamental rights.[103]

Whilst conceptually within the reach of the citizenship and equal treatment provisions found in the Treaties, and despite significant potential advantages, however, 'such a step [could not] be taken unilaterally by the Court,' as it 'would involve introducing an overtly federal element into the structure of the EU's legal and political system'. That was too far a step, politically, for the Court to take out of its own motion:

> A change of that kind would alter, in legal and political terms, the very nature of fundamental rights under EU law. It therefore requires both an evolution in the case-law and an unequivocal political statement from the constituent powers of the EU (its Member States), pointing at a new role for fundamental rights in the EU.[104]

Further reading

In the next chapter, we turn to the free movement of goods. Ask yourself: should there be a coherent approach to the legal regulation of all four Internal Market freedoms? Yes, absolutely, argues Nic Shuibhne, suggesting that this is a key constitutional responsibility of the CJEU: *The Coherence of EU Free Movement Law: Constitutional Responsibility and the Court of Justice* (Oxford University Press 2013).

The rise (and fall) of citizenship of the EU as a powerful conceptual tool to overcome the traditional limitations of free movement law is traced in B Anderson, '"Heads I Win, Tails You Lose": Migration and the Worker Citizen' (2015) 68 Current Legal Problems 179.

Free movement (rightly or wrongly) was a key topic of debate in the run-up to Brexit. Has the time come to replace it with 'fair movement' (i.e. more managed migration)? See C Barnard and S Fraser Butlin, 'Free Movement vs. Fair Movement: Brexit and Managed Migration' (2018) 55(2) CML Rev 203.

---

[103] *Ruiz Zambrano* [163].

[104] *Ruiz Zambrano* [171]–[173].

CHAPTER 10

Sex Dolls, Beer, and *Keck*

Free Movement of Goods and the Internal Market

The Internal Market sits at the very core of the European project. Whilst there is little to suggest this pre-eminence on the face of the Treaties, the commitment to liberalising the movement of goods, persons, services, and capital has been elevated by the CJEU to nothing less than a 'fundamental' freedom,[1] providing the impetus to kickstart European integration and to regain momentum when the process stalled.[2]

The Internal Market, the Commission ambitiously proclaimed in the 1980s, was to be completed in 1992.[3] Three decades on, its development continues at full pace.[4] The free movement of goods has played a central role in shaping the contours of the Internal Market, organised around two deceivingly straightforward questions: what national rules and practices count should count as prohibited trade barriers? And what space, if any, should be left to Member States to justify such measures?

What started out as a battle against obscure national standards – from cone-shaped butter to minimum alcohol content for fruit liqueurs – has today morphed into a much broader set of debates surrounding national values, regulatory competence, and the ever-present tension between economic freedoms and broader, 'non-market' concerns. Whilst these challenges play out across nearly all domains of Union law, there is no better place for a comprehensive overview than the very origins of the Internal Market.

[1] S Weatherill, *The Internal Market as a Legal Concept* (Oxford University Press 2017), especially Chapters 2 and 3.

[2] With both the CJEU and individual traders playing a notable role in breaking the deadlock created by political inaction: P Craig, 'Once upon a time in the west: Direct effect and the federalization of EEC law' (1992) 12(4) OJLS 453.

[3] Commission, 'Completing the Internal Market: White paper from the Commission to the European Council' [1986] COM/85/310.

[4] See, e.g., M Monti, 'A new strategy for the single market: At the service of Europe's economy and society' (European Commission, 9 May 2010), https://perma.cc/9BU3-XFS6.

Debate 1

What kind of market?

Before we delve into a detailed analysis of these (legal) questions, we need to appreciate the fundamental (economic and political) debate that shapes them. What kind of market is EU law trying to achieve? This is a debate which has never been fully resolved – and its tensions, twists, and turns are therefore key to understanding the meandering case law of the CJEU.

(A) The Benefits of Free Trade

Why trade? Schuman's original aim was clear: establish peace in a war-torn continent through collaborative trade in the means of war, *viz* the coal and steel required for industrial-scale production of armaments. Central to the European Coal and Steel Community was 'solidarity in production', designed to ensure 'that any war between France and Germany becomes not merely unthinkable, but materially impossible'.[5] Seventy years on, that goal has certainly been achieved. So we must ask anew: why is the Internal Market at the very core of the European project?

Economics 101: Comparative Advantage, Economies of Scale, and Increased Consumer Choice

'If there is one proposition with which virtually all economists agree', *The Economist* proclaimed at the turn of the millennium, 'it is that free trade is almost always better than protection'.[6] At the foundation of this bold commitment lies Ricardo's *Theory of Comparative Advantage*, first espoused over two centuries ago: by focusing manufacturing in line with a country's relative advantage and engaging in trade with others, overall productivity (and thus societal welfare) is increased for all.[7] Ricardo illustrated his point with trade in wine and cloth between England and Portugal. The maths is somewhat counterintuitive, but the upshot is simple: specialisation and trade will yield more wine and cloth than 'autarky', where each state is left to fend for itself.

Over time, patterns of trade can allow countries to specialise in exports that make the most of their natural and human resources ('production factors' to economists), whilst importing goods that would be more difficult and expensive to make.[8] The benefits of trade are not limited to increased production:

---

[5] European Union, 'The Schuman Declaration – 9 May 1950', https://perma.cc/ZVJ5-93RB.

[6] 'Special report: Why trade is good for you' *The Economist* (London, 1 October 1998), https://www.economist.com/special-report/1998/10/01/why-trade-is-good-for-you.

[7] D Ricardo, *On the Principles of Political Economy and Taxation*, 3rd edn (John Murray 1821).

[8] This is developed in the so-called *Heckscher-Ohlin* theorem: M Blaug, 'The Heckscher-Ohlin theory of international trade' in M Blaug, *The Methodology of Economics – Or How Economists Explain*, 2nd edn (Cambridge University Press 2009).

once no longer shackled to small domestic markets, companies will be able to engage in intensive competition with each other, innovating and becoming more efficient. Producers furthermore enjoy 'economies of scale', where the average cost of producing each unit falls as more are produced. These benefits are passed on to (or at least shared with) consumers, who will be able to enjoy a wider range of products at lower prices, whilst sustaining long-term economic growth.[9]

Explaining these benefits to the governments of ECSC Member States, the Belgian Foreign Minister Paul-Henri Spaak warned in 1956 that any attempt to ensure Europe's successful development would quickly 'run into the too narrow limits of Europe's separate markets.'[10] As a result, the creation of a common market was nothing short of an 'absolute necessity' to ensure a 'powerful unit of production', 'an accelerated rise in living standards', and, crucially, the 'development of harmonious relations between the countries it brings together'.[11]

Achieving Free Trade in Europe

What precisely did Spaak mean by the 'too narrow limits' of separate markets? Economist have identified a wide range of obstacles or barriers to free trade – from tariffs to diverging product standards. *Tariffs* (sometimes also known as customs duties) are taxes levied when goods cross borders. At the time of writing, for example, the United States of America levy a tariff of 25 per cent on wines from a number of major EU countries (who just happen to be key players in the Airbus consortium).[12] The negative impact on trade is straightforward: every $10 bottle of Malvasia is $2.50 more expensive than a similarly priced Californian Pinot Blanc, creating a strong incentive for American oenophiles to stick to local produce.

Obstacles to trade are by no means limited to tariffs. A wide range of so-called *non-tariff barriers* can have a functionally similar impact.[13] Countries might impose complete embargoes or quotas (rice imports from Vietnam into the EU, for example, are limited to 80,000 tonnes per year)[14] or find more subtle ways to harass traders, such as long-winded customs checks at the border

[9] World Trade Organisation (WTO), 'Understanding the WTO: Basics – The case for open trade', https://perma.cc/T9P4-CAN2.

[10] Comité Intergouvernemental crée par la Conférence de Messine, 'Rapport des Chefs de Délégation aux Ministres des Affaires Etrangères' (Secrétariat, 21 April 1956), https://perma.cc/XM9A-VE6E, p. 10.

[11] Comité Intergouvernemental crée par la Conférence de Messine, 'Rapport des Chefs de Délégation aux Ministres des Affaires Etrangères', p. 13.

[12] C Mercer, 'Champagne avoids US tariffs over French digital tax' (*Decanter*, 16 July 2020), https://perma.cc/97ME-Y98U.

[13] WTO, 'Understanding the WTO: The agreements – Non-tariff barriers: red tape, etc', https://perma.cc/KAJ8-UAQC.

[14] 'Rice exports to EU remain modest due to limited quota' (*Voice of Vietnam*, 8 June 2020), https://perma.cc/JWM2-55ZH.

(a 17-km traffic jam at the Turkish–Bulgarian border can delay imports by more than 30 hours, at an estimated cost of €3 billion per year[15]).

Trade barriers may even exist 'behind the border'.[16] Neutral tax regimes can have a disproportionate impact on imported goods – for example, where a traditionally beer-drinking country taxes wine at higher rates. So-called *technical barriers to trade* include a wide range of 'regulations, standards, testing and certification procedures'. From requiring safety equipment on woodworking machines to specifying minimum alcohol contents for fruit liqueurs, technical barriers can be 'a nightmare for manufacturers and exporters'.[17]

Free trade, finally, may also be hindered or distorted by a wide range of other barriers driven by states or private actors – from government subsidies for particular industries and the deliberate 'dumping' of cheap goods into a foreign market to fluctuating exchange rates and the burning of Spanish strawberries by irate French farmers.[18]

Put together, the cost of these barriers (or the 'cost of non-Europe', as several reports have styled it) can be vast, whether in terms of lost opportunities for GDP growth or job creation.[19] Removing them can be legally and politically tricky (more on which soon), which explains the dynamic evolution of the Internal Market. Economic integration is not a binary choice. Free trade can have many different flavours, depending on how many types of barriers we are willing to abolish for it – from merely waving tariffs to adopting a single currency and fiscal policy.[20]

To get a sense of the choices made by the Member States in setting up the Internal Market, let us take a closer look at how the Treaties tackle (some, but by no means all) of the potential barriers we have just identified. Border tariffs, or customs duties on imports and exports, as well as charges having equivalent effect are clearly illegal under Article 30 TFEU. Tariffs no longer exist within

---

[15] M Srivastava and A Barker, 'Turkey border gridlock hints at pain to come for Brexit Britain' (*Financial Times*, London, 16 February 2017), https://perma.cc/KZ8H-GGZ4.

[16] J Francois and B Hoekman (eds), *Behind-the-Border Policies: Assessing and Addressing Non-tariff Measures* (Cambridge University Press 2019).

[17] WTO, 'Understanding the WTO: The agreements – Standards and safety', https://perma.cc/QRL7-5QRE.

[18] Case C-265/95 *Commission v France* [1997] ECR I-6959.

[19] Though difficult to quantify: for an early attempt, see P Cecchini, M Catinat, and A Jacquemin, *The European Challenge 1992: The Benefits of a Single Market* (Gower Publishing 1988); more recently, European Parliamentary Research Service, 'The cost of non-Europe in the single market: I – Free movement of goods' (European Parliament, September 2014), https://perma.cc/WHY8-F27T.

[20] Political economists think of these different arrangements along a gradated spectrum, from mere Free Trade Areas through to Political Union: AM El-Agraa, *The European Union: Economics and Policies*, 9th edn (Cambridge University Press 2011), Chapter 1. See also T Heller and J Pelkmans, 'The federal economy: Law and economic integration and the positive state – The U.S.A. and Europe compared in an economic perspective' in M Cappelletti and others (eds), *Integration Through Law: Europe and the American Federal Experience. A Political, Legal and Economic Overview* (De Gruyter 1985).

the Union – although you have already encountered them in one high-profile case; *Van Gend en Loos*.[21] The prohibition has been construed widely so as to catch other charges and levies that might indirectly burden cross-border traders, such as attempts to pass on the cost of phytosanitary inspections.[22] As we shall explore in detail below, the Treaties also forbid all quantitative restrictions on imports and exports, including quotas and complete embargoes.

The Internal Market does not stop at the frontier: EU law also carefully scrutinises what goes on *inside* national markets, at least where there is an impact on cross-border trade. 'Internal taxation', for example, is tackled by Article 110 TFEU. Even where Member States do not *explicitly* tax foreign goods at a higher rate, they may well end up doing so indirectly by enacting supposedly neutral rules that end up favouring domestic producers. A country with a long tradition of brewing beer domestically but importing most of its wine could charge much higher rates of tax on wine – even though, as the Court of Justice drily pointed out, 'the two beverages in question were capable of meeting identical needs'.[23] As a result, the UK's 'tax system [had] the effect of subjecting wine imported from other Member States to an additional tax burden so as to afford protection to domestic beer production … [by] stamp[ing] wine with the hallmarks of a luxury product'.[24] Most importantly, Articles 34 and 35 TFEU also catch 'all measures having equivalent effect' to quantitative restrictions. Designed to eliminate 'behind the border' trade barriers, the interpretation of this provision has become highly controversial in defining the scope of the Internal Market.

It is important to remember, finally, that free movement rules are not alone in creating the Internal Market. Distinct areas of EU law – from detailed provisions on state-aid through to intricate fiscal rules for the Eurozone – set out to achieve Spaak's vision. At the same time, we are far from harmonisation, even in crucial trade-related areas such as value-added tax (VAT), which can vary dramatically across different Member States.[25] Just ask Swedish consumers, who have to rely on 'booze cruises' and similarly adventurous routes to dash across to Denmark, Germany, or the Baltics to evade high domestic taxes on alcohol. Half of all domestically consumed spirits are procured that way.[26]

---

[21] Case 26-62 *NV Algemene Transport–en Expeditie Onderneming van Gend en Loos v Netherlands Inland Revenue Administration* [1963] ECR 2.

[22] See, e.g., Case 87-75 *Conceria Daniele Bresciani v Amministrazione Italiana delle Finanze* [1976] ECR 129. Member States are allowed to recover costs which result from inspections mandated by the Union: Case 18/87 *European Commission v Germany* [1988] ECR 5427.

[23] Case 170/78 *Commission v United Kingdom* [1983] ECR 2265 [8]. Cf., on similar facts, Case C-167/05 *Commission v Sweden* [2008] ECR I-2127.

[24] *Commission v United Kingdom* [27].

[25] Although there is a complicated coordination regime: Council Directive 2006/112/EC of 28 November 2006 on the common system of value added tax [2006] OJ L347/1.

[26] D Crouch, 'Sweden's strict controls drive "booze-cruise" economy' (*Financial Times*, London, 22 February 2017), https://perma.cc/89JX-U3D7.

(B) The Cost of Free Trade

The success story of free trade which we have seen thus far has by no means gone unchallenged.[27] When enthusiastically presented with the benefits of liberalised markets, we should be careful also to remember the potential cost of unlocking any such gains – and thus the importance of appropriate regulatory mechanisms to strike the right balance.

The Dark Side of the Moon

Perhaps the single most important challenge to Ricardo's rosy picture of free trade is that his model is completely agnostic as to how the additional gains from cosmopolitan trade are distributed. The focus is on 'growing the size of the pie', rather than divvying it up into equal slices, even though it is obvious that the gains of free trade do not accrue uniformly.[28] In the basic comparative advantage model, shareholders who have invested in setting up cloth factories in the North of England will stand to gain handsomely, whereas Portuguese weavers find themselves out of a job and livelihood.

The negative impact on workers employed to produce goods in which their country does not enjoy a comparative advantage is not necessarily limited to factory restructurings: they will also suffer from downward pressures on wages, and the unintended side effects of innovation. The orthodox assumption that free trade will always increase the pie for workers, at the very least by making cheaper and more diverse products available to them, does not necessarily hold true either. If there is persistent downward pressure on real wages, even cheap imported goods will ultimately become unaffordable.[29] Furthermore, rapid advancements in innovation and productivity may stoke technological unemployment, as jobs across the socioeconomic spectrum are threatened by automation and the rise of artificial intelligence.[30]

The negative aspects of free trade regimes are by no means limited to these redistributive questions (which could, in principle at least, be addressed through taxation and wealth transfers). Consumers will suffer where trade liberalisation opens up markets to unhealthy or downright dangerous products. Think of the much-decried US practice of washing chicken meat with chlorinated water, which is explicitly banned on health grounds in the EU.[31] Excessive

---

[27] At the global level, see, e.g., H-J Chang, *Bad Samaritans: The Guilty Secrets of Rich Nations and The Threat to Global Prosperity* (Random House 2008).

[28] AS Blinder, 'The free-trade paradox: The bad politics of a good idea' (*Foreign Affairs*, New York, January/February 2019), https://perma.cc/WTY6-68LB.

[29] PA Samuelson, 'Where Ricardo and Mill rebut and confirm arguments of mainstream economists supporting globalization' (2004) 18(3) J Econ Perspect 135.

[30] C Estlund, 'What should we do after work? Automation and employment law' (2018) 128(2) Yale LJ 254. A further, related dimension is the free movement of workers across Member States with vastly different wage levels, as discussed in Chapter 9, Debate 1.

[31] EFSA AFC Panel, 'Opinion of the AFC Panel on a request from the Commission related to treatment of poultry carcasses with chlorine dioxide, acidified sodium chlorite, trisodium phosphate and peroxyacids' (2005) 297 EFSA Journal 1; EFSA BIOHAZ Panel, CONTAM Panel and AHAW Panel, 'Scientific opinion on the public health hazards to be covered by inspection of meat (poultry)' (2012) 10(6) EFSA J 2741.

production levels also go hand in hand with so-called externalities – unseen costs not born by the producer, most notably including environmental pollution.

At the macro-economic level, liberalised trade may even end up *discouraging* competition by allowing large multinational players to emerge at the expense of small and medium-sized enterprises – harming consumers both directly through monopoly exploitation, and indirectly through regulatory capture and arbitrage. These risks are particularly high where individual Member States or local areas retain some regulatory flexibility, for example when it comes to enforcing environmental standards. They might be tempted to skew the playing field in their favour, leading to regulatory competition and a 'race to the bottom' where the lowest standard prevails.

Last, but by no means least (depending on your dietary habits, at least), are real concerns that trade rules attack some of the more attractive national quirks and niches embedded in centuries of local market regulation – from kipferl to croissants.

Saving Sicilian Salami

The fact that liberalised trade has its problems should not tempt us into agreeing with Donald Trump, who proudly proclaims to be 'a Tariff Man'.[32] Instead, we need to ask the more important (and complex) question as to how the Union's legal system should deal with 'non-market values'.[33] Not every obstacle to trade is necessarily a bad thing. No one wants poisonous food or dangerous toys to circulate freely. Workers must be protected against discriminatory dismissals and the environment against waste dumping and pollution. We might even want countries to protect genuine national traditions and quirks (to a point!).

EU law has developed a series of tools to balance free trade in the Internal Market against competing considerations. For present purposes, this means in particular the justification mechanism to which we will return in Debate 3: Article 36 TFEU opens the way to Member States justifying practices where they restrict trade in a proportionate manner. This mechanism has been extended by the CJEU to cover a wide range of considerations, from consumer protection to fundamental (human) rights.[34] Whilst the scope of Articles 34 and 35 TFEU is key in *challenging* trade barriers, the interpretation of Article 36 TFEU provides the crucial counterweight in balancing the benefits of liberalisation against its dangers.

[32] Donald Trump, 'I am a Tariff Man' (*Twitter*, 4 December 2018), https://twitter.com/realdonaldtrump/status/1069970500535902208.

[33] B de Witte, 'Non-market values in Internal Market legislation' in N Nic Shuibhne (ed), *Regulating the Internal Market* (Edward Elgar 2006).

[34] Case 120/78 *Rewe-Zentral AG v Bundesmonopolverwaltung für Branntwein* [1979] ECR 649 (*Cassis de Dijon*).

Just as the creation of the Internal Market is not left to free movement rules alone, the protection of competing interests is visible throughout the Treaties.[35] We have already encountered one key device in Chapter 2: Article 114 TFEU is designed to establish EU-wide standards. It is joined by specific competences, ranging from the common agricultural policy,[36] environmental and labour regulation, and consumer protection, through to major areas of Union regulatory activity, such as competition law (designed to deal with inappropriate state aid), and abuses of market concentration). There is even a special scheme of 'geographical indications'[37] to celebrate and protect a veritable smorgasbord of national (culinary) treasures – from Croatia's *Paški sir*[38] (a hard sheep cheese from northern Dalmatia) to Lithuania's hard and crumbly *Džiugas*.[39]

(C) A Market Without Internal Frontiers

This, then, is the fundamental tension which continues to shape the development of the Internal Market. Article 26 TFEU sets out a clear commitment to free cross-border trade, defining the Internal Market as 'an area without internal frontiers in which the free movement of goods, persons, services and capital is ensured'.[40] At the same time, Article 3(3) TEU reminds us that the market is not an end in itself:

> [It] shall work for the sustainable development of Europe based on balanced economic growth and price stability, a highly competitive social market economy, aiming at full employment and social progress, and a high level of protection and improvement of the quality of the environment.

---

[35] Though the inclusion of equal pay in the EEC Treaty was primarily a way of protecting France from unfair competition: J Snell, 'The Internal Market and the philosophies of market integration' in C Barnard and S Peers (eds), *European Union Law*, 3rd edn (Oxford University Press 2020).

[36] Remember how many of the cases you encountered in the (early) constitutional debates of the EU revolved around such mesmerising questions as the cold-storage of pig meat, compulsory recycling of milk powder, and distillation of surplus wine? Revisit them in the light of this debate – does the Court strike the right balance?

[37] European Parliament and Council Regulation (EU) No 1151/2012 of 21 November 2012 on quality schemes for agricultural products and foodstuffs [2012] OJ L343/1. A full list can be found in '*e*Ambrosia – the EU geographical indications register' at https://ec.europa.eu/info/food-farming-fisheries/food-safety-and-quality/certification/quality-labels/geographical-indications-register.

[38] Commission Implementing Regulation (EU) 2019/1940 of 15 November 2019 entering a name in the register of protected designations of origin and protected geographical indications 'Paški sir' (PDO) [2019] OJ L303/25.

[39] Commission Implementing Regulation (EU) 2019/972 of 7 June 2019 entering a name in the register of protected designations of origin and protected geographical indications ('Džiugas' (PGI)) [2019] OJ L157/1.

[40] TFEU, Article 26(1).

Can the narrow definition of Article 26 TFEU deliver on Article 3 TEU's ambitious goals?[41] It is easy in principle to assert that the emphasis in EU law is on ensuring free *cross-border* trade (rather than free, unlimited trade) as an end in and of itself – and that careful definitions of illegal trade barriers and the justification mechanism provide clear lines to protect domestic regulatory choices.

The reality, of course, is much messier – not least because companies will frequently try to push trade law to its limits (and beyond) in challenging domestic rules. In the *Sunday Trading* saga,[42] for example, a UK do-it-yourself and home improvement chain sought to overturn a domestic law closing their stores on Sundays by arguing that this resulted in lower sales – including of products imported from other Member States.

Have you spotted the red herring? By focusing on their impact on *cross-border trade volume*, domestic rules look like they should have been caught by Article 34 TFEU: Sunday closure means that British consumers will buy fewer Spanish tiles. Taken to its logical extremes, however, this would mean that just about *any* form of national regulation – from minimum wage laws to bans on the sale of alcohol to children – could be a trade barrier and *prima facie* illegal. If we look at the same rules through a *discrimination* lens, it quickly becomes obvious that imported and domestic goods suffer equally: British charcoal and German chainsaw sales will take the same hit.

Ultimately, markets are state constructs, and free trade is not the only goal. This is a tension which we already encountered in Chapter 2. Let us now return to it in the context of the two key debates in free movement law: How should we define trade barriers (i.e. which national rules should be scrutinised)? And when might they nonetheless be justified (thus opening a space for domestic consumer and environmental protection, labour rights, and cultural sensitivities)?

Debate 2

What is a trade barrier?

Articles 34 and 35 TFEU are perhaps the single most important tools in the Internal Market's regulatory arsenal, stipulating that

> Quantitative restrictions on imports/exports and all measures having equivalent effect shall be prohibited between Member States.

Behind this apparent simplicity hides a host of interpretative difficulties. Remember how barriers to trade range from the blindingly obvious

[41] I Lianos, 'Shifting narratives in the European Internal Market: Efficient restrictions of trade and the nature of "economic" integration' (2010) 21(5) Eur Bus L Rev 705.

[42] Case C-145/88 *Torfaen BC v B&Q Plc* [1989] ECR 3851; Case C-169/91 *Stoke-on-Trent CC v B&Q Plc* [1992] ECR I-6635.

(a complete ban on imports of a particular foreign good) to difficult and controversial 'behind-the-border' obstacles (such as a food safety rules)? The scope of Articles 34 and 35 TFEU is key in determining how far EU trade law will go to combat them – and yet the bare-bones wording creates space for a vast range of competing interpretations. It is not surprising, then, that the definition of a trade barrier continues to evolve, driven by intense controversies, particularly as regards the outer boundaries.[43] Think of the following categories as spheres expanding outwards – starting with an uncontroversial core of quantitative restrictions and direct discrimination, surrounded by a broader category of neutral requirements with disparate impacts, and extending to the contentious domain of 'general' market regulation, including the use and marketing of products.

(A) Easy Cases: Quantitative Restrictions and Measures of Equivalent Effect

The inner core of Article 34 TFEU is pretty straightforward. Quantitative restrictions have been defined by the Court of Justice as any measure that amounts to 'a total or partial restraint of, according to the circumstances, imports, exports or goods in transit'.[44]

That said, they are not unheard of. On occasion, Member States have tried to ban the import of particular products, such as pork into Italy[45] or French turkeys into the UK.[46] Export bans are even rarer, as they are unlikely to be in a country's economic interests, but again there have been exceptions: Spain, for example, used to limit the export of bulk (unbottled) Rioja wine to 600 hectolitres;[47] more recently, export bans were imposed on personal protective equipment and medical supplies during the early stages of the COVID-19 pandemic.[48]

Article 34 TFEU also covers the stoppage of goods in transit – such as the overzealous customs officer at Heathrow airport, who, in October 1982, seized

[43] This development has primarily taken place in the context of Article 34 TFEU, the interpretation of which will therefore form the bulk of our discussion. The scope of Article 34 TFEU was long held to be narrower by an emphasis on explicit discrimination in Case 15/79 *P.B. Groenveld BV v Produktschap voor Vee en Vlees* [1979] ECR 3409; but see now Case C-205/07 *Lodewijk Gysbrechts and Santurel Inter BVBA* [2008] ECR I-9947.

[44] Case 2/73 *Riseria Luigi Geddo v Ente Nazionale Risi* [1973] ECR 865 [7].

[45] Case 7/61 *Commission v Italy* EU:C:1961:31.

[46] Case 40/82 *Commission v United Kingdom* [1982] ECR 2793.

[47] Case C-47/90 *Établissements Delhaize frères and Compagnie Le Lion SA v Promalvin SA and AGE Bodegas Unidas SA* [1992] ECR I-3669 (*Delhaize*).

[48] Bundesministerium für Wirtschaft und Energie, Anordnung von Beschränkungen im Außenwirtschaftsverkehr mit bestimmten Gütern vom: 04.03.2020 (BAnz AT 04.03.2020 B1) (DE); Bundesministerium für Wirtschaft und Energie, Anordnung von Beschränkungen im Außenwirtschaftsverkehr mit bestimmten Gütern vom: 12.03.2020 (BAnz AT 04.03.2020 B1) (DE).

several crates of erotic paraphernalia[49] – as well as state inaction. The French government's persistent failure to reign in angry farmers attacking Spanish imports was caught by Article 34 TFEU,[50] as was the Austrian government's authorisation of a demonstration on the Brenner motorway, a key trade route between Italy and Germany.[51]

In addition to quantitative restrictions, Article 34 TFEU also covers provisions that directly discriminate against goods on grounds of their origin ('distinctly applicable' rules). While not quantitative restrictions as such, they can be hidden attempts to achieve a similar outcome (i.e. boost the sale of domestic goods at the expense of imported ones). To put it in Treaty terms, they are 'measures of equivalent effect' (MEQRs). Classic illustrations of MEQRs include schemes to entice citizens (even if indirectly and unsuccessfully) to 'Buy Irish'[52] or to label goods with their country of origin (enabling customers 'to assert any prejudices which they may have against foreign products').[53]

The CJEU's definition of MEQRs, however, is not limited to scenarios of outright discrimination. Indeed, the iconic definition of MEQRs explicitly eschews the notion. In *Dassonville*, a father and son duo had been charged with forgery in breach of a Belgian law that required fine Scotch whisky to be sold with a certificate of origin. Importing Scotch from France, rather than directly from the UK, meant that they had been unable to procure the relevant certificates and invented their own labels instead. Their defence was to invoke Article 34 TFEU, arguing that the Belgian rules involved a 'strict walling-off of markets' and should therefore be characterised as an MEQR. The Court of Justice readily agreed, in the process laying down a formula which continues to resonate to this day:

> All trading rules enacted by Member States which are capable of hindering, directly or indirectly, actually or potentially, intra-Community trade are to be considered as measures having an effect equivalent to quantitative restrictions.[54]

The *Dassonville* formula has been praised for its 'magnificent sweep'.[55] It is hard to overstate the breadth and depth of its potential reach: focusing on a measure's *impact* on cross-border trade, and including indirect as well as potential obstacles, the Court's approach is 'best appreciated as a calculated wrench away from a mere anti-discrimination norm … a major choice with

---

[49] Case 121/85 *Conegate Ltd v HM Customs & Excise* [1986] ECR 1007.

[50] Case C-265/95 *Commission v France* [1997] ECR I-6959.

[51] Case C-112/00 *Eugen Schmidberger, Internationale Transporte und Planzüge v Austria* [2003] ECR I-5659.

[52] Case 249/81 *Commission v Ireland* [1982] ECR 4005.

[53] Case 207/83 *Commission v United Kingdom* [1985] ECR 1201.

[54] Case 8/74 *Procureur du Roi v Benoît and Gustave Dassonville* [1974] ECR 837 (*Dassonville*) [5].

[55] Lord Cockfield, 'Address to the Beama Symposium on the Internal Market' (The Beama Seminar, London, 22 February 1988), https://perma.cc/ZF72-3JPJ.

immense implications for the shape of the Internal Market.'[56] In concrete terms, just about any kind of market regulation could be caught in its cross-hairs, including more recent attempts to set minimum unit prizes for the sale of Scotch whisky and other alcoholic beverages.[57] That is good news, insofar as decades (or even, as we are about to see, centuries) of frankly bizarre regulatory deadwood are concerned. But it is also potentially disastrous when we think about important counterweights to trade liberalisation.

(B) Indistinctly Applicable Rules: Technical Standards

In the short term, the CJEU was undeterred in expanding the scope of Article 34 TFEU. The next frontier was so-called indistinctly applicable rules or measures. The *cause célèbre* proved to be Article 100(3) of Germany's *Branntweinmonopolgesetz*, which stipulated a minimum alcohol content of 32 per cent for spirits to be sold in the Federal Republic. Rewe, a major German supermarket chain, sought to import French liqueurs – including (much to the chagrin of saccharophobic professors of EU law) a sickly-sweet red blackcurrant liqueur called *Cassis de Dijon*, with an alcohol content of 15 to 25 per cent. When Rewe were denied permission to import Cassis, they invoked Article 34 TFEU: 'the fixing by the German rules of a minimum alcohol content leads to the result that well-known spirits products from other Member States of the Community cannot be sold in the Federal Republic of Germany'.[58] Once more, the Court enthusiastically sided with the traders: 'disparities between the national laws relating to the marketing of ... products', it asserted without much further explanation, result in '[o]bstacles to movement within the Community'.[59] The message is clear: even 'neutral' product standards that do not single out products produced in a particular country can cause serious disruption to the Internal Market – for example, where they require different manufacturing or packaging setups – and will therefore be caught by EU law.

Cassis de Dijon was enthusiastically embraced by the Union institutions and traders alike.[60] There ensued a veritable bonfire of domestic regulations, not without a serious whiff of national stereotyping. Think German laws on beer purity (the medieval *Reinheitsgebot* limiting ingredients to water, barley, hops,

---

[56] S Weatherill, *Law and Values in the European Union* (Oxford University Press 2016), p. 315.

[57] Case C-333/14 *Scotch Whisky Association and ors v The Lord Advocate and the Advocate General for Scotland* EU:C:2015:845. At the same time, even in *Dassonville* (n 54) itself, the Court acknowledged that there could be space for consumer protective rules as long as they were 'reasonable' – i.e. 'not act as a hindrance of trade [and] be accessible to all [Union] nationals' [6].

[58] *Cassis de Dijon* (n 34) [4].

[59] *Cassis de Dijon* [8]. That is not the end of the story, of course: we will return to *Cassis de Dijon* in the next debate.

[60] L Gormley, '*Cassis de Dijon* and the Communication from the Commission' (1981) 6 EL Rev 454.

and yeast),[61] the shape of wine bottles,[62] and fair advertising (the space taken up by a promotional message extolling 10 per cent free extra content of ice-cream bars, which could not exceed the proportionate amount of packaging).[63] French rules specifying a minimum fat content of 40 per cent before cheese can be marketed as Edam,[64] and the safe construction of woodworking machines.[65] A Belgian law demanding that margarine be sold in cube shapes only.[66] Greek laws requiring professional baking setups before supermarkets can sell bread.[67] Italian rules on chocolate (no vegetable fat),[68] vinegar (fermented wine only, never from cider),[69] and of course, pasta (100 per cent durum wheat, if you please).[70] The list goes on and on.

Much of this is to be welcomed. Why should German consumers not be free to try a fine British ale or a Belgian sour beer? Why not let Italians decide what they think about black bean pasta or cider vinegar? (As for cube-shaped margarine, we cannot work it out either.) At the same time, however, the readier we are to recognise trade barriers, the closer we get to overexpanding market liberalisation. It is easy to make fun of bottle shapes and minimum alcohol contents, but what about limits on preservatives which might be carcinogens[71] or, indeed, Sunday trading?

(C) Generic Obstacles to Trade

It was the *Sunday Trading* saga that proved to be the straw that (possibly) broke the camel's back, having triggered extensive criticism in the literature. A broad interpretation of Article 34 TFEU, built on an analysis of the effect on trade levels irrespective of cross-border differences, risks drawing the CJEU into commercial disputes and value judgments far beyond the scope of Article 26 TFEU.[72] By late 1993, the time had come for the Court to recognise 'the increasing tendency of traders to invoke Article [34 TFEU] as a means of challenging any rules whose effect is to limit their commercial freedom even where such rules are not aimed at products from other Member

---

[61] Case 178/84 *Commission v Germany* [1987] ECR 1227.

[62] Case 16/83 *Criminal proceedings against Karl Prantl* [1984] ECR 1299.

[63] Case C-470/93 *Verein gegen Unwesen in Handel und Gewerbe Köln e.V. v Mars GmbH* [1995] ECR I-1923.

[64] Case 286/86 *Ministère public v Gérard Deserbais* [1988] ECR 4907.

[65] Case 188/84 *Commission v France* [1986] ECR 419.

[66] Case 261/81 *Walter Rau Lebensmittelwerke v De Smedt PVBA* [1982] ECR 3961.

[67] Case C-58/04 *Antje Köhler v Finanzamt Düsseldorf-Nord* [2005] ECR I-8219.

[68] Case C-14/00 *Commission v Italy* [2003] ECR I-513.

[69] Case 788/79 *Criminal proceedings against Herbert Gilli and Paul Andres* [1980] ECR 2071.

[70] Case 407/85 *3 Glocken GmbH and Gertraud Kritzinger v USL Centro-Sud and Provincia autonoma di Bolzano* [1988] ECR 4233.

[71] Case 53/80 *Officier van justitie v Koninklijke Kaasfabriek Eyssen BV* [1981] ECR 409 (*Kaasfabriek Eyssen*).

[72] E White, 'In search of the limits to Article 30 of the EEC Treaty' (1989) 26(2) CML Rev 235; L Gormley, 'Recent case law on the free movement of goods: Some hot potatoes' (1990) 27(4) CML Rev 825.

States', as a result of which it was 'necessary to re-examine and clarify [the] case-law on this matter'.[73]

This turn in the jurisprudence was triggered by the case of Messieurs *Keck and Mithouard*, who found themselves prosecuted for illegal sales at a loss – a common commercial strategy to get customers into shops. Their defence was inspired by the Dassonvilles', some 40 years earlier: the French prohibition, they contented, was incompatible with Article 34 TFEU.[74]

This time, however, the Court was much more careful in its scrutiny of domestic rules:

> By contrast [to Cassis de Dijon], contrary to what has previously been decided, the application to products from other Member States of national provisions restricting or prohibiting certain selling arrangements is not such as to hinder directly or indirectly, actually or potentially, trade between Member States within the meaning of the Dassonville judgment [...], so long as those provisions apply to all relevant traders operating within the national territory and so long as they affect in the same manner, in law and in fact, the marketing of domestic products and of those from other Member States.[75]

This two-pronged test looks like a marked retrenchment: out goes the emphasis on trade volume and in comes a reassertion of discrimination or differential impact. Mere selling arrangements, *viz* the application of a rule which does not prevent 'access to the market or [...] impede[s] access any more than it impedes the access of domestic products', were to fall outside the scope of Article 34 TFEU.[76] Upon closer inspection, however, it is not clear even on its own wording that *Keck* elevates discrimination over market access. Once more, what looks like a clean distinction drawn in principle would be much harder to enforce in practice: rather than completely excluding considerations of trade volume impact, the formulation in *Keck* readily invited clever arguments about the effect, *in fact*, of any given market regulation.

(D) Market Access: Having Your *Keck* and Eating It?[77]

In retrenching the scope of Article 34 TFEU in *Keck*, the Commission declared in 1993 that the CJEU had 'completed its case law'.[78] Well, not quite. Nearly

[73] Joined Cases C-267/91 and C-268/91 *Criminal proceedings against Bernard Keck and Daniel Mithouard* [1993] ECR I-6097 (*Keck*) [14].

[74] *Dassonville* (n 54) [3].

[75] *Keck* (n 73) [16].

[76] *Keck* [17].

[77] The ruling in *Keck* gave rise to a number of fine puns in the literature, including C Barnard, 'What the Keck? Balancing the needs of the single market with state regulatory autonomy' (2012) 2 Eur J Const L 201; and E Spaventa, 'Leaving Keck behind? The free movement of goods after the rulings in *Commission v. Italy* and *Mickelsson and Roos*' (2009) 34(6) EL Rev 914, from where this subtitle is taken.

[78] European Commission, 'Communication on management of the mutual recognition of national rules after 1992' [1993] OJ C353/4.

three decades on, that is hardly the case. Spurred on by traders and the Commission alike, the Court continues to define (and expand) the scope of its understanding of a trade barrier. The waters to be chartered are treacherous: draw the circle too narrowly, and markets will continue to be unnecessarily partitioned; draw it too widely, and risk becoming a tool for untrammelled deregulation. The Court's approach, broadly speaking, has been to 'cast the scope of Article [34 TFEU] as widely as the *Keck* framework will allow'.[79]

The first context in which *Keck* became the subject of intense scrutiny were domestic advertising restrictions, such as Sweden's *Alkoholreklamlagen*, which bans alcohol ads with the specific intent to reduce overall sales and consumption. However, the Swedish government insisted, pursuant to *Keck*, that the ban was not an obstacle to trade: the impact on domestic and foreign alcohol was the same, in law and in fact.[80] AG Jacobs, a long-standing (but hitherto unsuccessful) critic of the narrow approach taken in *Keck*,[81] was not convinced: given that consumers are creatures of habit, he argued, the 'role of advertising is primordial in launching a new product or in penetrating a new market.'[82] The Court agreed: 'in the case of products like alcoholic beverages, the consumption of which is linked to traditional social practices and to local habits and customs, a prohibition of all advertising [...] is liable to impede access to the market by products from other Member States more than it impedes access by domestic products, with which consumers are instantly more familiar'.[83] This can be characterised as holding onto to the elements in *Keck* which emphasise discrimination – but there is also a resurgence of market access itself as the key criterion.[84]

Another field in which the application of *Keck* has caused significant difficulty are so-called product use restriction cases – specifically, an Italian ban on motorbike-towed trailers and a Swedish ban on 'personal watercraft' (i.e. jet-skis). Relying on *Keck* by analogy, a large group of Member States argued that such rules should clearly fall outside the scope of Article 34 TFEU: all economic operators, and thus products, were affected equally.[85] Advocates General continued to diverge in their preferred approaches,[86] but the Court was clear:

[79] P Oliver and S Enchelmaier, 'Free movement of goods: Recent developments in the case law' (2007) 44(3) CML Rev 649, 683.

[80] Case C-405/98 *Konsumentombudsmannen v Gourmet International Products AB* [2001] ECR I-1795 (*GIP*) [14]–[15].

[81] See, e.g., his opinion in Case C-412/93 *Société d'Importation Edouard Leclerc-Siplec v TF1 Publicité SA and M6 Publicité SA* [1995] ECR I-179.

[82] *GIP* (n 80), Opinion of AG Jacobs [36].

[83] *GIP* [21].

[84] See A Biondi, 'Advertising alcohol and the free movement principle' (2001) 26(6) EL Rev 616.

[85] Case C-110/05 *Commission v Italy* [2009] ECR I-519 [22] (*Moped Trailers*).

[86] Compare the arguments of AG Kokott in Case C-142/05 *Åklagaren v Percy Mickelsson and Joakim Roos* [2009] (Alfa Vita) ECR I-4273, and AGs Léger and Bot in *Moped Trailers*. Cf. also AG Poiares Maduro in Joined Cases C-158/04 and C-159/04 *Alfa Vita Vassilopoulos AE and Carrefour Marinopoulos AE v Elliniko Dimosio and Nomarchiaki Aftodioikisi Ionninon* [2006] ECR I-8135 (*Alfa Vita*). For more on *Moped Trailers'* unusual procedural history, see R Grahn, 'Free movement of goods, motorcycle trailers, product use and road safety: Case C-110/05' (*EU Law Blog*, 16 February 2009), https://perma.cc/K6HN-G7MP.

both use prohibitions fell within the scope of Article 34 TFEU. Italy's ban had 'a considerable influence on the behaviour of consumers, which, in its turn, affects the access of that product to the market of that Member State'. This suppression of consumer demand was a clear hindrance of trailer importation,[87] as was the lack of waterways on which jet-skis could be enjoyed in Sweden.[88]

Where does this leave us? Barnard suggests that '*Trailers* and *Mickelsson* send out a strong message that the market access test has returned to Article 34 TFEU'.[89] Spaventa is less sure 'whether the cases ... have substituted the *Keck* exception in favour of a unified market access test'. Does it matter that the Grand Chamber was trying to 'have its *Keck*' and eat it? That depends, she argues: from 'a practical viewpoint, the choice ... might not make much difference', not least given a potentially more generous approach to justifications. When it comes to legal certainty, and even more importantly, the ultimate question as to what we mean by 'market access', and thus our broader conception of the internal market, on the other hand, 'the choice ... is of fundamental importance and one might be excused to feel a certain sense of frustration at the Grand Chamber's lack of clarity'.[90]

Debate 3

When can a trade barrier be justified?

Establishing a trade barrier is not the end of the story. Member States may still be able to justify local regulation, demonstrating that it constitutes a proportionate means of achieving a legitimate aim. In the final debate, we thus turn to look at the range of available justifications. Broadly speaking, we will discover two categories: the narrow exceptions contained in Article 36 TFEU; and (at least in the case of nondiscriminatory trade barriers, although the long-mooted distinction between directly and indirectly applicable measures is increasingly muddled[91]) so-called mandatory requirements – from consumer protection to fundamental rights.

As you work your way through the justifications, think back to the first debate in this chapter. The kind of justifications we are willing to accept tell us a lot about what market we want. More broadly, the interplay between trade barriers and justifications also takes us back to the underlying issue of the scope of EU law and Member States' regulatory competence.[92] On the face of it,

---

[87] *Moped Trailers* (n 85) [56]–[57].

[88] C-617/10 *Åklagaren v Hans Åkerberg Fransson* [2013] ECR I-9011 [25]–[28].

[89] C Barnard, *The Substantive Law of the EU: The Four Freedoms*, 6th edn (Oxford University Press 2019), p. 101.

[90] Spaventa, 'Leaving Keck behind?' (n 77), 921–22.

[91] This distinction has occasionally been challenged; see, e.g., Case C-379/98 *PreussenElektra AG v Schhleswag AG* [2001] ECR I-2099, Opinion of AG Jacobs; but to no avail. In reality, Barnard has suggested, the distinction is becoming less important, not least as a result of *Moped Trailers* (n 85) (Barnard, *The Substantive Law of the EU* (n 89), p. 146).

[92] Cf. Chapter 2, Debate 2.

there is no difference in outcome if we adopt an extensive definition of trade barriers and then accept the Member State's justification, or simply find a domestic measure not to come within the scope of Article 34 TFEU at all.[93] In practice, however, the former approach will require intensive scrutiny of domestic choices, putting domestic regulators on the back foot in having to explain themselves.

(A) Article 36 TFEU

EU law has always recognised *some* limits to trade, even within the Internal Market. The original vehicle to achieve this balance is Article 36 TFEU:

> The provisions of Articles 34 and 35 shall not preclude prohibitions or restrictions on imports, exports or goods in transit justified on grounds of public morality, public policy or public security; the protection of health and life of humans, animals or plants; the protection of national treasures possessing artistic, historic or archaeological value; or the protection of industrial and commercial property. Such prohibitions or restrictions shall not, however, constitute a means of arbitrary discrimination or a disguised restriction on trade between Member States.

We should note two things: first, the list of exceptions; and second, the explicit caution against 'arbitrary discrimination' and 'disguised restrictions'. As regards the specific exemptions, the list is short and substantively narrow. It is rare – but not impossible – for a Member State to rely successfully on Article 36 TFEU: derogations from Treaty rights have consistently been interpreted narrowly. Public policy, 'one of the most misunderstood of the justifications', is to be construed particularly narrowly;[94] it could not, for example, 'be extended so as to include … consumer protection'.[95] Public and environmental health arguments have had somewhat more purchase: it makes sense to protect endangered bee species,[96] ban the import of poultry meat during infectious outbreaks,[97] or limit sales of muesli bars with added vitamins due to concerns about excess consumption.[98] That said, public morality has been invoked successfully to justify the seizure of pornographic material, with the Court allowing a certain amount of discretion for Member States to determine their 'own scale of values'.[99]

---

[93] Compare, albeit in the context of the Free Movement of Services, the Opinion of AG Van Gerven and the Court's decision in C-159/90 *SPUC Ireland Ltd v Stephen Grogan and ors* [1991] ECR I-4685.

[94] L Gormley, *EU Law of Free Movement of Goods and Customs Union* (Oxford University Press 2009), paragraph 11.65.

[95] Case 177/83 *Th. Kohl KG v Ringelhan & Rennett SA and RIngelhan Einrichtungs GmbH* [1984] ECR 3651 [19].

[96] Case C-67/97 *Criminal proceedings against Ditlev Bluhme* [1998] ECR I-8033.

[97] *Commission v UK* (n 46).

[98] Case 174/82 *Criminal proceedings against Sandoz BV* [1983] ECR 2445.

[99] Case 34/79 *R v Maurice Donald Henn and John Frederick Ernest Darby* [1979] ECR 3795 [15].

Even where a justification is applicable in principle, however, the Court will be careful to ensure that it does not serve to camouflage arbitrary discrimination. It is not possible to justify the seizure of consignments of 'Love Love Dolls' and 'Sexy Vacuum Flasks' on public morality grounds when similar items can freely be manufactured and marketed domestically.[100] The same is true for disguised restrictions: upon closer scrutiny, the UK ban on poultry imports we encountered in the previous debate turned out to be primarily targeted at the sale of French turkeys at Christmas.[101] That said, public health arguments have occasionally been helped along by the so-called precautionary principle:[102] due to the scientific uncertainty about the impact of a particular preservative in cheese, for example, the Netherlands were permitted to limit its use – not least given the 'dietary habits of their own population'.[103]

(B) Mandatory Requirements

The narrow design of Article 36 TFEU makes sense in principle: states should only be allowed to engage in explicit discrimination in very limited circumstances, lest the Internal Market be undone. Drafted as an exhaustive list, the CJEU was understandably reluctant to widen its scope.[104] At the same time, however, the Court has continued to push the definition of trade barriers far beyond outright discrimination, potentially catching a much wider range of measures. This, in turn, necessitated an expanded list of potential justifications.

We have already encountered the watershed case of *Cassis de Dijon*. Whilst disparities between national standards could fall within the scope of Article 34 TFEU, the Court recognised that such obstacles 'must be accepted in so far as those provisions may be recognized as being necessary in order to satisfy ***mandatory requirements***.'[105] The translation is clumsy – Weatherill suggests that 'compelling interests' would be a more appropriate rendition of ***zwingende Erfordernisse*** or ***exigences imperatives***[106] – but the label has stuck, and the principle is clear enough. If domestic rules 'serve a purpose which is in the general interest', they are allowed 'to take precedence over the requirements of the free movement of goods'.[107]

In *Cassis de Dijon*, the Court suggested that mandatory requirements could include 'the effectiveness of fiscal supervision, the protection of public health,

---

[100] *Conegate* (n 49), Opinion of AG Slynn [11].

[101] *Commission v UK* (n 46) [24], [40].

[102] On the ensuing game of 'precaution spotting', see E Fisher, 'Precaution, precaution everywhere: Developing "common understanding" of the precautionary principle in the European community' (2002) 9 Maastricht J Eur Comp L 7.

[103] *Kaasfabriek Eyssen* (n 71) [14].

[104] Case 113/80 *Commission v Ireland* [1981] ECR 1625 [7].

[105] *Cassis de Dijon* (n 34) [8] [emphasis added].

[106] Weatherill, *Law and Values* (n 56), p. 331.

[107] *Cassis de Dijon* (n 34) [14].

the fairness of commercial transactions and the defence of the consumer'.[108] The list has continued to expand ever since, notably to include 'the protection of the environment'.[109] Perhaps the most significant addition, however, was the recognition of human rights as mandatory requirements.

The Union's fundamental (economic) freedoms were pitched directly against fundamental (human) rights in *Schmidberger*, when the Austrian government sought to justify the closure of the Brenner motorway by reference to protesters' 'freedoms of expression and assembly, since fundamental rights are inviolable in a democratic society'.[110] The Court was receptive. Having rehearsed its well-established commitment to fundamental rights as general principles of EU law, it concluded that

> since both the [EU] and its Member States are required to respect fundamental rights, the protection of those rights is a legitimate interest which, in principle, justifies a restriction of the obligations imposed by [EU] law, even under a fundamental freedom guaranteed by the Treaty such as the free movement of goods.[111]

In combination with Article 36 TFEU, the mandatory requirements thus open up a not insignificant space for domestic obstacles to trade. *Cassis*, suggests Nicolaïdis, was 'most importantly about widening the Article 36 TFEU gaps in the net through which fishy state regulations would be able to escape the rigours of liberalisation.'[112] End of story? Not necessarily. Mandatory requirements only justify trade barriers ***in principle***: there is one more hurdle to overcome.

(C) Proportionality

The final step takes place under the broad banner of proportionality, although precise formulations and the intensity of the enquiry are variable. Is the impugned measure in fact capable of achieving its purported aims? Could it be achieved with less restrictive measures? The answer is a question of fact – to be decided by the CJEU in infringement proceedings or the referring court in preliminary references.[113]

---

[108] *Cassis de Dijon* [8].

[109] Case 302/86 *Commission v Denmark* [1988] ECR 4607 [9]. The Court has also accepted particularly sensitive constitutional traditions, such as Austria's ban on noble titles in Case 208/09 *Ilonka Sayn-Wittgenstein v Landeshauptmann von Wien* EU:C:2010:806.

[110] *Schmidberger* (n 51) [17].

[111] *Schmidberger* [71]–[74].

[112] K Nicolaïdis, 'Kir forever? The journey of a political scientist in the landscape of mutual recognition' in MP Maduro and L Azoulai (eds), *The Past and Future of EU Law: The Classics of EU Law Revisited on the 50th Anniversary of the Rome Treaty* (Hart 2010), p. 449.

[113] Though the Court cannot always resist the temptation to offer its own analysis: see, e.g., *Schmidberger* (n 51) [81] ff.

The most spectacular illustration of how to get this wrong can be found in *Cassis de Dijon* itself. Remember how the *Branntweinmonopolgesetz* laid down a *minimum* alcohol content of 25 per cent for fruit liqueurs, thus excluding weaker French products? This, the German government proffered, was designed to protect public health by avoiding 'the proliferation of alcoholic beverages on the national market, in particular alcoholic beverages with a low alcohol content, since ... such products may more easily induce a tolerance towards alcohol than more highly alcoholic beverages'.[114] Unsurprisingly, the Court was not impressed: German consumers were, after all, indulging in 'an extremely wide range of weakly or moderately alcoholic products', and consuming a large proportion of the stronger stuff 'in a diluted form'.[115]

In practice, litigation often turns on whether a legitimate aim could be achieved in a less restrictive manner. To protect the poor German consumers against beers brewed in more adventurous ways than those envisaged by the medieval *Reinheitsgebot*, for example, the Court suggested the 'compulsory affixing of suitable labels'. Consumer protection was fine, but it could be achieved by providing information rather than outright bans.[116] Similar considerations, *mutatis mutandis*, were lethal to the Greek bakery laws we encountered – justified in part as protection lest consumers be duped by 'bake-off' breads.[117] The theme that emerges is a strong opposition to excessively paternalistic regulation, and a trust in Europe's consumers to be 'reasonably circumspect' and not easily fooled by flashy chocolate wrappers.

That is not to say, of course, that justifications are never successful: France was able to defend its rules requiring additional safeguards for woodworking machines on the basis that operators were not formally trained in their use (as their German counterparts had to be), thus requiring additional protection in case of mechanical malfunctions.[118] Italy convinced the Court that its ban on moped trailers was required to ensure road safety: whilst the burden of proof was firmly on the government, it could not 'be so extensive as to require the Member State to prove, positively, that no other conceivable measure could enable that objective to be attained under the same conditions'.[119] And in *Schmidberger*, the Court's extensive scrutiny of the Austrian authorities' actions concluded that they 'were reasonably entitled, having regard to the wide discretion which must be accorded to them in the matter, to consider that the

[114] *Cassis de Dijon* (n 34) [10].
[115] *Cassis de Dijon* [11].
[116] *Commission v Germany* (n 61) [35].
[117] *Alfa Vita* (n 86) [22]–[27]. Similarly, in *Delhaize* (n 47), the Court found that Spain could not rely on the DOC scheme to insist on bottling Rioja locally, as 'bottling of the wine in question in the region of production was [not] an operation which endowed it with particular characteristics or was essential in order to maintain the specific characteristics acquired by it' [19].
[118] *Commission v France* (n 65) [10]–[23].
[119] *Moped Trailers* (n 85) [66].

legitimate aim of that demonstration could not be achieved in the present case by measures less restrictive of intra-[EU] trade.'[120]

CONCLUSION: 'YOU CANNOT FALL IN LOVE WITH THE SINGLE MARKET'

'You cannot fall in love with the single market', Jacques Delors, then-President of the Commission, famously quipped in his 1989 address to the European Parliament.[121] We disagree. The few sparse words of Articles 34 to 36 TFEU have become an endless source of fascinating and entertaining cases and, more importantly, continue to provide an important microcosm in which to better understand European integration, and to study the tensions we encountered in our opening debate in this chapter. Is *Cassis de Dijon* really a 'supranational conspiracy uniting the Court, the Commission and big business ... that simply cannot be stopped'?[122] Or should we face up to 'the sad truth ... that over the years plenty of regulating authorities ... have run it close by wasting the Court's time, and that of traders and consumers, by trying to rely on shoddy argument to protect worthless trade restrictions'?[123]

In working out what you think, remember that the removal of trade barriers is but one of several mechanisms in developing the Internal Market. Revisit, in particular, the broad legislative competence of Article 114 TFEU, which we encountered in Chapter 2. As Delors reminded the European Parliament, it was not enough to stress the need 'for a frontier-free area': what mattered just as much was the careful design of 'flanking policies' (including, in particular, social policy and environmental protection) 'which will open up new horizons for the men and women who make up this Community of ours'.[124]

FURTHER READING

If you are interested in the Economics that underpin Debate 1, try R Baldwin and C Wyplosz, *The Economics of European Integration*, 6th edn (McGraw Hill 2020) for an overview that is (relatively) light on complex equations.

To understand the intricacies of free movement law, it can be very helpful to draw out the different categories in the case law as a flow chart or diagram. For detailed illustrations, we particularly like C Barnard, *The Substantive Law of the EU: The Four Freedoms*, 6th edn (Oxford University Press 2019). See, e.g., 'QRs, MEEs, and CSAs after *Trailers*', page 133.

Market access continues to play a crucial role in defining the scope of Article 34 TFEU. But what vision of the market does it actually subscribe to? That is unclear – if

[120] *Schmidberger* (n 51) [93].

[121] Jacques Delors, 'Address to the European Parliament' (Strasbourg, 17 January 1989), https://perma.cc/S3WM-A6X4.

[122] Nicolaïdis (n 112), 'Kir forever?', p. 450.

[123] Weatherill, *Law and Values* (n 56), p. 335. Remember also the tensions that surfaced in Chapter 9.

[124] Delors, 'Address to the European Parliament' (n 121).

anything, the concept might camouflage the need to make important choices, argues J Snell: 'The Notion of Market Access: A Concept or a Slogan?' (2010) 47(2) CML Rev 437.

Critics have long argued that, despite cases like *Schmidberger*, the Internal Market will always prioritise economic aims over social and political ones at end of the day. For a powerful defence of the CJEU's work (and an explanation of key missteps), see S Weatherill, 'The EU Internal Market Perspective' in M Freedland and J Prassl (eds), *EU Law in the Member States: Viking, Laval, and Beyond* (Hart 2015).

The construction of the Internal Market took place over many decades – but not at the same pace for all Member States. S Bogojević and M Drenovak-Ivanović use EU enlargement as a lens through which to explore how new Member States agree on possible market structures, interventions, and derogations – from 'two extra lorry loads of Bulgarian strawberry jam [to] an extra 12 kilos of Slovak ham per Member State per day': 'Environmental Protection Through the Prism of Enlargement: Time for Reflection' (2019) 56(4) CML Rev 949.

CHAPTER 11

Back to the Future

A Union Ready for the Challenges Ahead?

The Great Debates identified throughout this book are not new. For more than 60 years, EU law has grappled with questions concerning the scope of law-making competences and powers allocated to the central authority, the judicial and political arrangements of a polycentric but 'ever-closer' Union, the relationship between social and economic interests, and the need to protect and preserve national procedural space at the same time as safeguarding individual rights uniformly across a growing number of Member States. The Union, furthermore, does not exist in a vacuum isolated from external upheavals – whether it is the fall of the Soviet Union, the financial crash of 2008, or Europe's persistent migration crisis. As a result, we have to keep asking many of the questions we have encountered and revisit longstanding debates in order to determine what kind of Union is possible, and what kind of Union is desirable.

In the evolution of the new legal order, the Treaties act as blueprints, or planning permits, for what the Union can create and constitute. European integration is an open-ended project, and the Treaties are revised whilst this building-work is carried out, which can make it difficult to offer neat narratives about EU law and governance.[1] That is why EU law can sometimes appear messy, Pollockian. Its architecture is fragmented and in a constant state of development.

At the same time, this dynamic is what makes the study of EU law so exciting. As the Union evolves, we are able to revisit long-standing debates and evaluate their impact on emerging challenges to plot a path forward. In this concluding chapter, we briefly identify three areas in which major disruption looms: the resurgence of the nation state, the climate crisis, and rapid digitalisation. When it comes to revision, we invite you to work through each of these (global) challenges, and ask yourself how each of the Great Debates should play out to ensure a Union fit for the future.

[1] E Fisher, 'EU environmental law and legal imagination' in P Craig and G du Búrca (eds), *The Evolution of EU Law*, 3rd edn (Oxford University Press forthcoming) explores this in the context of environmental law.

Challenge 1
The return of the nation-state

In the ruins of World War II, Western Europe decided to engage with the political world economy by closing ranks. The EU's legal order was to be built on negotiations, mutuality, and interconnectedness.[2] Fast forward 60 years and this *modus operandi* is coming under threat by the return of the nation-state where populism is on the rise, the rule of law is undercut, and mutual trust is increasingly overshadowed by state-centred interests. What role does this leave for the EU, which is dependent on the Member States for its powers? And what rights protection may individuals under threat of national populist politics find under EU law?

(A) Populism

Populism is a slippery concept, veering between ideology and political strategy[3] and encompassing both left- and right-wing ideologies,[4] but it is undoubtedly on the rise – from the *gilets jaunes* in France and Brexit in the UK to Poland's attempt to overhaul its judiciary and the Hungarian government's unabashed attack on the media and minorities.[5]

A key feature of populist politics is that it draws a distinction between 'the people', which it purports to represent, and 'the elite', which is cast as the people's antagonist.[6] Although it is often obscure *who* exactly the people are, the view is always 'anti-pluralist' and – in the case of right-wing populism in Europe – it conjures up a group of 'culpable others (immigrants)', who supposedly do not work but 'live like parasites off the work of others'.[7] As such, the focal point of populist politics is in the defence of national, political, social, and economic ways of life 'against external actors who penetrate the state by migrating, exchanging goods or exerting rule'.[8]

Xenophobia of this kind runs directly against the idea of an ever-closer union of peoples, and the transnational belonging that the EU offers. Remember the commitments in Article 2 TEU:

---

[2] See, e.g., V Bornschier (ed.), *State-Building in Europe: The Revitalization of Western European Integration* (Cambridge University Press 2000).

[3] C Mudde and C Rovira Kaltwasser, *Populism: A Very Short Introduction* (Oxford University Press 2017), pp. 2–9.

[4] P Taggert, *Populism* (Oxford University Press 2000), p. 2.

[5] D Adamski, 'The social contract of democratic backsliding in the "new EU" countries' (2019) 56(3) CML Rev 623.

[6] J-W Müller, *What Is Populism?* (Penguin 2017), p. 40.

[7] A Noury and G Roland, 'Identity politics and populism in Europe' (2020) 23 Ann Rev Polit Sci 421, 423.

[8] L Hooghe and G Marks, 'Cleavage theory meets Europe's crises: Lipset, Rokkan, and the transnational cleavage' (2018) 25(1) J Eur Public Policy 109, 110.

> The Union is founded on the values of respect for human dignity, freedom, democracy, equality, the rule of law and respect for human rights, including the rights of persons belonging to minorities. These values are common to the Member States in a society in which pluralism, non-discrimination, tolerance, justice, solidarity and equality between women and men prevail.

But what *legal* bite, if any, do these values have? Can the EU prevent democratic backsliding in the Member States? And if so, on what grounds?

(B) The EU as a Protector of the Rule of Law

Populism seeks to erode the rule of law by undercutting expertise, deliberative processes, and legal institutions.[9] Protecting the values set out in Article 2 TEU thus requires a robust defence – politically and legally – of its core values, including not least the independence of domestic judiciaries.

In terms of political mechanisms, Article 7 TEU sets out a procedure to identify and sanction serious breaches of the rule of law. The Council, with the European Parliament's consent, may impose sanctions such as the suspension of voting rights where a Member State is in serious and persistent breach of Article 2 TEU.[10] In cases where the Council finds a clear *risk* of a serious breach of these values, it may issue recommendations for preventative measures.[11] There is also a newly established Rule of Law Framework – an early-warning tool adopted by the Commission to prevent the erosion of the rule of law through targeted dialogues with a Member State to address systematic threats,[12] as well as rule of law conditionality in the use of EU funds.[13] These are complemented by legal mechanisms ranging from infringement proceedings to preliminary references sent off by national courts.

The Commission's actions against Poland in the wake of its judicial reforms, which subjected regular judges to disciplinary investigations and sanctions, and forcefully retired senior members of the judiciary, provide a useful illustration of the interplay of these different avenues. The Union's first step in addressing this threat to the rule of law was to open a dialogue with the Polish government in 2016 under the Rule of Law Framework. As no progress was made at this stage, the Commission activated Article 7 TEU in 2017 – for the first time

---

[9] N Lacey, 'Populism and the rule of law' (2019) 15 Ann Rev L Soc Sci 79.

[10] TEU, Article 7(3). The European Parliament may also take the initiative, as it did in the case of Hungary in 2018: J Sargentini, 'Report on a proposal calling on the Council to determine, pursuant to Article 7(1) of the Treaty on European Union, the existence of a clear risk of a serious breach by Hungary of the values on which the Union is founded (2017/2131(INL))' (European Parliament, 4 July 2018), https://perma.cc/3LUW-QHU4. Hungary sought an annulment: Case C-650/18 *Hungary v European Parliament* EU:C:2019:438.

[11] TEU, Article 7(1).

[12] Commission, 'Communication from the Commission to the European Parliament and the Council: A new EU Framework to strengthen the rule of law' [2014] COM/2014/0158 final.

[13] At the time of writing, the regulation is still in draft form: https://perma.cc/XQS2-EEKG.

ever.[14] The following year, the Commission initiated the same procedure with regard to Poland's restructuring of its judiciary.[15] In both cases, an interim measure was granted.[16]

The Commission has also relied on infringement proceedings to safeguard the independence of judiciaries across Europe. The Court of Justice has been clear that even where a Member State is not 'implementing' EU law it will be required to respect the rule of law – particularly judicial independence.[17] This creates a powerful instrument in scrutinising any degradation of the rule of law: in contrast to Article 7 TEU, the Court's rulings cannot be blocked by political veto. Thus, in *Commission v Poland*, the Grand Chamber found a violation of the requirements of judicial independence in the new rules on removal of judges.[18] Intensive political and legal activity continues to develop at pace in rule of law litigation and political enforcement actions: the challenge is not limited to a specific area, with related issues cropping up in the context of environmental protection,[19] migration, and EU financial policy.[20]

Bogdandy suggests that the breadth of Article 2 TEU allows values to feature prominently in the Court's case law, and that judicial action can thus be seen 'as a veritable steppingstone towards a "Union of values", on par with the Court's constitutionalizing jurisprudence in *van Gend en Loos* and *Costa*'.[21] How does this tie in, for example, with debates surrounding the role of the CJEU (Chapter 7, Debate 1), challenges to policy decisions taken 'in Brussels' (Chapter 3, Debate 2), and the role of the European Union as a guarantor of fundamental rights (Chapter 8, Debate 1)?

Challenge 2

The climate crisis

The climate crisis, the UN suggests, is 'the single most important issue' we face today.[22] The EU has long been at the forefront of international climate change action, rallying support for the Kyoto Protocol's emission reductions and

---

[14] Commission Recommendation (EU) 2018/103 of 20 December 2017 regarding the rule of law in Poland complementary to Recommendations (EU) 2016/1374, (EU) 2017/146 and (EU) 2017/1520 [2018] OJ L17/50.

[15] Case C-619/18 R *Commission v Poland* EU:C:2019:531.

[16] Orders C-619/18 R *Commission v Poland* EU:C:2018:1021; Case C-791/19 R *Commission v Poland* EU:C:2020:277.

[17] Case C-64/16 *Associação Sindical dos Juízes Portugueses v Tribunal de Contas* EU:C:2018:117 [29].

[18] Case C-192/18 *Commission v Poland* EU:C:2019:924; *Commission v Poland* (n 15).

[19] S Bogojević, 'The erosion of the rule of law: How Populism threatens environmental protection' (2019) 31(3) JEL 389.

[20] See, e.g., F Bignami, *EU Law in Populist Times: Crises and Prospects* (Cambridge University Press 2020).

[21] A von Bogdandy, 'Principles of a systemic deficiencies doctrine: how to protect checks and balances in the Member States' (2020) 57(3) CML Rev 705, 712–13.

[22] UN Secretary General Antonio Guterres, 'Secretary-General's remarks at opening ceremony of UN Climate Change Conference COP25' (Madrid, 2 December 2019), https://perma.cc/RTG9-MDTR.

establishing an emissions trading scheme,[23] as well as taking unilateral action on aviation when international appetite was lacking.[24] The Union's citizens, recent MEP elections suggest, overwhelmingly approve.[25]

But who should decide on the direction of travel? Ambitious environmental protection is a paradigm polycentric issue, requiring serious trade-offs with other policy areas – not least in budget-constrained times, where Member States are, for example, planning for a recovery after COVID-19. So who should decide the appropriate level of ambition at the Union level: the Commission? The Member States? Should NGOs and individuals have a say? And which forum would be most appropriate – the legal or political?

(A) Governance Models

The climate crisis challenges us to rethink nature and our relationship with it. Latour argues that nature is no longer a mere silhouette from which resources can be extracted for human benefit; rather, it is an active agent in the future of our planet.[26] This demands an integral framework to consider multiple voices in understanding the dependency of societies upon nature. How can this fit with EU governance?

At the institutional level, the Union appears increasingly receptive to ambitious participation models in revising its climate change objectives. Take the proposed European Climate Law as an example.[27] The goal is to achieve climate neutrality by 2050, led by a 'European Climate Pact' that gives 'everyone a voice and space to design new climate actions, share information, launch grassroots activities and showcase solutions that others can follow'.[28]

Broad public participation does not guarantee *better* environmental laws, of course.[29] Questions remain as to how new participatory models can fit into existing legislative structures. Will individuals be granted a firmer role in the political process? Or will formalised civic influence remain limited to climate matters? How will competing views be reconciled?

At the level of individual rights protection, climate litigation has mushroomed globally, offering a platform for marginalised voices. The CJEU, on the other hand, has been more reluctant to hear related cases. Remember *Carvalho* in Chapter 8, where the General Court – whilst acknowledging the

---

[23] S Bogojević, *Emissions Trading Schemes: Markets, State and Law* (Hart 2013), chapter 3.

[24] J Scott and L Rajamani, 'EU climate change unilateralism' (2012) 23(2) EJIL 469.

[25] M Pearson and W Rudig, 'The Greens in the 2019 European elections' (2020) 29(2) Environ Polit 336.

[26] B Latour, *Down to Earth: Politics in the New Climate Regime* (Polity 2018).

[27] Proposal for a Regulation of the European Parliament and of the Council establishing the framework for achieving climate neutrality and amending regulation (EU) 2018/1999 (European Climate Law) [2020] COM/2020/80 final.

[28] Commission, 'European climate pact', https://perma.cc/X9FJ-8HN4.

[29] A Russell Hochschild, *Strangers in Their Own Land: Anger and Mourning on the American Right* (The New Press 2016).

urgency of the climate crisis – refused to change the restrictive standing rules we encountered in Chapter 4. The Treaty requirement of 'individual concern' could not be reconciled with the fact that 'every individual is likely to be affected one way or another by climate change'.[30]

(B) A 'Green Recovery'

The ensuing tensions are likely to become even starker as a result of ballooning public debt levels in the wake of the COVID-19 pandemic.[31] Can the economic recovery be a 'green' one? Yes, according to the Commission, which has put forward a comprehensive rescue package geared towards delivering 'a more sustainable, resilient and fairer Europe for the next generation'[32] – a proposal subsequently adopted by the Council.[33] One pillar of this package is a 'European Green Deal', promising to make the EU's economy 'resource efficient and competitive' and climate neutral by 2050.[34]

One of the challenges ahead is figuring out how exactly climate action, and environmental protection more broadly, features in debates about rebuilding the Internal Market. COVID-19 and the climate crisis are both framed as externalities – market failures that require state intervention in the form of fiscal stimuli.[35] From this perspective, any recovery plan is about 'fixing' the market. This sounds straightforward enough in the abstract, but what does it mean in concrete terms?

Does 'recovery' entail rescuing the petrochemical industry – which is at risk of becoming a stranded asset on the road to a low-carbon economy[36] – just as the banking sector was bailed out in the 2008 crisis? Can we expect more frequent exemptions from state aid rules for the aviation and maritime industry, which are under continued strains of the pandemic?[37] And what about subsidies for fossil

---

[30] Case T-330/18 *Armando Carvalho and ors v European Parliament and Council* EU:T:2019:324 (on appeal) [50].

[31] As discussed in S Bogojević, 'COVID-19, climate change action, and the road to green recovery' (2020) 32(3) JEL 355.

[32] Commission, 'Communication from the Commission to the European Parliament, the European Council, the Council, the European Economic and Social Committee and the Committee of the Regions on "Europe's Moment: Repair and Prepare for the Next Generation"' [2020] COM/2020/456 final, p. 2.

[33] European Council, 'Special meeting of the European Council (17, 18, 19, 20 and 21 July 2020) – Conclusions' [2020] EUCO/10/20.

[34] Commission, 'Communication from the Commission to the European Parliament, the European Council, the Council, the European Economic and Social Committee and the Committee of the Regions on "The European Green Deal"' [2019] COM/2019/640 final, 2. See also F Timmermans, 'Speech on the European Green Deal as a growth strategy at the Bruegel Annual Meetings' (Brussels, 1 September 2020), https://perma.cc/5V4J-Z9QS.

[35] C Hepburn and others, 'Will COVID-19 fiscal recovery packages accelerate or retard progress on climate change?' (2020) 36(S1) Oxford Rev Econ Policy S359.

[36] See, e.g., S Felt and C Muffett, *Pandemic Crisis, Systemic Decline: Why Exploiting the COVID-19 Crisis Will Not Save the Oil, Gas, and Plastic Industry* (CIEL 2020).

[37] The many state aid exemptions made during the COVID-19 pandemic are available online at https://ec.europa.eu/competition/state_aid/what_is_new/COVID_19.html.

fuels, fisheries, and farming? These are sectors that often support small and remote communities – how should that be weighed against their damaging impact on the environment? The *gilets jaunes* protests are a powerful reminder of just how difficult so-called market fixes can turn out to be.

In insisting on a 'just and inclusive'[38] transition, the Commission seems to be tuned into these dangers, even if its labelling of the European Green Deal as a 'growth' strategy does little to explain who will inevitably have to make painful (even if fair) adjustments, and on what grounds.[39] In thinking about how an eventual balance should be struck, consider our discussions on polycentricity in Union policy-making (Chapter 3, Debate 3). When it comes to the roles of individuals, does the climate crisis provide further impetus for arguments in favour of abandoning the CJEU's narrow approach to standing (Chapter 4, Debate 1)? Might the concept of EU citizenship provide added arguments for expanding individual rights (Chapter 9, Debate 3)?

Challenge 3
Digitalisation

The rapid pace of technological innovation and the ensuing widespread digitalisation of our world are a third major challenge facing the EU in the years ahead. As opposed to radical populism and the climate crisis, however, digitalisation also provides significant opportunities. A well-regulated digital single market, recent studies suggest, could unlock economic benefits in excess of €175 billion for citizens and businesses across the Member States.[40]

From the explosive growth of social networking platforms, online commerce, and the gig economy to the datafication of finance, healthcare, and industry – digitalisation is bringing about fundamental changes in the organisation of the Common Market and individuals' lives. Consumers benefit from the seemingly unlimited availability and swift delivery of products and services. At the same time, their every move online is tracked and mined for information, creating vulnerabilities for targeted advertising and subtle price manipulation.[41] Workers can tap into the flexibility of the gig economy, whilst also risking being caught in precarious, low-paid work.[42] The ensuing challenges are further exacerbated by the fact that a small number of large corporations claim an overwhelming market share.[43]

[38] Commission, Communication on the European Green Deal (n 34), p. 2.
[39] Timmermans (n 34), 'Speech on the European Green Deal'.
[40] Directorate-General for Internal Policies of the Union, 'The European digital single market: Delivering economic benefits for citizens and businesses' (European Parliament, 28 October 2020), https://perma.cc/7WQ8-X9FJ.
[41] ME Stucke and A Ezrachi, 'How pricing bots could form cartels and make things more expensive' (*Harvard Business Review*, 27 October 2016), https://perma.cc/C5EJ-2FLU.
[42] J Prassl, *Humans as a Service: The Promise and Perils of Work in the Gig Economy* (Oxford University Press 2018).
[43] M Sandbu, 'FT collections: The economics of big tech', https://perma.cc/QJN3-JKTH.

(A) The Digital Single Market

The EU has been active in regulating technological innovation for several decades: the digital single market (DSM) developed out of comparatively mundane questions of industrial policy,[44] beginning with the 'Television without Frontiers' Directive in 1989.[45] The broad regulatory pattern is familiar: emphasis on removing (national) rules that impede cross-border markets is combined with targeted (re-)regulation.

The DSM is thus an evolution of the single market which we saw in the preceding chapter – designed, in addition to the four fundamental freedoms, to ensure that 'individuals and businesses can seamlessly access and engage in online activities under conditions of fair competition, and a high level of consumer and personal data protection, irrespective of their nationality or place of residence.'[46] A key priority of the Juncker Commission, elements of the DSM include increased access to digital technologies, creating a level playing field for innovation, and maximising economic growth.[47]

The DSM strategy is complemented by several fundamental rights guaranteed in the Charter, as well as a series of specific legislative measures. We have already encountered Article 8 CFR, an innovative commitment to Data Protection,[48] and the Court's robust defence of that right in *DRI*.[49] In *Schrems I* and *Schrems II*, a similar approach ensured the extraterritorial protection of Union citizens' rights: in the absence of appropriate safeguarding regimes, platforms such as Facebook could not export user data to the United States.[50]

Perhaps the highest-profile measure in the Union's digital regulatory arsenal is the General Data Protection Regulation of 2016, enacted on the basis of Art 16 TFEU and designed to protect citizens against the unlawful collection

---

[44] For a more extensive overview, see A Harcourt, 'The EU's digital single market' (*UK in a Changing Europe,* 20 December 2016), https://ukandeu.ac.uk/explainers/the-eus-digital-single-market.

[45] Harcourt, 'The EU's digital single market'; Council Directive 89/552/EEC of 3 October 1989 on the coordination of certain provisions laid down by law, regulation or administrative action in Member States concerning the pursuit of television broadcasting activities [1989] OJ L298/23 (no longer in force).

[46] Commission, 'Shaping the digital single market', https://perma.cc/V9EZ-TDMM.

[47] Ranging from rules on cross-border data storage and platform trading practices to a ban on geo-blocking: European Commission, 'A Digital Single Market for the benefit of all Europeans', https://perma.cc/BU2K-WBWC.

[48] O Lynskey, 'Article 8: The right to data protection' in M Bobek and J Adams-Prassl (eds), *The EU Charter of Fundamental Rights in the Member States* (Hart 2020).

[49] Joined Cases C-293/12 and C-594/12 *Digital Rights Ireland Ltd v Minister for Communications and ors* [2014] ECR I-238.

[50] Case C-362/14 *Maximillian Schrems v Data Protection Commissioner* EU:C:2015:650; M Van der Sluis and L Azoulai, 'Institutionalizing personal data protection in times of global institutional distrust: *Schrems*' (2016) 53(5) CML Rev 1343; Case C-311/18 *Data Protection Commissioner v Facebook Ireland Ltd and Maximillian Schrems* EU:C:2020:559; M Rotenberg, '*Schrems II*, from Snowden to China: Toward a new alignment on transatlantic data protection' [2020] (1-2) ELJ 141.

and processing of their data (as well as inflicting no end of cookie warnings on us).[51] A host of other regulations and directives address more specific issues – from trading standards on online marketplaces[52] to basic rights for gig economy workers.[53] The broader challenges of market domination by a small number of multinational players – including Google, Amazon, Apple, and Microsoft – have been the subject of repeated competition law actions by the Commission.[54]

(B) Towards a European Digital Strategy

This plethora of measures is promising. Only concerted action can achieve successful regulation: there are no silos in a digitalised world. At the same time, however, the current approach raises the danger of 'kaleidoscopic data-related enforcement', where different substantive provisions and levels of enforcement at the national and European level collide.[55]

A related danger is that the DSM might reopen many of the conflicts between economic and social regulatory goals we have encountered in preceding chapters. In *Uber*, for example, the eponymous gig economy platform sought to characterise itself as a digital services provider, with a view to avoiding a host of domestic regulatory obligations.[56] The Court of Justice disagreed: Uber is just another taxi service, even though it uses an app to dispatch its cars. *AirBnB*, on the other hand, succeeded with broadly similar arguments several months later.[57] Some have perceived this as an unwelcome shift in tech regulation 'from maximizing economic benefits to minimizing social and political

[51] European Parliament and Council Regulation (EU) 2016/679 of 27 April 2016 on the protection of natural persons with regard to the processing of personal data and on the free movement of such data, and repealing Directive 95/46/EC (General Data Protection Regulation) [2016] OJ L119/1.

[52] European Parliament and Council Regulation (EU) 2019/1150 of 20 June 2019 on promoting fairness and transparency for business users of online intermediation services [2019] OJ L186/57 (P2B Regulation).

[53] European Parliament and Council Directive (EU) 2019/1152 of 20 June 2019 on transparent and predictable working conditions in the European Union [2019] OJ L186/105 (TPWC). For a detailed analysis, see B Bednarowicz, 'Delivering on the European pillar of social rights: The new directive on transparent and predictable working conditions in the European Union' (2019) 48(4) ILJ 604.

[54] Editorial comments, 'Special advice on competition policy for the digital era' (2020) 57(2) CML Rev 315.

[55] A Arnbak, W Geursen, and S Yakovleva, 'Kaleidoscopic data-related enforcement in the digital age' (2020) 57(5) CML Rev 1461.

[56] Case C-434/15 *Asóciacion Profesional Elite Taxi v Uber Systems Spain SL* EU:C:2017:981. The current version of the relevant legislation is European Parliament and Council Directive (EU) 2015/1535 of 9 September 2015 laying down a procedure for the provision of information in the field of technical regulations and of rules on Information Society services [2015] OJ L241/1.

[57] Case C-390/18 *Criminal proceedings against X* EU:C:2019:1112.

costs';[58] others are impressed by the Court's commitment to a level playing field for digital and traditional industries alike.[59]

With the rapid commercialisation of 'artificial intelligence' (i.e. machine learning algorithms which can process vast quantities of data at hitherto unprecedented speed and scale), the challenges identified are quickly becoming turbo-charged – creating an urgent need for new and fully integrated regulatory frameworks. The European Digital Strategy launched in February 2020 provides a first glimpse of measures to come, setting out four pillars around which Europe's digital future will be shaped: 'technology that works for people'; a 'fair and competitive digital economy'; an 'open, democratic and sustainable digital society'; and 'Europe as a global digital player'.[60]

These are lofty ambitions, and it remains to be seen whether and how they will be achieved. Take the Commission's White Paper on Artificial Intelligence as an example: whilst it recognises a need to build an 'ecosystem of trust' and protect fundamental rights and consumers' rights' – in particular for artificial intelligence systems operated in the EU that pose a 'high risk' – the overarching emphasis is on harnessing economic benefits.[61] A long-mooted moratorium on facial recognition, on the other hand, was quietly shelved at the last minute.[62]

Whether it is balancing citizens' rights with economic growth (Chapter 10, Debate 1), ensuring responsible innovation in the face of global competition whilst operating within the limits of conferred competences (Chapter 2, Debate 1), or the role of the Charter in regulating relationships between internet users and service providers (Chapter 6, Debate 2), the discussion is set to continue.

Conclusion: Looking Back, Going Forward

On 11 March 2020, the WHO declared a global pandemic.[63] COVID-19 provided an unexpected boost for the nation-state: borders returned within the EU, the right to free movement was restricted, and protectionist economic measures resurrected.[64] Across Europe, Member States varied greatly in

[58] D Adamski, 'Lost on the digital platform: Europe's legal travails with the Digital Single Market' (2018) 55(3) CML Rev 719.

[59] J Prassl, 'The Internal Market goes digital: How will it grapple with the future of work?' in F Amtenbrink and others (eds), *The Internal Market and the Future of European Integration: Essays in Honour of Laurence W. Gormley* (Cambridge University Press 2019).

[60] European Commission, 'The European digital strategy', https://perma.cc/ZX5A-R92P.

[61] Commission, 'White Paper on artificial intelligence: A European approach to excellence and trust' [2020] COM/2020/65 final, 3.

[62] J Espinoza and M Murgia, 'EU backs away from call for blanket ban on facial recognition tech' (*Financial Times*, London, 11 February 2020).

[63] WHO Director-General Dr Tedros Adhanom Ghebreyesus, 'WHO Director-General's opening remarks at the media briefing on COVID-19 – 11 March 2020' (Geneva, 11 March 2020), https://perma.cc/5TUA-7BSM.

[64] See, e.g., the list of state aid exemptions at https://ec.europa.eu/competition/state_aid/what_is_new/COVID_19.html..

responding to the crisis, creating a divided Union with limited central leadership. It is against this setting that the challenges of populism, climate change, and digitalisation will have to be resolved.

The EU is both driven – and hampered – by the political willpower of its Member States. When nations look inward, the EU is relegated to the margins. As a Union built on legal pluralism, key tenets can suddenly look fragile. Is it right to insist on policing rule of law violations, for example, whilst Member States rely on states of emergency to infringe on basic civil liberties to protect citizens from harm?[65] What is, and what ought to be, the role of EU law in addressing the pandemic, whilst safeguarding liberal democracy?

Dealing with these challenges will not be easy. To explore what kind of Union is possible, what kind of Union we want and need, legal imagination is required: 'the abstract language of legal concepts need to be applied to specific circumstances [... as] part of a process of inquiry, individual or collective, in which any particular interpretation or understanding of a law needs to be tested to see how appropriate it is'.[66]

We hope to have introduced you to some of the many ways in which EU law is such an imaginative legal order. There are clear principles (from direct effect and supremacy to the rule of law) and plenty of interests to be balanced against one another (from the effective protection of individual rights to Member State sovereignty). As the Union turns to tackle the challenges of the twenty-first century, resort to its imaginative enterprise and an openness to the Great Debates which have shaped the new legal order will be more important than ever.

FURTHER READING

Many challenges lay ahead, as explored in a special issue of the German Law Journal: '20 Challenges in the EU in 2020' (2020) 21 German LJ 1. Is there a commonality between these and is the EU equipped to deal with them? If not, what legal changes may be needed, and why?

Should the EU be concerned with preventing democratic backsliding in the Member States? Why, or why not? See, e.g., JW Müller, 'Should the EU Protect Democracy and the Rule of Law Inside Member States?' (2015) 21(2) Eur LJ 141.

Climate change has been described as legally disruptive in the way that it gives rise to disputes and problems not easily addressed by existing legal doctrines and frameworks (see E Fisher, E Scotford and E Barritt, 'The Legally Disruptive Nature of Climate Change' (2017) 80(2) MLR 173). How is climate change disruptive of the EU legal order? What legal challenges does this create for EU law?

The challenges raised by digitalisation are by no means limited to the Internal Market. Consider, for example, the impact on fundamental rights protection, as explored in the European Law Journal's special issue on 'Internet and Human Rights Law' (2019) 25 Eur LJ 119.

---

[65] Verfassungsblog, 'Debate: COVID-19 and states of emergency', https://verfassungsblog.de/category/debates/COVID-19-and-states-of-emergency-debates.

[66] Fisher (n 1), 'EU environmental law and legal imagination'.

Index